OVER THE FENCE IS OUT!

The Larry Walker Story
and more of
Canada's Baseball Legends

Jim Shearon

Malin Head Press
Canada

Published in Canada by:
Malin Head Press
79 Tiffany Place
Kanata, Ontario
Canada K2K 1W5
Telephone: (613) 592-4453
Email: jimshearon@sympatico.ca

Elizabeth Shore, *Editor*
Neil Munro, *Statistics*
Algrove Publishing Limited, *Graphic Design*

Front cover photo: Larry Walker, by Al Behrman, Associated Press

Also by Jim Shearon
Canada's Baseball Legends
ISBN 0-9698039-0-7

Library and Archives Canada Cataloguing in Publication

Shearon, Jim, 1936-
      Over the fence is out : The Larry Walker story and more of Canada's baseball legends / Jim Shearon.

Includes index.
ISBN 978-0-969803-93-5

      1. Baseball players--Canada--Biography. 2. Baseball players--Canada--Statistics. 3. Walker, Larry, 1966-. I. Title.
GV865.A1S444 2009   796.357092'271   C2008-907347-9

#1/01/09

About the Cover

When he hit the pitch, Jon Nunnally thought it was a deep fly ball. When he saw Larry Walker still backing up, he thought it was going to be a home run. Then Walker jumped and Nunnally said, "Oh, no, he's not going to catch that!" Larry reached above and beyond the eight-foot fence to catch the ball, and over the fence was out.

Associated Press photographer Al Behrman, who took the picture in Cincinnati, said he wasn't sure Walker would catch the ball. "I shot when he went up for it, thinking I would either get a photo of him catching it, or just missing a home run." Behrman used a Nikon F45 camera with a 500mm lens at 1/1000th of a second.

Dedication

To my wife Joan; our children, Brian, Mary, Catherine, Michael, David and Melanie; and our grand-children Braden, Julie, Adam, Dylan and Joshua; and to Uncle Barney, who took me and my brother Jackie to Ebbets Field, the Polo Grounds and Yankee Stadium when we visited every summer.

Acknowledgements

Sincere thanks for assistance and encouragement to Bill Atkinson, Michael Bowie, Ed Carson, Scott Crawford, Randall Scott Echlin, Mary Lee Eno, Elizabeth Farrell, Bill Humber, Beth Kaplan, Murray King, Peter Loyello, Alan Mann, Neil Munro, Elizabeth Shore, Tom Valcke, the Canadian Baseball Hall of Fame at St. Marys, Ontario, the National Baseball Hall of Fame Library, Cooperstown, New York, and the University of Toronto Summer Writing School.

About the Author

Former sports announcer with CFRA and CBO in Ottawa, Jim Shearon was 10 years old when he saw Jackie Robinson play for the Montreal Royals. He saw his first major league game at Ebbets Field in Brooklyn in 1949.

In writing this book, Jim Shearon visited and interviewed players and their families. He researched records and photos at the National Baseball Hall of Fame and Museum in Cooperstown, New York and newspaper files at the National Library of Canada and the Boston Public Library.

Author, Jim Shearon.

Table of Contents

5. The 1950s and '60s 151

6. The Modern Era 185

7. For The Record 217

Index 256

Chapter 1

Larry Walker

A Story in Three Parts

THE EXPOS YEARS
THE COLORADO ROCKIES
THE ST. LOUIS CARDINALS

Larry Walker, Simply the Best!

The first time I met Larry Walker, I wanted to tell him to go to Jericho, or some other warm place. But I bit my tongue and waited ... and waited.

It was in March 1991, at the Montreal Expos spring training complex in West Palm Beach, Florida. I was on assignment for CBC Radio's *In Town and Out* program in Ottawa to interview the only Canadian in the Expo lineup.

I got to the ballpark two-and-a-half hours before the game to be sure I had lots of time. Larry Walker was already out on the field, preparing for batting practice. I introduced myself and said I would like to do an interview whenever he was free. "I'll see you after batting practice," was his reply.

I sat on a bench behind the batting cage and watched for the next half hour as the players took their turns. When he was through batting, Larry picked up his glove, and ran right past me to the outfield, where he spent about 40 minutes catching fly balls and throwing to each of the bases. Next, he did some sprints and then sat on the grass, talking with some of the Atlanta players.

Just as the ground crew starting marking the white lines and laying down clean bases, Larry jogged up to me and said, "Make this quick, I have to change for the game."

That's when I wanted to tell him where to go; but after waiting an hour-and-a-half, I smiled instead, and turned on my tape recorder. It was well worth the wait.

Larry talked about his hockey career as a teenage goalkeeper trying out for the Regina Pats. He spoke about the pressure of being the only Canadian on the Expos, and he answered all my questions directly and honestly.

When I first interviewed him, Larry had played one full season with the Expos. His batting average was .241; but the Expos saw promise of better things. Walker, himself, never had any doubts.

Larry wasn't cocky; he was self-assured. He was an instinctive base runner, and had become an excellent fielder with an outstanding arm; and each year Larry became a better hitter.

Walker's batting average rose from .241 to .290, then .301, and, ultimately, three consecutive years of .366, .363 and .379. Larry won three National League batting championships. He hit 390 career home runs and was named the Most Valuable Player in 1997.

Larry Walker always knew he was going to be great, and he proved it. I interviewed Larry many times during his career and he was always gracious, always proud to say he is a Canadian and always interesting to talk to. Looking back on the achievements of Canadians in baseball, Larry Walker was simply the best.

I'm glad I didn't tell him where to go that first time.

Author, Jim Shearon, with Larry Walker.

I Would Have Done Anything
To Have Played in the NHL!

"I'm very happy I chose baseball. I've had a great career playing baseball," Larry Walker said. Then he made this startling confession, "At the same time I miss hockey. It's the greatest game in the world and I would have done anything to have played in the NHL."

How did a boy who wanted to be an NHL goalie wind up as a candidate for the Baseball Hall of Fame? Larry Walker was just 16 years old when he left his home in Maple Ridge, British Columbia, to attend the Regina Pats training camp in Saskatchewan in September 1983. The Pats are the oldest major junior hockey franchise in Canada, three-time winners of the Memorial Cup as national champions. Billy Hicke, Doug Wickenheiser and Clark Gillies are former Pats who played in the NHL.

Larry was six feet tall and two months away from his 17th birthday when he put on the goalie pads in the Regina dressing room for the twice-a-day workouts. He was one of six goalkeepers among the 46 players who took part in the annual Blue and White intra-squad game that marked the end of training camp.

Larry was the starting goalie for the White team. He handled 12 shots and allowed two goals.

"One was a screened shot from the point and the other was a deflection. I had no chance on either," he recalled. Two days later, Larry was one of 25 players cut from the team.

I asked him if he thought about what might have happened if he had made the team with the Regina Pats. "What I think about most," Larry answered, "is the team in Swift Current, where I had an offer to play Junior B, after I didn't make Regina. For some reason, I said, 'No' and turned away from it, and that was the last I ever saw of hockey."

One year after turning his back on Swift Current, Larry was back in Saskatchewan but in a baseball uniform trying out for the national youth team at Kindersley. Earl Berard, one of the organizers of the Kindersley tournament, smiled as he remembered Larry Walker when I spoke to him at Earl's induction into the Saskatchewan Baseball Hall of Fame.

"Larry was a big kid playing first base," said Earl. "He was kind of awkward but he looked awesome when he caught hold of a ball. He hit a couple of home runs that were just colossal."

Larry also remembered Kindersley, "That's where the Expos first saw me," he said. "Two weeks later, I played in a college tournament. Until then, I never thought of doing anything in baseball."

In November 1984, two weeks before Larry's 18th birthday, the Expos offered him a contract with a $1,500 bonus, and assigned him to Utica, New York, for the 1985 season.

Utica was the first step on a tall ladder that would eventually lead to Montreal, Denver, St. Louis and the World Series. As the following pages disclose, Larry Walker's progress to the major leagues was not easy but the young man from Maple Ridge never had any doubt that he would go all the way to the top.

Larry Walker is Headed for the Hall

They've already got a space reserved for him in St. Marys, Ontario, but Larry Walker might want to save one of his silver bats for Cooperstown because the Canadian Baseball Hall of Fame may not be his only destination.

Larry Walker is not simply the greatest Canadian-born baseball player of all time; he is one of the best players ever, period. A confident hitter, an exceptional outfielder with a strong, accurate throwing arm and one of the best base runners of the modern era, Walker has legitimate credentials to join Ferguson Jenkins as the only Canadians in the National Baseball Hall of Fame at Cooperstown, New York.

During his 16 years in the major leagues, Larry Walker grew from a raw youth into a disciplined, powerful force who was compared to some of the greatest outfielders in the game.

Felipe Alou, former manager of the Montreal Expos, said Walker made him think of Willie Mays and Roberto Clemente.

"He is one of the best I have ever seen," said Alou, "a challenging, daring kind of outfielder."

That opinion was shared by Jim Leyland, who managed Larry with the Colorado Rockies. "He's one of the best players in baseball. He's a five-tool player. He can beat you with his legs on offence or on defence; he can beat you with his arm. He can beat you at the bat with power. He can beat you running the bases. He can do it all. He's just a great player."

After winning the National League's Most Valuable Player award and leading the league with 49 home runs in 1997, Larry won the National League batting championship in 1998 and again in 1999. In doing so, Walker became the first player in 70 years to bat over .360 three years in a row. Larry batted .366 in 1997, .363 in 1998 and .379 in 1999. The last player to do that was Al Simmons of the Philadelphia Athletics, and he's in the Hall of Fame.

Jim Fanning, former general manager of the Expos, said he knew Larry Walker was an outstanding prospect when he first signed him to a contract as a teenager.

"He needed direction but Larry had the build and the power to be a great player. You can teach a smaller man some of the refinements of the game but size, instinct and power is something you can't teach. Larry had all those."

It took Larry Walker five years to climb from Class A, through double A and triple A into the major leagues, and a knee injury almost ended Larry's career before he made it to the top.

It happened in 1987. Larry played for Jacksonville of the Southern League and was chosen to the all-star team. When the season ended, the Expos sent him to play winter ball in the Mexican League. He tore knee ligaments sliding into home plate and there was a concern that he might never play again.

"I was told that my career might end," says Larry, "but I never thought about the negative part of it. I was thinking positive all the time and how good I was going to be when I came back."

Larry had lots of time to think positive. He missed the entire 1988 season because of the knee injury and when he joined Indianapolis for the 1989 season, he had to wear a knee brace. For Walker that was no big deal.

As a hockey player, Larry was used to putting on pads before a game. He said it was the same for baseball, "I just flip the brace on and go out and play." Walker batted .270 and stole 36 bases at Indianapolis before being called up to Montreal.

LARRY WALKER

THE EXPOS YEARS
Local boy makes good; leaves town.

The Expos Years

Larry Walker was the ideal player for the Montreal Expos: young, talented but still undeveloped. Like the Expos, Larry was the promise of good things to come. That he was a Canadian was a marketing bonus.

The Montreal media and Larry Walker were made for each other. The Montreal media machine is insatiable when it comes to sports heroes, and Larry was brash and outspoken. Larry talked a lot but he didn't just "talk the talk," he also "walked the walk." Year by year he became a better player. In time, Larry would become one of the finest hitters in the game but he was always an outstanding fielder.

Larry Walker made his Expo debut August 16, 1989, against the San Francisco Giants. He had a perfect day at the plate with a single off Mike LaCoss, and three walks. He also scored two runs as the Expos won 4-1. The next day Larry drove in his first run with an infield single, and the following day he had three hits and two more runs batted in against San Diego. He also made a sensational running catch.

After four games, Larry was batting .600, with six hits in 10 at bats and three runs batted in. He was optioned to Indianapolis August 29th but returned to the Montreal lineup when the rosters expanded on September 1st. Larry finished the year with eight hits in 47 times at bat for a batting average of .170.

When Larry Walker batted against Steve Wilson June 26, 1990, in Chicago, it was the first time a Canadian batter had batted against a Canadian pitcher since September 1977 when Bill Atkinson of the Expos pitched to Terry Puhl of the Houston Astros.

Wilson and Walker are both from the Vancouver area and were well acquainted with each other. Wilson came into the game in the top of the ninth inning, replacing Les Lancaster who gave up a lead-off home run to Jerry Goff. The tall lefthander from New Westminster retired Dave Martinez and Spike Owens on fly balls, and then struck out Larry Walker on four pitches.

After the game, Wilson said to Walker, "One Canuck to another; don't take it personal. It's my job to get you out."

Larry played 133 games in 1990 and tied Andre Dawson's team record of 19 home runs by a rookie. He stole 21 bases and played well in the outfield but he batted only .241.

The turning point in Larry Walker's career was the 1991 season, a year that started badly. Larry was recovering from chicken pox when he reported for spring training. Then he dove for a ball and hurt his shoulder. He had only five hits in 18 games in Florida and was batting just .125 but Expos pitching coach Larry Bearnarth insisted Walker was going to do well.

Larry Walker was the promise of better things to come with the Montreal Expos.
(Courtesy Montreal Expos)

"He has to learn how to adjust to a couple of pitches," Bearnarth told me; "mainly the inside fast ball, and once he learns to deal with them a bit he's probably going to be a star along the lines of Barry Bonds."

The opening game in 1991 was at Pittsburgh, where Bonds was playing for the Pirates. Larry doubled his first time at bat, singled the next two times and walked on his fourth appearance. He also made two outstanding catches in right field to help Dennis Martinez preserve a one-hit shutout. Larry played 137 games in 1991 and raised his batting average to .290.

Walker was determined to ask for a big raise in 1992 but even he was surprised when Dan Duquette, the Expos general manager, offered a five-fold increase with a contract for $975,000 (US), equal to 1.17 million Canadian dollars.

Larry became the Expos clean-up batter in 1992 and he responded to the big raise in pay by batting .301 with 23 home runs and 93 runs batted in. Walker's fielding percentage of .993 surpassed Andre Dawson's club record, and he finished the season by playing 61 consecutive games without an error.

Larry demonstrated his quickness in the field and his strong arm by throwing out Tony Fernandez at first base on July 4, 1992. The San Diego shortstop had hit an apparent single to right field but took his time running to the base. Walker charged the ball and rifled a throw to first base to retire the batter and take away a hit.

Larry did the same thing later in the year when pitcher Tim Wakefield hit a ground ball to right field. Word got around and batters learned to run to first base if they hit the ball to the Expos right fielder.

In 1993, Larry became the first Canadian to hit 20 home runs and steal 20 bases in the same season. He wound up with 22 home runs and 29 stolen bases and for the second year in a row, he won a golden glove for his fielding. The stage was now set for what would have been the greatest year in Montreal sports history - the 1994 season when the Expos were the best team in baseball.

The Expos and Larry Walker avoided arbitration by agreeing to the richest contract in club history. Larry signed a one-year deal for $4.025 million (US), the equivalent of $5.2 million Canadian. It was more than a million dollars higher than his 1993 contract but Walker said he was disappointed that the Expos had not agreed to a multi-year contract. He told the Canadian Press, "It hurts my chances of being in an Expos' uniform next year."

Early in the season, Larry Walker found himself on the nightly highlight reel. It happened April 24 at Dodger Stadium in Los Angeles. In the third inning, with one man out and Jose Offerman the runner at first base,

Larry Walker tied Andre Dawson's Expo record for home runs by a rookie. (Courtesy Montreal Expos)

Mike Piazza hit a foul ball down the right field line. Walker easily made the catch near the grandstand and, thinking it was the third out, handed the ball to a little boy sitting in the first row.

As he started to jog to the Expos dugout, Larry saw Offerman running around second base and realized there were only two out. Walker ran back to the little boy, got the ball back and threw to third base. The next batter, Tim Wallach, hit a home run so Larry's miscalculation had no effect on the final score. When he came out for the fourth inning, Larry brought a new ball with him and handed it to the little boy.

By early June, Walker was hitting well but playing the outfield became an ordeal because of an inflamed right shoulder. Larry was reduced to flipping the ball underhand. After a game in St. Louis, June 22, he told Jeff Blair of the Montreal Gazette, "I can't throw 50 feet."

Walker missed the next four games while undergoing treatment. Moises Alou replaced Larry in right field. When Walker returned to the lineup June 28 against Atlanta in Montreal he was at first base, displacing Cliff Floyd. Larry had a double and three singles and drove in two runs as the Expos rallied to beat Atlanta. Walker stayed at first base and continued to hit well for the final 35 games of what turned out to be a strike-shortened season.

Larry's final game in Montreal was on August 4, 1994, against the St. Louis Cardinals. The Players Union had announced that unless agreement was reached with the owners on a new collective agreement, a strike would begin August 12. Among the crowd of 39,000 spectators there was a sprinkling of signs; "NO STRIKE", said one. "SAVE OUR SEASON" read another.

Walker hit two home runs against Bob Tewksbury, in the seventh inning and in the ninth. His last hit in Montreal was a home run. The Expos finished the season in Pennsylvania, sweeping three from the Phillies and winning three of four in Pittsburgh. Larry Walker's last hit as an Expo was a single off Denny Neagle of the Pirates. His last time at bat in a Montreal uniform, on August 10, was a tribute to his growing stature. Larry was given an intentional walk in the ninth inning with a runner on second base and two out. In 103 games, the equivalent of two-thirds of a season, Larry batted .322 with 19 home runs and 86 runs batted in.

On August 12, the strike began. Nobody knew how long it would last. Expos manager Felipe Alou said later he thought the players would be out a week and then everything would be back to normal. Instead, after 33 days, with no settlement in sight, the owners cancelled the rest of the season.

LARRY WALKER

THE COLORADO ROCKIES

*A new team with deep pockets
made Larry rich and famous.*

Welcome to Colorado

The baseball strike and lockout that ended the 1994 season also marked the end of Larry Walker's association with the Montreal Expos. As a free agent at the end of the year, Larry was able to go wherever he could make the most money. He insists that he hoped the Expos would try to keep him but Expos management knew it could not compete against American teams who were ready to put big dollars on the line. It was not just a case of Larry Walker.

Bill Stoneman, Vice-President of baseball operations and Kevin Malone, Director of player personnel, had to make difficult decisions about a number of key players. The list included pitchers Pedro Martinez, Jeff Fassero, Ken Hill, and John Wetteland, catcher Darrin Fletcher, and outfielders Cliff Floyd, Moises Alou, and Marquis Grissom, as well as Larry Walker.

The Expos had only so much salary money and a lot of players to satisfy. Moreover, Walker's frequent criticism of Montreal management as "cheap" meant nobody would make a special effort to speak up for him.

Larry Walker's first major league contract in 1988 was for $62,500. In 1991, his breakout year as an Expo, he earned $185,000. Larry's salary had risen to $3 million in 1993, and in 1994, the Expos right fielder was earning $4.025 million. If Montreal wanted to keep him, they would have to offer a multi-year contract averaging five million dollars a year or more.

In the end, the Expos decided not to enter the bidding for Walker. They also unloaded Marquis Grissom to Atlanta, Ken Hill to St. Louis and John Wetteland to the Yankees. Larry says the Expos decision hurt him deeply.

"Maybe I would have opted for some other club but I was very disappointed that they didn't even try to keep me in Canada."

If the Expos weren't interested, the Colorado Rockies, an expansion franchise, in last place, and with a brand new stadium, had no hesitation in pursuing Walker.

On April 8, 1995, the Rockies announced Larry Walker had signed a four-year contract worth $22 million. Larry was now a rich man and the Rockies believed they had just bought one of the best hitters in baseball. They were not to be disappointed.

In the first game played at Denver's new Coors Field, Larry Walker hit three doubles and drove in three runs as the Rockies beat the Mets on opening day. Larry batted .306 for the season and reached new heights with 36 home runs and 101 runs batted in.

Larry Walker had reason to smile when he signed a $22-million contract with the Colorado Rockies. (Courtesy Colorado Rockies)

On the last day of the season, Walker had a double, a two-run home run and batted in three runs as the Rockies beat San Francisco to win the National League wild card and their first trip to the playoffs against Atlanta.

The Braves won the first two games in Denver, behind Greg Maddux and Tom Glavine. Walker hit a home run with two men on base off Glavine to tie the score at 3-3 in the second game but Atlanta scored four runs in the ninth to win 7-4. Manager Don Baylor moaned that the Rockies should have been leading 2-0 when they left for Atlanta but the bullpen had failed to save the lead in both games.

The Rockies roughed up John Smoltz in game three to win 7-5; but in game four, despite an early 3-0 lead and 10 hits off Greg Maddux, the Rockies lost 10-4. Colorado pitching simply wasn't up to the same standard as the batters.

Larry's first year in Denver was a success in every way. No other Canadian player had ever hit so many home runs in one year, and Larry's batting average and run production were only a hint of even greater things to come. Walker was generous with his time in making public appearances and he won community respect for a joint donation with the Rockies of $3,333,333 to children's organizations in British Columbia and Colorado.

Larry's second year in Colorado started off in spectacular fashion. He hit a home run his first time at bat and hit safely in 10 consecutive games, including home runs on three successive days. On May 21, Walker set a club record with a double, a triple and two home runs for 13 total bases and six runs batted in.

The next day, Larry set a National League record of six consecutive extra-base hits; adding two triples and a double to his total. His torrid hitting came to a sudden stop. On June 9, Larry slammed into the fence at Coors Field trying to catch a line drive by Jeff Blauser of the Braves.

Walker broke his collarbone and was out of action for two months. He returned to the lineup August 15 and hit four home runs in the next two weeks but on August 18 he suffered a left shoulder spasm that limited him to just 14 times at bat in the final month. For the year, he played 83 games, slightly more than half a season, and hit 18 home runs, with 58 runs batted in and an average of .276.

Ballplayers dream of having a season like Larry Walker had in 1997. His first hit of the year was a home run in Cincinnati, April 2. He hit home runs in each of the next two games. On April 5 at Olympic Stadium in Montreal, Larry hit three consecutive home runs in the fourth, sixth and seventh innings against three different pitchers. He tied the league record for home runs in April with 11 and all season long he batted at a phenomenal pace.

In 1997, Larry Walker became the first Canadian to hit more than 40 home runs and was named Most Valuable Player in the National League. (Courtesy Colorado Rockies)

Walker was over .400 until July 19 and ended the season with 208 hits, 49 home runs and 130 runs batted in. It was the most outstanding batting performance in Canadian baseball history, and Larry Walker made sure everybody knew he was a proud Canadian.

During the 1997 season, when he talked to reporters in the Rockies' dressing room, Larry Walker always wore a white T-shirt with the name Canada in black letters, and a red maple leaf flag over the final "a".

Larry was promoting Canada and encouraging Canadian kids to follow his lead. "I hope I do a lot of good things for this country," Larry said. "I want to open a lot of eyes for some young kids. If they work hard and listen to their coaches, they could have a career in sports too."

If he had hit 50 home runs in 1997, Walker would have joined a very exclusive club. Larry hit his 49th home run on the last Friday of the season but he was unable to play in the final two games. Larry's right elbow was so sore, he could not swing a bat. After the season he had surgery to remove bone chips. If Larry had hit a 50th home run, he would have joined Babe Ruth and Hack Wilson as the only players in history with 200 hits and 50 home runs in the same season.

Christmas came early for Larry Walker in 1997. On November 13, the Baseball Writers of America named Larry as the National League's Most Valuable Player. He received 22 of a possible 28 first-place votes. Walker's 409 total bases were the highest in the major leagues in almost 50 years. The last man to hit for more total bases was Stan Musial, with 429 in 1948.

Neil Munro, author of the Canadian Players Encyclopedia, says Larry Walker's performance in 1997 may have been the greatest single season by any player in National League history. Honus Wagner, Rogers Hornsby, Chuck Klein, Hack Wilson, Joe Medwick, Stan Musial and Hank Aaron are the only others whose single season dominance approached Larry Walker's 1997 numbers; and all of them are in the Hall of Fame.

Larry's 33 stolen bases made him only the third player ever with 40 home runs, 200 hits and 30 stolen bases in the same season. In the field, Walker made just two errors all year, and he set a club record by playing 128 consecutive games without an error.

A play he made in Cincinnati on August 20, was symbolic of Walker's incredible year. Larry jumped above and reached beyond the eight-foot fence to take a home run away from Jon Nunnally. Then, he threw to first base to complete a double play. The picture on the cover of this book shows that amazing catch.

How do you top an MVP season? In 1998, Larry Walker became the first Canadian in the 20th century to win a batting championship. He hit safely in 49 of the Rockies' first 56 games but elbow soreness held him to only one home run in April. In May, Larry hit a pinch-hit grand slam home run at Philadelphia and had a 20-game hitting streak. A sprained finger and back spasms kept Walker out of the lineup at times but he played in 130 games.

Larry took the batting lead September 2 in Milwaukee and batted over .500 for the month of September to win the title with an average of .363.

The only other Canadian to win a batting championship was "Tip" O'Neill of Woodstock, Ontario, who played for the St. Louis Browns in 1887.

After signing a six-year contract extension, Larry Walker missed opening day for the first time in 11 years. Larry strained a muscle on the right side of his rib cage in the last week of March 1999. When he returned to the lineup April 14th, Walker began a torrid hitting streak with a double in his first time at bat. He hit safely in 26 of his next 27 games, including a career-high 21 consecutive games from April 25 to May 21.

Larry hit three home runs in one game, and drove in eight runs in another game. He hit safely in 18 consecutive games, including home runs in five successive games.

By mid-September, Walker was so far ahead of his nearest batting rival that he played his last game September 24th and underwent arthroscopic knee surgery. In Larry's words, "They just go in and clean them out; kind of like your brake pads need changing. I need to get some dust out of my knees."

Larry won his second straight batting championship with an average of .379. He also had the best on-base percentage, .459 and the highest slugging average, .710.

Walker was the first National League player to lead in all three averages since Stan Musial in 1948 and the first in the major leagues since George Brett of Kansas City in 1980.

After playing nearly 140 games in each of the three previous seasons, Larry played in only 87 games in 2000. He was on the disabled list twice with an irritated right elbow, and in early September, he had surgery to remove bone spurs from the elbow.

Despite the nagging injuries, Walker set new records. In April, at Arizona, Larry singled against Brian Anderson for his 1,448th hit, surpassing Jeff Heath as the all-time leader among Canadian-born players.

On August 13, 2000, in Montreal, the Canadian Baseball Hall of Fame presented Larry Walker with a shield recognizing him as the all-time Canadian champion in base hits, doubles, home runs, runs scored and runs batted in. The Hall of Fame wanted to make a pre-game presentation at home plate, but lingering bitterness between Walker and the Expos management doomed the ceremony to a space under the grandstand, near the umpires' dressing room.

Rebounding from elbow surgery, Larry Walker won his third batting championship in 2001 with a .350 average. He hit 38 home runs and had 123 runs batted in while playing in 142 games. He won his sixth gold glove, hit his 300th home run and stole his 200th base.

Asked how a .260 hitter turned into a three-time batting champion, Walker replied, "I think you learn as a hitter. If a pitcher pitches you away, you hit the ball the other way. Little things like taking a base on balls, things that help your average. I've matured over the last few years."

Maturing also meant getting older. As he turned 35, Walker told me, "I'd like to play till I'm 40, but I've had some surgery and some broken bones. I still want to play and I still want to win. It all comes down to how I am physically."

Larry played 136 games in 2002. He batted .338 with 26 home runs and 104 runs batted in but he angered some of the Rockies by having laser eye surgery before the end of the season.

He missed three of the team's final six games while trying to adjust to playing without contact lenses. Walker said he scheduled the surgery because the Rockies had been eliminated from the playoffs. Larry's age, 36, his $12.6 million salary and a feeling he was not showing a good example by missing games may have prompted the Rockies to try to trade him after the 2002 season.

It turned out to be a messy business. The Rockies negotiated a deal to send Walker to the Arizona Diamondbacks for third baseman Matt Williams but the deal blew up when first Williams, and then Walker, refused to approve the trade. Larry stayed in Colorado but his days in Denver were numbered and his contribution in 2003 was well below standard.

After six straight years in the upper atmosphere of batting, Walker dropped to .284, with a similar power decline to 16 home runs and 79 runs batted in. In the three previous seasons, Walker had come to bat with runners in scoring position, either second or third base, an average of 125 times per season and had batted .360, .374 and .391 respectively in those situations. In 2003, he came to bat 134 times with runners in scoring position and made 41 hits for an average of .306, a significant drop in performance.

Part of the reason may have been Walker's position in the batting order. In the previous five seasons, Larry had batted third most of the time and either third or fourth 94% of the time; but in 2003 he batted fifth in 105 of the 131 games he started in right field.

Larry admitted that his physical condition may have been a factor. He hurt his left shoulder during the first week of the season diving for a fly ball, and his knee also bothered him.

"Toward the end of the season, I let myself go," Walker said. He was overweight and probably out of shape when he ended the season at about 255 pounds.

At 37, with two years left of his contract, Larry had to decide whether the time had come to retire.

Larry Walker hit 259 home runs while playing for Colorado. (Colorado Rockies)

"I was miserable," Larry told Troy Renck of the Denver Post. "I was doing badly. The team was struggling. Retirement was close," said Walker. "My wife and I talked about it." Larry decided to try again. He had surgery on his shoulder and knee and did regular exercises and weight-lifting throughout the winter. When he reported for spring training, he was lighter and slimmer and ready to work hard.

Another injury slowed Larry's return. He strained a groin muscle running out a hit in March and was on the disabled list when the season began. Walker was starting his 15th year as a full-time major league player. He had never played for a pennant winner; never played in the World Series and the prospects of doing so in the near future weren't good.

Larry didn't play his first game in 2004 until June 22 at Milwaukee. He hit a double his first time at bat. Three days later, at Jacobs Field in Cleveland, Walker had a perfect day at the plate and showed all of his old-time power. Larry blasted three home runs. He also had a double and two walks. Walker's third home run, with a man on base, won the game in the 10th inning.

On June 30 at Denver, Larry doubled in the fourth inning for the 2,000th hit of his career, the first Canadian ever to reach that plateau. After 38 games, on August 5, 2004, Walker appeared fully recovered. He was batting .324 and was equally successful at home and away. He was hitting .328 in Denver and .317 in all other parks.

Walker was doing well, but the Rockies were sinking fast. The Rockies were in fourth place, 17fi games behind the Dodgers. August 6 was a turning point. The Rockies announced they had traded Larry Walker to the St. Louis Cardinals for three minor-league pitchers. General Manager Dan O'Dowd said the trade was made, in part, to give Walker a chance to get to the World Series. "Larry has had a great career and has accomplished so much in a Rockies uniform," said O'Dowd. "It really is bittersweet. This is the best opportunity to put him somewhere with a chance to win." Overnight, Larry Walker went from fourth place to first place. His new team, the Cardinals, was leading the Central Division with the best record in baseball.

LARRY WALKER

THE ST. LOUIS CARDINALS
*In the World Series spotlight,
and shining.*

Meet Me in St. Louis

Larry Walker began his Cardinal career at Busch Stadium, on August 7, as a pinch-hitter in a tie game with the New York Mets. He struck out in the bottom of the seventh inning with runners on first and second base. Larry stayed in the game and the score was still tied in the ninth inning. Walker came to bat with two on and two out. He was walked intentionally to load the bases. The next batter, Yadier Molina, singled to drive in the winning run.

Larry Walker's first hit as a Cardinal was a double off Al Leiter of the Mets August 8. He hit his first St. Louis home run August 12 in Florida against A.J. Burnett of the Marlins.

Larry played 44 games for the Cardinals. He batted .280 and had 11 home runs and 27 runs batted in for St. Louis. His combined totals for the season were a batting average of .298, with 17 home runs and 47 runs batted in. The best was still to come.

October took on a new meaning as a member of the St. Louis Cardinals. For the first time since 1995, Larry was in the playoffs. The first game of the division series against Los Angeles was in St. Louis, Tuesday afternoon October 5. Woody Williams started for the Cardinals against Odalis Perez of the Dodgers. In the third inning, with two out Walker hit a towering home run to make the score 2-0. In the seventh inning, Larry hit his second home run off Giovanni Carrara. St. Louis won the opener 8-2.

The Cardinals won the second game 8-3 against Jeff Weaver. Walker was hit by a pitch and hit a double. In the third game at Los Angeles, Jose Lima pitched a five-hit shutout and struck out Walker twice as the Dodgers won 4-0. Larry broke out in the fourth game. He had two hits and two walks, stole a base and scored three runs as St. Louis won 6-2 to wrap up the series.

The League Championship Series against Houston began in St. Louis October 13. Craig Biggio led off with a single and Carlos Beltran followed with a home run to put Houston into a quick lead. In the bottom of the first, Walker tripled to centre field and Pujols tied the score with a home run. The teams were tied 4-4 after five innings but the Cardinals scored six runs in the sixth and won 10-7. Larry had three hits and scored three runs.

In the second game, Houston took a 3-0 lead but St. Louis scored four in the fifth inning on a pair of two-run home runs by Walker and Scott Rolen. The Cardinals won 6-4.

The next three games were played in Houston and the Astros won them all. Roger Clemens won the third game 5-2, despite home runs by Walker and Jim Edmonds. In game four, Carlos Beltran broke a 5-5 tie with his fourth home run of the series.

Larry Walker went from fourth place to first place when he joined the St. Louis Cardinals in 2004. (Canadian Baseball Hall of Fame)

Game five was a brilliant pitching duel between Woody Williams and Brendan Backe. Each man allowed just one hit. In the bottom of the ninth, the game was still scoreless. With one out and two on, Jeff Kent hit a home run against Jason Isringhausen to send the Astros to St. Louis with a 3-2 lead in the series. Game six went into extra innings. In the 12th, Albert Pujols led off with a single and Jim Edmonds blasted a home run to tie the series at three games each.

Roger Clemens and Jeff Suppan were the starting pitchers for the final game at Busch Stadium. Each pitched six innings. Clemens gave up a home run to Scott Rolen and left the game trailing 4-2. Larry Walker drove in the final run with an eighth inning single. St. Louis won 5-2 and advanced to the World Series.

The Boston Red Sox won the American League championship by sweeping four in a row from the New York Yankees after losing the first three games. Boston was determined to erase the "Curse of the Bambino" which had haunted them ever since they won the World Series in 1918 and then sold "Babe" Ruth to the Yankees. The Red Sox had spent the past 86 years in the wilderness.

The 2004 World Series opened at Fenway Park, October 23. The game was a free-swinging slugfest with 24 hits. Larry Walker homered for St. Louis; David Ortiz and Mark Bellhorn homered for Boston. The Red Sox scored twice in the bottom of the eighth to win 11-9.

Boston won the second game 6-2. Curt Schilling allowed one run in six innings and struck out Larry Walker twice.

Pedro Martinez pitched the third game for Boston and allowed just three hits and no runs in seven innings. Larry Walker hit a home run off Keith Foulke for the Cardinals' only run.

The Red Sox finally put the "Babe" to rest October 27, 2004, in St. Louis behind the pitching of Derek Lowe, who gave up just three hits. Boston won 3-0 to complete an incredible eight-game sweep after losing the first three games in the league championship series.

Larry Walker finally got to play in the World Series. He had five hits in 14 times at bat, for a .357 average including two home runs and three runs batted in, but it was all swept aside by an irresistible Boston tidal wave.

The 2005 season was something of an anti-climax for Larry Walker. After losing to Boston, the Cardinals were anxious for another chance at the World Series. Walker had three hits on opening day at Houston, including a home run. Larry had hit streaks of six games and five games between April 23 and May 12 but a herniated disk in his neck kept him uncomfortable or in pain for most of the season.

Larry Walker belts a home run against Roger Clemens of the Houston Astros, October 16, 2004. (AP Photo by Sue Ogrocki)

Walker had periodic cortisone shots but missed a month between July 22 and August 20. He played exactly 100 games and hit 15 home runs with 52 runs batted in and a batting average of .289. In the playoffs, he had three hits in 28 at-bats. Roy Oswalt, who was on the mound when Houston lost the seventh game in 2004, won two games in the 2005 championship series, including the deciding game in St. Louis.

Walker doubled against Oswalt in the sixth inning of the final game.

Larry's last time at bat in baseball was against Dan Wheeler, leading off the ninth inning. He took a called third strike. Moments later, Yadier Molina flied to right field and the Cardinals' dream of World Series revenge was ended. Larry Walker said he knew right away that his career was over. "The emotions were so high. I couldn't even breathe," he told the St. Louis Post-Dispatch. "I'm not coming back."

Injuries Take Their Toll!

Terry Puhl, the graceful outfielder from Melville, Saskatchewan, who played 14 seasons with the Houston Astros, said, "Injuries happen to guys who stay around for a lot of years. The fields take a toll; the schedule takes a toll."

That was certainly true of Larry Walker. A list of Larry's injuries during his baseball career might almost serve as a catalogue of optional courses at medical school. Injuries to the knee, shoulder, ankle and elbow and many parts in between were the cause of missed games.

During 16 years in the big leagues, Larry Walker missed the equivalent of more than three full seasons: a total of 536 regular season games. In 1996, 2000 and 2004, when he played 83, 87 and 82 games, respectively, Larry essentially missed half of each season. Walker never played an entire season.

The only time Walker played close to a full season was in 1997. That year, he played 153 of 162 games for Colorado. Larry batted .366, led the league with 49 home runs and was chosen the Most Valuable Player in the National League. What more records might Larry Walker have broken if he had played those missed games?

In June 2005, Walker admitted his age and numerous surgeries were forcing him to consider retirement. "I've had eight surgeries and a reconstructed knee," he said. "I'm just trying to make it through this year and contribute as much as I can." To the end, Larry Walker played the game the only way he knew - full speed ahead.

Walker in Good Company in Canada's Sports Hall of Fame

In October 2007, two years after his retirement from baseball, Larry Walker was inducted into Canada's Sports Hall of Fame. At the ceremony in Toronto, Larry was joined by five other great Canadian athletes and two builders.

The other athletes inducted into Canada's Sports Hall of Fame that night were:

- **Cassie Campbell**, captain of two Olympic Champion hockey teams, the first Canadian woman hockey player in the Hall of Fame;

- **Beckie Scott**, who won an Olympic gold medal in cross-country skiing in the 2006 Games in Italy;

- New York Islanders star **Mike Bossy**, who set an NHL record by scoring at least 50 goals in nine consecutive seasons;

- Olympic wrestler **Daniel Igali**, a refugee from Nigeria, who became a Canadian and won a gold medal at the 2000 Games in Sydney;

- Quarterback **Doug Flutie**, six-time Most Valuable Player in the Canadian Football League. Flutie was the first non-Canadian to be inducted into Canada's Sports Hall of Fame. Doug Flutie said, "I never enjoyed myself as much as when I played in the CFL."

The Sports Hall of Fame inducted two pioneers in 2007:

- The late **Sam Jacks** invented the game of ringette in 1963 while he was director of parks and recreation in North Bay, Ontario;

- **Robert Steadward**, of Eston, Saskatchewan, was the driving force in the Paralympic movement for athletes with disabilities.

Larry Walker, who started out as a hockey goaltender, told a news conference, "Hockey was always in my blood. I have a baseball card called 'Idols,' and it asks 'Who was your idol growing up?' My card says Mike Bossy."

Larry Walker was the ninth baseball player or executive inducted into Canada's Sports Hall of Fame. In chronological order of induction, the other baseball members and their birthplaces are:

- **George Gibson**, London, Ontario, catcher and manager of the Pittsburgh Pirates;

- **Phil Marchildon**, Penetanguishene, Ontario, 1940s pitching star of the Philadelphia Athletics;

- Pitcher **Ferguson Jenkins**, Chatham, Ontario, the only Canadian in the Baseball Hall of Fame at Cooperstown, New York;

- **Ron Taylor**, Toronto, Ontario, pitched in four World Series games and did not allow a hit or a run;

- **James "Tip" O'Neill**, Woodstock, Ontario, 19th-century batting champion with the Saint Louis Browns;

- **John Hiller**, Toronto, Ontario, set two major league records as a relief pitcher for the Detroit Tigers;

- **Claude Raymond**, St. Jean, Quebec, outstanding relief pitcher with Houston, Atlanta and the Montreal Expos;

- **Paul Beeston**, Welland, Ontario, former President of the Toronto Blue Jays, and major league baseball executive.

Six new members were inducted into Canada's Sports Hall of Fame in 2007. From left: Cassie Campbell, Beckie Scott, Mike Bossy, Daniel Igali, Larry Walker, and Doug Flutie. (The Canadian Press - Frank Gunn)

Larry Walker's Home Runs

Larry Walker hit a total of 390 home runs during a major league career that lasted 16 years. His first home run, on April 20, 1990, was a towering shot off Ron Darling of the New York Mets that travelled an estimated 435 feet to the scoreboard at Shea Stadium.

Walker hit another 389 home runs, including five home runs in league championship playoffs and two home runs in the World Series. His best year was 1997 when he hit 49 home runs but had to miss the last two games of the season because of an elbow injury.

During his career, Larry Walker hit home runs off 267 different pitchers of 27 teams in the National and American Leagues. Walker hit home runs against every one of the 16 National League teams and he hit home runs against 11 of the 12 American League teams that he played against. Larry never played against the Chicago White Sox or Baltimore Orioles. In six games against Detroit, Walker had seven hits but no home runs.

The details of when, where, and against whom Larry Walker hit all those home runs are listed, year by year, in the following pages.

Larry Walker hitting against the New York Mets. (Montreal Expos)

Note: RH = right-hand pitcher; LH = left-hand pitcher.

Larry Walker's Home Runs 1989

Walker played 20 games in 1989. He did not hit any home runs.

Larry Walker's Home Runs 1990

April

1. April 20 at New York, Ron Darling, 2nd inn., 0-on, RH.

May

2. May 13 at San Diego, Calvin Schiraldi, 4th inn., 2-on,RH.
3. May 20 at San Francisco, John Burkett, 2nd inn., 0-on, RH

June

4. June 11 at Philadelphia, Darrel Akerfelds, 9th inn., 0-on, RH.
5. June 22 vs. Pittsburgh, Walt Terrell, 4th inn., 0-on, RH.
6. June 27 at Chicago, Jeff Pico, 8th inn., 0-on, RH.
7. June 29 vs. Atlanta, Tom Glavine, 8th inn., 0-on, LH.
8. June 30 vs. Atlanta, Charlie Leibrandt, 5th inn., 0-on, LH.

July

9. July 6 vs. Houston, Danny Darwin, 4th inn., 0-on, RH.
10. July 7 vs. Houston, Jim Deshaies, 3rd inn., 0-on, LH.
11. July 16 at Cincinnati, Chris Hammond, 2nd inn., 0-on, LH.

August

12. Aug. 3 at Chicago, Mike Harkey, 6th inn., 1-on, RH.
13. Aug. 4 at Chicago, Bill Long, 9th inn., 0-on, RH.
14. Aug. 21 at San Francisco, John Burkett, 6th inn., 1-on, RH.
15. Aug. 26 vs. San Diego, Bruce Hurst, 8th inn., 2-on, LH.
16. Aug. 29 vs. San Francisco, Kelly Downs, 1st inn., 1-on, RH.

September

17. Sep. 5 at St. Louis, Jose DeLeon, 5th inn., 1-on, RH.
18. Sept. 14 vs. Pittsburgh, Neal Heaton, 8th inn., 1-on, LH.

October

19. Oct. 3 vs. St. Louis, Ken Hill, 2nd inn., 0-on, RH.

Larry Walker's Home Runs 1991

May
1. May 6 vs. San Francisco, Rod Beck, 7th inn., 0-on, RH.
2. May 10 at San Diego, Craig Lefferts, 8th inn., 1-on, LH.
3. May 10 at San Diego, Wes Gardner, 10th inn., 1-on, RH.
4. May 17 at San Francisco, Mike LaCoss, 9th inn., 1-on, LH.

June
5. June 9 at Atlanta, Tom Glavine, 2nd inn., 2-on, LH.
6. June 22 at Cincinnati, Jack Armstrong, 5th inn., 1-on, RH.

July
7. July 15 vs. San Diego, Andy Benes, 3rd inn., 1-on, RH.
8. July 21 vs. San Francisco, Jeff Brantley, 9th inn., 0-on, RH.
9. July 29 at San Francisco, John Burkett, 2nd inn., 1-on, RH.

August
10. Aug. 2 vs. Philadelphia, Danny Cox, 4th inn., 0-on, RH.
11. Aug. 11 at Philadelphia, Bruce Ruffin, 6th inn., 1-on, LH.
12. Aug. 17 vs. St. Louis, Jose DeLeon, 4th inn., 0-on, RH.
13. Aug. 26 at Atlanta, Tony Castillo, 5th inn., 1-on, LH.

September
14. Sept. 12 at Philadelphia, Mike Hartley, 7th inn., 0-on, RH.
15. Sept. 15 at Chicago, Rick Sutcliffe, 2nd inn., 0-on, RH.
16. Sept. 17 at New York, Anthony Young, 4th inn., 0-on, RH.

Larry Walker's Home Runs 1992

April
1. April 14 vs. St. Louis, Donovan Osborne, 2nd inn., 0-on, LH.
2. April 15 vs. St. Louis, Cris Carpenter, 7th inn., 0-on, RH.
3. April 29 at San Diego, Greg Harris, 6th inn., 0-on, RH.
4. April 29 at San Diego, Greg Harris, 9th inn., 0-on, RH.
5. April 30 at San Diego, Andy Benes, 6th inn., 1-on, RH.

May
6. May 5 vs. San Diego, Greg Harris, 3rd inn., 0-on, RH.
7. May 16 at Atlanta, Alejandro Pena, 8th inn., 0-on, RH.
8. May 23 vs. Atlanta, Mike Stanton, 8th inn., 0-on, LH.
9. May 26 vs. Houston, Darryl Kile, 3rd inn., 1-on, RH.

June

10. June 7 vs. Chicago, Mike Morgan, 6th inn., 0-on, RH.
11. June 13 at Chicago, Frank Castillo, 6th inn., 1-on, RH.
12. June 28 vs. Pittsburgh, Randy Tomlin, 2nd inn., 0-on, LH.
13. June 28 vs. Pittsburgh, Denny Neagle, 8th inn., 1-on, LH.
14. June 30 at Philadelphia, Wally Ritchie, 6th inn., 0-on, LH.

July

15. July 7 at Los Angeles, Jim Gott, 8th inn., 1-on, RH.
16. July 9 at San Francisco, Francisco Olivares, 2nd inn., 0-on, RH.
17. July 21 vs. San Francisco, Bud Black, 3rd inn., 1-on, LH.
18. July 30 vs. Philadelphia, Greg Matthews, 1st inn., 1-on, LH.

August

19. Aug. 26 at Atlanta, Steve Avery, 5th inn., 0-on, LH.
20. Aug. 31 at Cincinnati, Tom Bolton, 4th inn., 1-on, LH.

September

21. Sept. 8 vs. St. Louis, Bob McClure, 7th inn., 2-on, LH.
22. Sept. 13 vs. New York, Anthony Young, 9th inn., 2-on, RH.
23. Sept. 25 vs. Chicago, Heathcliff Slocum, 10th inn., 0-on, RH.

....

Larry Walker's Home Runs 1993

April

1. April 5 at Cincinnati, Rob Dibble, 9th inn., 0-on, RH.
2. April 8 at Cincinnati, Tim Belcher, 2nd inn., 0-on, RH.
3. April 20 vs. Los Angeles, Tom Candiotti, 3rd inn., 1-on, RH.
4. April 24 vs. San Francisco, Dave Burba, 5th inn., 0-on, RH.
5. April 25 vs. San Francisco, Bill Swift, 2nd inn., 0-on, RH.

May

6. May 9 at Pittsburgh, Tim Wakefield, 6th inn., 0-on, RH.
7. May 13 vs. Florida, Jack Armstrong, 6th inn., 0-on, RH.

June

8. June 23 at New York, Frank Tanana, 6th inn., 1-on, LH.
9. June 29 vs. Pittsburgh, Dave Otto, 7th inn., 0-on, LH.
10. June 30 vs. Pittsburgh, Denny Neagle, 3rd inn., 1-on, LH.

July

11. July 7 vs. San Francisco, Greg Brummett, 2nd inn., 0-on, RH.
12. July 11 vs. San Diego, Mark Davis, 6th inn., 0-on, LH.
13. July 22 at San Diego, Andy Benes, 4th inn., 1-on, RH.

August

14. Aug. 4 vs. New York, Sid Fernandez, 3rd inn., 0-on, LH.
15. Aug. 8 at Atlanta, Steve Avery, 7th inn., 0-on, LH.
16. Aug. 21 at Cincinnati, John Roper, 1st inn., 3-on, RH.

September

17. Sept. 1 at Colorado, Kent Bottenfield, 1st inn., 1-on, RH.
18. Sept. 6 vs. Colorado, Kent Bottenfield, 2nd inn., 0-on, RH.
19. Sept. 8 vs. Colorado, Armando Reynoso, 1st inn., 1-on, RH.
20. Sept. 11 vs. Cincinnati, Scott Ruskin, 8th inn., 0-on, LH.
21. Sept. 16 at St. Louis, Bob Tewksbury, 3rd inn., 0-on, RH.

October

22. Oct. 1 vs. Pittsburgh, Paul Wagner, 6th inn., 0-on, RH.

....

Larry Walker's Home Runs 1994

April

1. April 5 at Houston, Doug Drabek, 6th inn., 1-on, RH.
2. April 12 vs. Cincinnati, Tim Pugh, 6th inn., 0-on, RH.
3. April 22 at Los Angeles, Tom Candiotti, 2nd inn., 0-on, RH.

May

4. May 9 vs. New York, Frank Seminara, 3rd inn., 1-on, RH.
5. May 14 vs. St. Louis, John Habyan, 8th inn., 1-on, RH.
6. May 29 vs. Colorado, Bruce Ruffin, 10th inn., 0-on, LH.

June

7. June 1 at Cincinnati, Pete Schourek, 9th inn., 0-on, LH.
8. June 4 at Chicago, Willie Banks, 1st inn., 1-on, RH.
9. June 13 vs. Pittsburgh, Rick White, 6th inn., 2-on, RH.
10. June 20 at St. Louis, Rob Murphy, 7th inn., 0-on, LH.
11. June 22 at St. Louis, Bob Tewksbury, 1st inn., 2-on, RH.
12. June 30 at San Francisco, Brad Brink, 6th inn., 0-on, RH.

July

13. July 1 at San Francisco, John Burkett, 3rd inn., 2-on, RH.
14. July 3 at San Francisco, Mark Portugal, 5th inn., 2-on, RH.
15. July 4 at Los Angeles, Omar Daal, 8th inn., 0-on, LH.
16. July 9 at San Diego, Scott Sanders, 6th inn., 1-on, RH.

August

17. Aug. 4 vs. St. Louis, Bob Tewksbury, 7th inn., 0-on, RH.
18. Aug. 4 vs. St. Louis, Bob Tewksbury, 9th inn., 1-on, RH.
19. Aug. 9 at Pittsburgh, Jon Lieber, 6th inn., 0-on, RH

PLAYERS' STRIKE AND OWNER'S LOCK-OUT ENDED SEASON

· ·

Larry Walker's Home Runs 1995
(His first year with the Colorado Rockies)

April

No home runs. Did not play first game until April 26.

May

1. May 7 vs. Los Angeles, Hideo Nomo, 5th inn., 0-on, 0-out, RH.
2. May 10 vs. San Francisco, Mark Leiter, 3rd inn., 1-on, 2-out, RH.
3. May 11 vs. San Francisco, Terry Mulholland, 1st inn., 2-on, 0-out, LH.
4. May 12 at Miami, Yorkis Perez, 8th inn., 0-on, 1-out, LH.
5. May 13 at Miami, Bobby Witt, 6th inn., 1-on, 2-out, RH.
6. May 18 at Atlanta, Greg McMichael, 8th inn., 0-on, 0-out, RH.
7. May 22 vs. Chicago, Jaime Navarro, 3rd inn., 2-on, 1-out, RH.
8. May 23 vs. Chicago, Kevin Foster, 5th inn., 0-on, 0-out, RH.
9. May 31 at St. Louis, Mark Petkovsek, 6th inn., 0-on, 0-out, RH.

June

10. June 3 vs. Pittsburgh, Jon Lieber, 2nd inn.. 0-on, 0-out, RH.
11. June 3 vs. Pittsburgh, Jon Lieber, 4th inn., 0-on, 0-out, RH.
12. June 4 vs. Pittsburgh, Mike Dyer, 7th inn., 0-on, 1-out, RH.
13. June 11 at Chicago, Steve Trachsel, 2nd inn., 0-on, 0-out, LH.
14. June 12 vs. Cincinnati, Michael Jackson, 7th inn., 0-on, 0-out, RH.
15. June 14 vs. Cincinnati, Pete Schourek, 5th inn., 0-on, 2-out, LH.
16. June 20 vs. Florida, Terry Matthews, 6th inn., 0-on, 2-out, RH
17. June 25 at San Diego, Scott Sanders, 1st inn., 1-on, 2-out, RH.

July

18. July 3 vs. Houston, Jim Dougherty, 8th inn., 0-on, 2-out, RH.
19. July 7 vs. Montreal, Gabe White, 2nd inn., 1-on, 1-out, LH.
20. July 9 vs. Montreal, Pedro Martinez, 6th inn., 0-on, 1-out, RH
21. July 18 vs. Philadelphia, Curt Schilling, 4th inn., 0-on, 1-out, RH.
22. July 18 vs. Philadelphia, Curt Schilling, 6th inn., 1-on, 1-out, RH.
23. July 28 at Montreal, Ugueth Urbina, 3rd inn., 1-on, 0-out, RH.

August

24. Aug. 2 vs. Los Angeles, Pedro Astacio, 9th inn., 0-on, 2-out, RH.
25. Aug. 3 vs. Los Angeles, Ramon Martinez, 3rd inn., 0-on, 1-out, RH.
26. Aug. 4 vs. San Diego, Fernando Valenzuela, 3rd inn., 0-on, 2-out, LH.
27. Aug. 12 at Atlanta, Matt Murray, 7th inn., 2-on, 0-out, RH.
28. Aug. 24 vs. Pittsburgh, Jason Christiansen, 7th inn., 2-on, 0-out, LH.
29. Aug. 30 at Pittsburgh, John Ericks, 2nd inn., 0-on, 0-out, RH.

September

30. Sept. 11 vs. Atlanta, Brad Clontz, 8th inn., 0-on, 2-out, RH.
31. Sept. 16 vs. Florida, Willie Banks, 3rd inn., 1-on, 2-out, RH.
32. Sept. 18 at San Diego, Joey Hamilton, 5th inn., 0-on, 1-out, RH.
33. Sept. 26 at Los Angeles, Tom Candiotti, 4th inn., 0-on, 1-out, RH.
34. Sept. 26 at Los Angeles, Tom Candiotti, 6th inn., 1-on, 0-out, RH.
35. Sept. 30 vs. San Francisco, Sergio Valdez, 7th inn., 0-on, 2-out, RH.

October

36. Oct. 1 vs. San Francisco, Joe Rosselli, 3rd inn., 1-on, 1-out, LH.
A NEW CANADIAN RECORD: 36 HOME RUNS

Post-season

Division Series
1. Oct. 4 vs. Atlanta, Tom Glavine, 6th inn., 2-on, 1-out, LH.

....

Larry Walker's Home Runs 1996

April

1. Apr. 2 at Philadelphia, Sid Fernandez, 1st inn., 1-on, 2-out, LH.
2. Apr. 11 vs. New York, Dave Mlicki, 1st inn., 2-on, 0-out, RH.
3. Apr. 12 vs. New York, Mark Clark, 6th inn., 1-on, 2-out, RH.
4. Apr. 14 vs. New York, Pete Harnisch, 2nd inn., 0-on, 0-out, RH.
5. Apr. 19 at New York, Pete Harnisch, 5th inn., 0-on, 2-out, RH.
6. Apr. 24 vs. Philadelphia, Rich Hunter, 3rd inn., 0-on, 2-out, RH.

May

7. May 3 vs. Florida, Matt Mantei, 7th inn., 1-on, 0-out, RH.
8. May 4 vs. Florida, Chris Hammond, 1st inn., 1-on, 0-out, LH.
9. May 18 vs. St. Louis, Mike Morgan, 6th inn., 0-on, 0-out, RH.
10. May 21 vs. Pittsburgh, Matt Ruebel, 1st inn., 1-on, 2-out, LH.
11. May 21 vs. Pittsburgh, Jason Christiansen, 7th inn., 1-on, 2-out, RH.
12. May 27 at St. Louis, Todd Stottlemyre, 1st inn., 0-on, 1-out, RH.

June

13. June 8 vs. Atlanta, Tom Glavine, 2nd inn., 0-on, 0-out, LH.
14. June 8 vs. Atlanta, Brad Clontz, 6th inn., 0-on, 2-out, RH.
June 9-30, did not play; on disabled list with broken clavicle.

July

Did not play; on disabled list with broken clavicle.

August

Aug. 1-14, did not play; on disabled list with broken clavicle.
15. Aug. 16 at Cincinnati, Hector Carrasco, 9th inn., 0-on, 0-out, RH.
16. Aug. 17 at Cincinnati, Giovanni Carrara, 3rd inn., 1-on, 1-out, RH.
17. Aug. 19 at Cincinnati, Scott Service, 3rd inn., 0-on, 1-out, RH.
18. Aug. 25 vs. Pittsburgh, Dan Miceli, 4th inn., 1-on, 2-out, RH.

· ·

Larry Walker's Home Runs 1997

April

(Tied National League record for home runs in April (11).
1. Apr. 2 at Cincinnati, Dave Burba, 2nd inn., 0-on, 0-out, RH.
2. Apr. 3 at Cincinnati, Stan Belinda, 7th inn., 0-on, 0-out, RH.
3. Apr. 4 at Montreal, Anthony Telford, 6th inn., 0-on, 0-out, RH.
4. Apr. 5 at Montreal, Anthony Telford, 4th inn., 0-on, 2-out, RH.
5. Apr. 5 at Montreal, Omar Daal, 6th inn., 0-on, 2-out, LH.
6. Apr. 5 at Montreal, Dave Veres, 7th inn., 0-on, 2-out, RH.
7. Apr. 12 vs. Montreal, Jim Bullinger, 2nd inn., 1-on, 1 out, RH.
8. Apr. 15 at Chicago, Kevin Foster, 1st inn., 1-on, 1 out RH.
9. Apr. 15 at Chicago, Larry Casian, 8th inn., 0-on, 1-out, LH.
10. Apr. 25 at St. Louis, Alan Benes, 5th inn., 0-on, 1-out, RH.
11. Apr. 30 vs. Chicago, Kevin Foster, 4th inn., 0-on, 0-out, RH.

May

12. May 8 vs. Pittsburgh, Esteban Loaiza, 1st inn., 1-on, 2-out, RH.
13. May 9 at Philadelphia, Calvin Maduro, 6th inn., 0-on, 0-out, RH.
14. May 16 at New York, Greg McMichael, 8th inn., 1-on, 1-out, RH.
15. May 29 at Florida, Alex Fernandez, 6th inn., 0-on, 1-out, RH.

June

16. June 5 vs. San Diego, Sterling Hitchcock, 1st inn., 0-on, 2-out, LH.
17. June 5 vs. San Diego, Terry Burrows, 11th inn., 1-on, 1-out, LH.
18. June 7 vs. Florida, Rick Helling, 1st inn., 0-on, 1-out, RH.
19. June 14 at Oakland, Carlos Reyes, 7th inn., 0-on, 0-out, RH.
20. June 15 at Oakland, Ariel Prieto, 3rd inn., 0-on, 0-out, RH.
21. June 21 at San Diego, Rich Batchelor, 9th inn., 0-on, 1-out, RH.
22. June 24 at Los Angeles, Pedro Astacio, 1st inn., 1-on, 1-out, RH.
23. June 28 vs. San Francisco, Dan Carlson, 4th inn., 0-on, 2-out, RH.
24. June 29 vs. San Francisco, Doug Henry, 9th inn., 0-on, 1-out, RH.
25. June 30 vs. Anaheim, Kevin Gross, 1st inn., 0-on, 1-out, RH.

July

26. July 10 vs. San Diego, Andy Ashby, 5th inn., 1-on, 1-out, RH.
27. July 17 at Atlanta, Greg Maddux, 1st inn., 0-on, 2-out, RH.
28. July 20 at Chicago Cubs, Kevin Foster, 5th inn., 1-on, 2-out, RH.
29. July 20 at Chicago Cubs, Mel Rojas, 9th inn., 1-on, 2-out, RH.
30. July 31 at Pittsburgh, Jason Schmidt, 6th inn., 0-on, 2-out, RH.

August

31. Aug. 1 at Pittsburgh, Esteban Loaiza, 1st inn., 0-on, 2-out, RH.
32. Aug. 1 at Pittsburgh, Ricardo Rincon, 9th inn., 0-on, 2-out, LH.
33. Aug. 2 at Pittsburgh, Francisco Cordova, 1st inn., 0-on, 2-out, RH.
34. Aug. 9 vs. Pittsburgh, Steve Cooke, 1st inn., 1-on, 1-out, LH.
35. Aug. 9 vs. Pittsburgh, Paul Wagner, 7th inn., 0-on, 2-out, RH.
36. Aug. 15 vs. New York Mets, Cory Lidle, 7th inn., 1-on, 2-out, RH.
37. Aug. 25 vs. Cincinnati, Scott Sullivan, 7th inn., 0-on, 1-out, RH.
38. Aug. 29 vs. Seattle, Ken Cloude, 3rd inn., 0-on, 1-out, RH.
39. Aug. 31 vs. Oakland, Mike Oquist, 3rd inn., 1-on, 2-out, RH.
40. Aug. 31 vs. Oakland, Mike Oquist, 5th inn., 0-on, 0-out, RH.

September

41. Sept. 2 at Anaheim, Jason Dickson, 3rd inn., 0-on, 1-out, RH.
42. Sept. 6 vs. St. Louis, Matt Morris, 8th inn., 1-on, 0-out, RH.
43. Sept. 10 vs. Houston, Ramon Garcia, 4th inn., 0-on, 0-out, RH.
44. Sept. 15 at Florida, Alex Fernandez, 7th inn., 0-on, 1-out, RH.
45. Sept. 16 at Florida, Antonio Alfonseca, 5th inn., 0-on, 0-out, RH.
46. Sept. 17 at San Diego, Andy Ashby, 1st inn., 2-on, 0-out, RH.
47. Sept. 17 at San Diego, Andy Ashby, 6th inn., 0-on, 0-out, RH.
48. Sept. 18 at San Diego, Tim Worrell, 8th inn., 1-on, 0-out, RH.
49. Sept. 26 vs. Los Angeles, Ismael Valdez, 4th inn., 0-on, 0-out, RH.

In 1997, Larry Walker was voted the National League's Most Valuable Player. He was the first Canadian-born player to win the MVP award.

Larry Walker's Home Runs 1998

April

1. Apr. 19 vs. Atlanta, Dennis Martinez, 2nd inn., 0-on, 0-out, RH.

May

2. May 2 at New York Mets, Masato Yoshii, 5th inn., 0-on, 2-out, RH.
3. May 5 at Philadelphia, Mike Grace, 5th inn., 0-on, 1-out, RH
4. May 6 at Philadelphia, Jerry Spradlin, 6th inn., 3-on, 2-out, RH.
5. May 20 at Atlanta, Kevin Millwood, 1st inn., 0-on, 2-out, RH.
6. May 29 vs. Houston, Doug Henry, 8th inn., 3-on, 2-out, RH.
7. May 30 vs. Houston, Pete Schourek, 1st inn., 1-on, 2-out, LH.

June

8. June 13 at Los Angeles, Darren Dreifort, 6th inn., 0-on, 0 out, RH.
9. June 14 at Los Angeles, Ramon Martinez, 3rd inn., 0-on, 2-out, RH.

July

10. July 13 vs. San Diego, Donne Wall, 7th inn., 0-on, 0-out, RH.
11. July 23 vs. Cincinnati, Pete Harnisch, 3rd inn., 1-on, 0-out, RH.
12. July 27 vs. Pittsburgh, Todd Van Poppel, 6th inn., 0-on, 1-out, RH.
13. July 28 vs. Pittsburgh, Jon Lieber, 2nd inn., 1-on, 1-out, RH.
14. July 28 vs. Pittsburgh, Jeff Tabaka, 5th inn., 0-on, 0-out, LH.

August

15. Aug. 7 vs. New York Mets, Rick Reed, 4th inn., 1-on, 1-out, RH.
16. Aug. 10 vs. Montreal, Carl Pavano, 6th inn., 0-on, 0-out, RH.
17. Aug. 16 vs. Philadelphia, Yorkis Perez, 8th inn., 0-on, 1-out, LH.
18. Aug. 28 vs. Chicago, Steve Trachsel, 1st inn., 0-on, 2-out, RH.
19. Aug. 29 vs. Chicago, Mark Clark, 1st inn., 0-on, 2-out, RH.
20. Aug. 30 vs. Chicago, Kevin Tapani, 4th inn., 0-on, 1-out, RH.

September

21. Sept. 7 vs. Florida, Livan Hernandez, 3rd inn., 0-on, 2-out, RH.
22. Sept. 7 vs. Florida, Livan Hernandez, 5th inn., 0-on, 0-out, RH.
23. Sept. 26 vs. San Francisco, Orel Hershiser, 6th inn., 0-on, 0-out, RH.

....

Larry Walker's Home Runs 1999

April

1. Apr. 28 at St. Louis, Jose Jimenez, 1st inn., 2-on, 0-out, RH.
2. Apr. 28 at St. Louis, Jose Jimenez, 2nd inn., 2-on, 2-out, RH.
3. Apr. 28 at St. Louis, Scott Radinsky, 7th inn., 1-on, 1-out, LH.
4. Apr. 30 at Pittsburgh, Pete Schourek, 1st inn., 1-on, 1-out, LH.
5. Apr. 30 at Pittsburgh, Pete Schourek, 3rd inn., 1-on, 2-out, LH.

May

6. May 2 at Pittsburgh, Jason Schmidt, 1st inn., 0-on, 2-out, RH.
7. May 7 vs. Philadelphia, Curt Schilling, 1st inn., 0-on, 2-out, RH.
8. May 9 vs. Philadelphia, Robert Person, 6th inn., 1-on, 1-out, RH.
9. May 17 vs. Cincinnati, Pete Harnisch, 9th inn., 0-on, 0-out, RH.
10. May 21 vs. Arizona, John Frascatore, 11th inn., 0-on, 1-out, RH.

June

11. June 4 vs. Milwaukee, Alberto Reyes, 7th inn., 1-on, 1-out, RH.
12. June 5 vs. Milwaukee, Mike Myers, 8th inn., 2-on, 1-out, LH.
13. June 8 vs. Seattle, Frankie Rodriguez, 3rd inn., 0-on, 0-out, RH.
14. June 15 vs. San Francisco, Chris Brock, 4th inn., 0-on, 1-out, RH.
15. June 18 vs. Florida, Matt Mantei, 9th inn., 0-on, 0-out, RH.
16. June 19 vs. Florida, Brian Edmondson, 8th inn., 1-on, 1-out, RH.
17. June 20 vs. Florida, Ryan Dempster, 1st inn., 2-on, 0-out, RH.
18. June 22 vs. Chicago Cubs, Scott Sanders, 6th inn., 1-on, 1-out, RH.
19. June 23 vs. Chicago Cubs, Dan Serafini, 8th inn., 1-on, 1-out, LH.
20. June 28 at San Diego, Will Cunnane, 9th inn., 1-on, 0-out, RH.

July

21. July 2 vs. San Diego, Sterling Hitchcock, 1st inn., 0-on, 2-out, LH.
22. July 3 (1) vs. San Diego, Woody Williams, 1st inn., 0-on, 2-out, RH.
23. July 3 (2) vs. San Diego, Heath Murray, 2nd inn., 1-on, 0-out, LH.
24. July 3 (2) vs. San Diego, Donne Wall, 8th inn., 0-on, 1-out, RH.
25. July 8 vs. Los Angeles, Chan Ho Park, 1st inn., 0-on, 2-out, RH.
26. July 17 at Cincinnati, Scott Williamson, 9th inn., 1-on, 2-out, RH.
27. July 19 at Oakland, Mike Oquist, 3rd inn., 1-on, 2-out, RH.
28. July 23 vs. St. Louis, Darren Oliver, 7th inn., 1-on, 1-out, RH.
29. July 25 vs. St. Louis, Manny Aybar, 9th inn., 0-on, 2-out, RH.
30. July 27 vs. Houston, Jose Lima, 6th inn., 0-on, 0-out, RH.

August

31. Aug. 18 vs. Atlanta, Kevin Millwood, 1st inn., 0-on, 2-out, RH.
32. Aug. 18 vs. Atlanta, John Rocker, 9th inn., 2-on, 0-out, LH.
33. Aug. 22 at Chicago, Steve Trachsel, 6th inn., 0-on, 1-out, RH.

September

34. Sept. 1 vs. Pittsburgh, Jason Schmidt, 3rd inn., 1-on, 1-out, RH.
35. Sept. 8 at Montreal, Dan Smith, 4th inn., 0-on, 0-out, RH.
36. Sept. 13 vs. New York Mets, Rick Reed, 4th inn., 0-on, 0-out, RH.
37. Sept. 17 vs. Dodgers, Ismael Valdez, 2nd inn., 2-on, 2-out, RH.

....

Larry Walker's Home Runs 2000

April

1. Apr. 23 at St. Louis, Andy Benes, 6th inn., 0-on, 0-out, RH.
2. Apr. 29 vs. New York Mets, Rick Reed, 1st inn., 1-on, 1-out, RH.

May

3. May 1 vs. Montreal, Matt Blank, 6th inn., 1-on, 0-out, LH.

June

4. June 10 vs. Texas, Esteban Loaiza, 1st inn., 2-on, 0-out, RH.

July

5. July 14 vs. Cincinnati, Pete Harnisch, 8th inn., 0-on, 2-out, RH.
6. July 17 vs. Oakland, Doug Jones, 4th inn., 1-on, 2-out, RH.
7. July 27 vs. L.A. Dodgers, Mike Fetters, 8th inn., 1-on, 0-out, RH.

August

8. Aug. 7 vs. Pittsburgh, Rich Loiselle, 7th inn. 0-on, 1-out, RH.
9. Aug. 11 at Montreal, Scott Forster, 7th inn., 3-on, 2-out, LH.

Larry Walker's Home Runs 2001

April

1. Apr. 2 vs. St. Louis, Mike James, 8th inn., 1-on, 2-out, RH.
2. Apr. 4 vs. St. Louis, Chad Hutchinson, 3rd inn., 1-on, 2-out, RH.
3. Apr. 8 vs. San Diego, Brian Tollberg, 1st inn., 1-on, 1-out, RH.
4. Apr. 9 at St. Louis, Andy Benes, 6th inn., 1-on, 1-out, RH.
5. Apr. 12 at St. Louis, Dustin Hermannson, 7th inn., 1-on, 1-out, RH.
6. Apr. 13 vs. Arizona, Randy Johnson, 1st inn., 1-on, 1-out, LH.
7. Apr. 17 at San Diego, Brian Lawrence, 7th inn., 1-on, 0-out, RH.
8. Apr. 18 at San Diego, Rodney Myers, 6th inn., 0-on, 2-out, RH.
9. Apr. 22 at Arizona, Armando Reynoso, 1st inn., 0-on, 2-out, RH.
10. Apr. 24 vs. Chicago Cubs, Kevin Tapani, 1st inn., 2-on, 0-out, RH.
11. Apr. 24 vs. Chicago Cubs, Todd Van Poppel, 5th inn., 1-on, 0-out, RH.

May

12. May 9 vs. New York Mets, Rick Reed, 6th inn., 0-on, 1-out, RH.
13. May 15 at Atlanta, John Burkett, 6th inn., 0-on, 0-out, RH.
14. May 16 at Atlanta, Tom Glavine, 3rd inn., 2-on, 2-out, LH.
15. May 20 at Florida, Ryan Dempster, 1st inn., 0-on, 2-out, RH.
16. May 22 vs. Los Angeles, Eric Gagné, 5th inn., 1-on, 0-out, RH.

June

17. June 1 vs. San Francisco, Kirk Rueter, 3rd inn., 0-on, 1-out, LH.
18. June 2 vs. San Francisco, Chad Zerbe, 9th inn., 1-on, 1-out, RH.
19. June 3 vs. San Francisco, Mark Gardner, 3rd inn., 1-on, 0-out, RH.
20. June 16 at Cincinnati, Hector Mercado, 7th inn., 1-on, 1-out, LH.
21. June 17 at Cincinnati, Elmer Dessens, 5th inn., 2-on, 1-out, RH.
22. June 21 vs. Arizona, Nick Bierbrodt, 3rd inn., 1-on, 2-out, LH.
23. June 22 vs. Arizona, Greg Swindell, 9th inn., 0-on, 1-out, LH.
24. June 25 vs. San Diego, Kevin Jarvis, 3rd inn., 1-on, 2-out, RH.
25. June 29 at Arizona, Greg Swindell, 9th inn., 0-on, 0-out, LH.

July

26. July 5 at San Diego, Adam Eaton, 3rd inn., 0-on, 1-out, RH.
27. July 6 vs. Anaheim, Mike Holtz, 7th inn., 1-on, 2-out, LH.
28. July 15 at Oakland, Cory Lidle, 1st inn., 0-on, 2-out, RH.

August

29. Aug. 5 vs. Pittsburgh, David Williams, 5th inn., 1-on, 2-out, LH.
30. Aug. 10 at Cincinnati, Hector Mercado, 8th inn., 2-on, 1-out, LH.
31. Aug. 19 vs. Florida, Jesus Sanchez, 1st inn., 0-on, 2-out, RH.
32. Aug. 24 at Milwaukee, Allen Levrault, 5th inn., 0-on, 2-out, RH.
33. Aug. 26 at Milwaukee, Ruben Quevedo, 5th inn., 2-on, 0-out, RH.

September

34. Sept. 23 at Montreal, Scott Stewart, 9th inn., 0-on, 0-out, RH.
35. Sept. 24 vs. San Diego, Kevin Jarvis, 1st inn., 0-on, 2-out, RH.
36. Sept. 24 vs. San Diego, Chuck McElroy, 5th inn., 0-on, 0-out, LH.
37. Sept. 25 vs. San Diego, Trevor Hoffman, 9th inn,, 0-on, 0-out, RH.

October

38. Oct. 5 at San Diego, Kevin Jarvis, 6th inn., 0-on, 2-out, RH.

....

Larry Walker's Home Runs 2002

April

1. Apr. 3 at St. Louis, Garrett Stephenson, 2nd inn., 2-on, 2-out, RH.
2. Apr. 8 vs. Houston, Roy Oswalt, 8th inn., 1-on, 0-out, RH.
3. Apr. 10 vs. Houston, Dave Mlicki, 4th inn., 0-on, 0-out, RH.
4. Apr. 12 vs. Arizona, Curt Schilling, 6th inn., 1-on, 1-out, RH.
5. Apr. 27 vs. Phila., Brandon Duckworth, 3rd inn., 1-on, 0-out, RH.

May

6. May 1 vs. Pittsburgh, Josh Fogg, 6th inn., 0-on, 0-out, RH.
7. May 8 at Montreal, Carl Pavano, 7th inn., 0-on, 0-out, RH.
8. May 12 at NY Mets, Kane Davis, 13th inn., 1-on, 0-out, RH.
9. May 21 vs. San Diego, Dennis Tankersley, 1st inn., 0-on, 2-out, RH.
10. May 23 vs. San Diego, Brett Tomko, 5th inn., 0-on, 0-out, RH.

June

11. June 3 vs. Los Angeles, Jesse Orosco, 8th inn., 0-on, 0-out, LH.
12. June 14 vs. Cleveland, Ryan Drese, 6th inn., 0-on, 0-out, RH.
13. June 15 vs. Cleveland, Chad Paronto, 7th inn., 1-on, 1-out, RH.
14. June 16 vs. Cleveland, Ricardo Rincon, 7th inn., 1-on, 2-out, LH.
15. June 19 vs. Yankees, Andy Pettitte, 4th inn., 0-on, 0-out, LH.
16. June 22 vs. Tampa Bay, Wilson Alvarez, 5th inn., 0-on, 1-out, LH.
17. June 28 at Seattle, Joel Pineiro, 4th inn., 0-on, 2-out, RH.

July

18. July 1 vs. San Francisco, Kirk Rueter, 1st inn., 2-on, 0-out, LH.
19. July 2 vs. San Francisco, Ryan Jensen, 5th inn., 0-on, 2-out, RH.
20. July 3 vs. S. Francisco, Livan Hernandez, 1st inn., 2-on, 0-out, RH.
21. July 21 vs. Milwaukee, Ben Sheets, 1st inn., 0-on, 2-out, RH.
22. July 28 at Milwaukee, Jamey Wright, 1st inn., 0-on, 2-out, RH.

August

23. Aug. 7 vs. Cincinnati, Joey Hamilton, 3rd inn., 2-on, 2-out, RH.
24. Aug. 18 at Atlanta, Greg Maddux, 7th inn., 0-on, 0-out, RH.
25. Aug. 18 at Atlanta, Kerry Ligtenberg, 9th inn., 1-on, 0-out, RH.

September

26. Sept. 1 at San Diego, Adam Eaton, 3rd inn., 1-on, 1-out, RH.

....

Larry Walker's Home Runs 2003

April

1. April 14 at Arizona, Steve Randolph, 7th inn., 2-on, 2-out, LH.
2. April 14 at Arizona, Mike Koplove, 9th inn., 0-on, 2-out, RH.
3. April 25 vs. Chicago Cubs, Mike Remlinger, 8th inn., 0-on, 1-out, LH.
4. April 29 vs. Cincinnati, Chris Reitsma, 4th inn., 0-on, 2-out, RH.

May

   NIL

June

5. June 7 vs. Kansas City, Chris George, 5th inn., 0-on, 0-out, LH.
6. June 12 at Minnesota, Kenny Rogers, 8th inn., 0-on, 2-out, LH.
7. June 23 at San Diego, Kevin Jarvis, 6th inn., 0-on, 1-out, RH.
8. June 24 at San Diego, Brian Lawrence, 6th inn., 1-on, 1-out, RH.

July

9. July 1 vs. Arizona, Andrew Good, 4th inn., 0-on, 0-out, RH.
10. July 25 vs. Milwaukee, Wes Obermueller, 4th inn., 0-on, 0-out, RH.

August

11. Aug. 16 at NY Mets, Jae Seo, 4th inn., 0-on, 1-out, RH.
12. Aug. 19 vs. Florida, Carl Pavano, 1st inn., 1-on, 1-out, RH.

September

13. Sept. 2 at San Francisco, Kevin Correia, 5th inn., 0-on, 0-out, RH.
14. Sept. 21 vs. San Diego, Adam Eaton, 2nd inn., 1-on, 0-out, RH.
15. Sept. 23 vs. Arizona, Brandon Webb, 1st inn., 3-on, 1-out, RH.
16. Sept. 27 at San Diego, Joe Roa, 5th inn., 0-on, 0-out, RH.

Larry Walker's Home Runs 2004

Larry Walker was on the disabled list from March 26 to June 21.

June

1. June 25 at Cleveland, Jason Davis, 2nd inn., 0-on, 0-out, RH.
2. June 25 at Cleveland, Jason Davis, 6th inn., 0-on, 0-out, RH.
3. June 25 at Cleveland, Jose Jimenez, 10th inn., 1-on, 1-out, RH.

July

4. July 15 vs. San Francisco, Jason Williams, 5th inn., 1-on, 1-out, RH.
5. July 19 vs. San Diego, Ismael Valdez, 2nd inn., 0-on, 0-out, RH.
6. July 24 at Arizona, Lance Cormier, 6th inn., 0-on, 0-out, RH.

August

Traded to St. Louis Cardinals, August 6
7. Aug. 12 at Florida, A.J. Burnett, 4th inn., 0-on, 0-out, RH.
8. Aug. 13 at Atlanta, Paul Byrd, 7th inn., 1-on, 2-out, RH.
9. Aug. 17 vs. Cincinnati, Danny Graves, 8th inn., 3-on, 2-out, RH.
10. Aug 22 vs. Pittsburgh, Brian Meadows, 8th inn., 3-on, 1-out, RH.

September

11. Sept. 1 vs. San Diego, Adam Eaton, 1st inn., 0-on, 1-out, RH.
12. Sept. 2 vs. San Diego, Blaine Neal, 7th inn., 0-on, 2-out, RH.
13. Sept. 12 at Los Angeles, Hideo Nomo, 1st inn., 0-on, 1-out, RH.
14. Sept. 12 at Los Angeles, Hideo Nomo, 4th inn., 1-on, 2-out, RH.
15. Sept. 19 vs. Arizona, Mike Gosling, 3rd inn., 1-on, 2-out, RH.
16. Sept. 22 at Milwaukee, Ben Sheets, 5th inn., 1-on, 2-out, RH.
17. Sept. 28 at Houston, Brendan Backe, 2nd inn., 0-on, 0-out, RH.

Larry Walker's Home Runs 2004 Post-Season

Division Series

1. Oct. 5 vs. Dodgers, W 5-3, Game 1, Odalis Perez, 3rd inning, 0-on, 2-out, LH.
2. Oct. 5 vs. Dodgers, W 5-3, Game 1, Giovanni Carrara, 5th inning, 0-on, 0-out, RH.

League Championship Series

1. Oct. 14 vs. Houston, W 6-4, Game 2, Pete Munro, 5th inning, 1-on, 2-out, RH.
2. Oct. 16 at Houston, L 2-5, Game 3, Roger Clemens, 1st inning, 0-on, 1-out, RH.

World Series

1. Oct. 23 at Boston, L 9-11, Game 1, Tim Wakefield,
   3rd inning, 0-on, 1-out, RH.
2. Oct. 26 vs. Boston, L 1-4, Game 3, Keith Foulke,
   9th inning, 0-on, 1-out, RH.

· ·

Larry Walker's Home Runs 2005

April

1. Apr. 5 at Houston, Russ Springer, 7th inn., 0-on, 2-out, RH.
2. Apr. 21 vs. Chicago Cubs, Mike Remlinger, 8th inn., 0-on, 1-out, LH.

May

3. May 7 vs. San Diego, Adam Eaton, 1st inn., 0-on, 1-out, RH.
4. May 8 vs. San Diego, Randy Williams, 2nd inn., 1-on, 2-out, LH.
5. May 21 at Kansas City, Jaime Cerda, 7th inn., 2-on, 1-out, RH.

June

6. June 14 at Toronto, Chad Gaudin, 1st inn., 1-on, 2-out, RH.
7. June 14 at Toronto, Chad Gaudin, 5th inn., 1-on, 0-out, RH.
8. June 29 vs. Cincinnati, Ramon Ortiz, 2nd inn., 1-on, 0-out, RH.
9. June 29 vs. Cincinnati, Ramon Ortiz, 3rd inn., 1-on, 0-out, RH.

July

10. July 8 at San Francisco, Jason Schmidt, 1st inn., 1-on, 2-out, RH.
11. July 16 vs. Houston, Roy Oswalt, 5th inn., 2-on, 1-out, RH.

August

12. Aug. 29 at Florida, A.J. Burnett, 3rd inn., 0-on, 0-out, RH.

September

13. Sept. 9 vs. New York Mets, Jae Seo, 8th inn., 0-on, 2-out, RH.

October

14. Oct. 1 vs. Cincinnati, Ramon Ortiz, 1st inn., 0-on, 1-out, RH.
15. Oct. 1 vs. Cincinnati, Ramon Ortiz, 4th inn., 0-on, 0-out, RH.

· ·

Larry Walker hit his final home run on the second-last day of the 2005 season against Cincinnati. Larry came to bat three times. He hit a home run in the first inning, and another home run to lead off the fourth inning. Larry walked and scored in the sixth inning. He was replaced at the end of the inning. Two weeks later, Larry Walker announced his retirement. It was the end of the greatest career in Canadian baseball history.

Larry Walker watches a home run against Houston. (AP photo by Al Behrman)

Alphabetical List of the Pitchers Against Whom Larry Walker Hit Home Runs

From Darrel Akerfelds of the Philadelphia Phillies to Chad Zerbe of the San Francisco Giants, Larry Walker hit 390 home runs against 267 different pitchers.

It was 11 years, five months, and two weeks between home runs against Tim Wakefield: from May 9, 1993 in Pittsburgh until October 23, 2004 in the World Series at Boston.

Here is the full list of 267 different pitchers.:

A

Akerfelds, Darrel
Alfonseca, Antonio
Alvarez, Wilson
Armstrong, Jack
Ashby, Andy
Astacio, Pedro
Avery, Steve
Aybar, Manny

B

Backe, Brendan
Banks, Willie
Batchelor, Rich
Beck, Rod
Belcher, Tim
Belinda, Stan
Benes, Alan
Benes, Andy
Bierbrodt, Nick
Black, Bud
Blank, Matt
Bolton, Tom
Bottenfield, Kent
Brantley, Jeff
Brink, Brad

Brock, Chris
Brummett, Greg
Bullinger, Jim
Burba, Dave
Burkett, John
Burnett, A. J.
Burrows, Terry
Byrd, Paul

C

Candiotti, Tom
Carlson, Dan
Carpenter, Cris
Carrara, Giovanni
Carrasco, Hector
Casian, Larry
Castillo, Frank
Castillo, Tony
Cerda, Jaime
Christiansen, Jason
Clark, Mark
Clemens, Roger
Clontz, Brad
Cloude, Ken
Cooke, Steve
Cordova, Francisco

Cormier, Lance
Correia, Kevin
Cox, Danny
Cunnane, Will

D

Daal, Omar
Darling, Ron
Darwin, Danny
Davis, Jason
Davis, Kane
Davis, Mark
DeLeon, Jose
Dempster, Ryan
Deshaies, Jim
Dessens, Elmer
Dibble, Rob
Dickson, Jason
Dougherty, Jim
Downs, Kelly
Drabek, Doug
Dreifort, Darren
Drese, Ryan
Duckworth, Brandon
Dyer, Mike

E

Eaton, Adam
Edmondson, Brian
Ericks, John

F

Fernandez, Alex
Fernandez, Sid
Fetters, Mike
Fogg, Josh
Forster, Scott
Foster, Kevin
Foulke, Keith
Frascatore, John

G

Gagné, Eric
Garcia, Ramon
Gardner, Mark
Gardner, Wes
Gaudin, Chad
George, Chris
Glavine, Tom
Good, Andrew
Gosling, Mike
Gott, Jim
Grace, Mike
Graves, Danny
Gross, Kevin

H

Habyan, John
Hamilton, Joey
Hammond, Chris
Harkey, Mike
Harnisch, Pete
Harris, Greg
Hartley, Mike
Heaton, Neal
Helling, Rick
Henry, Doug
Hermannson, Dustin

Hernandez, Livan
Hershiser, Orel
Hill, Ken
Hitchcock, Sterling
Hoffman, Trevor
Holtz, Mike
Hunter, Rich
Hurst, Bruce

J

Hutchinson, Chad
Jackson, Michael
James, Mike
Jarvis, Kevin
Jensen, Ryan
Jimenez, Jose
Johnson, Randy
Jones, Doug

K

Kile, Darryl
Koplove, Mike

L

LaCoss, Mike
Lawrence, Brian
Lefferts, Craig
Leibrandt, Charlie
Leiter, Mark
Levrault, Allen
Lidle, Cory
Lieber, Jon
Ligtenberg, Kerry
Lima, Jose
Loaiza, Esteban
Loiselle, Rich
Long, Bill

M

Maddux, Greg
Maduro, Calvin
Mantei, Matt
Martinez, Dennis

5, 4, 3, 2, 1 Blastoff! Andy Benes, John Burkettt, Adam Eaton, Tom Glavine, Pete Harnisch, as well as Pete Schourek each gave up five home runs to Larry Walker.

Martinez, Pedro
Martinez, Ramon
Matthews, Greg
Matthews, Terry
McClure, Bob
McElroy, Chuck
McMichael, Greg
Meadows, Brian
Mercado, Hector
Miceli, Dan
Millwood, Kevin
Mlicki, Dave
Morgan, Mike
Morris, Matt
Mulholland, Terry
Munro, Pete
Murphy, Rob
Murray, Heath
Murray, Matt
Myers, Mike
Myers, Rodney

N

Navarro, Jaime
Neal, Blaine
Neagle, Denny
Nomo, Hideo

O

Obermueller, Wes
Olivares, Francisco
Oliver, Darren
Oquist, Mike
Orosco, Jesse

Ortiz, Ramon
Osborne, Donovan
Oswalt, Roy
Otto, Dave

P

Park, Chan Ho
Paronto, Chad
Pavano, Carl
Pena, Alejandro
Perez, Odalis
Perez, Yorkis
Person, Robert
Petkovsek, Mark
Pettitte, Andy
Pico, Jeff
Pineiro, Joel
Portugal, Mark
Prieto, Ariel
Pugh, Tim

Q

Quevedo, Ruben

R

Radinsky, Scott
Randolph, Steve
Reed, Rick
Reitsma, Chris
Remlinger, Mike
Reyes, Alberto
Reyes, Carlos
Reynoso, Armando
Rincon, Ricardo
Ritchie, Wally
Roa, Joe
Rocker, John
Rodriguez, Frankie
Rogers, Kenny
Rojas, Mel
Roper, John
Rosselli, Joe
Ruebel, Matt

Rueter, Kirk
Ruffin, Bruce
Ruskin, Scott

S

Sanchez, Jesus
Sanders, Scott
Seo, Jae
Schilling, Curt
Schiraldi, Calvin
Schmidt, Jason
Schourek, Pete
Seminara, Frank
Serafini, Dan
Service, Scott
Sheets, Ben
Slocum, Heathcliff
Smith, Dan
Spradlin, Jerry
Springer, Russ
Stanton, Mike
Stephenson, Garrett
Stewart, Scott
Stottlemyre, Todd
Sullivan, Scott
Sutcliffe, Rick
Swift, Bill
Swindell, Greg

T

Tabaka, Jeff
Tanana, Frank
Tankersley, Dennis
Tapani, Kevin
Telford, Anthony
Terrell, Walt
Tewksbury, Bob
Tolberg, Brian
Tomko, Brett
Tomlin, Randy
Trachsel, Steve

U

Urbina, Ugueth

V

Valdez, Ismael
Valdez, Sergio
Valenzuela, Fernando
Van Poppel, Todd
Veres, Dave

W

Wagner, Paul
Wakefield, Tim
Wall, Donne
Webb, Brandon
White, Gabe
White, Rick
Williams, David
Williams, Jason
Williams, Randy
Williams, Woody
Williamson, Scott
Witt, Bobby
Worrell, Tim
Wright, Jamey

Y

Yoshii, Masato
Young, Anthony

Z

Zerbe, Chad

Five years in a row, from July 5, 2001 to May 7, 2005, Larry Walker hit one home run a year off Adam Eaton of the San Diego Padres.

Larry Walker Against the Top 10 Opposing Pitchers

During his career, Larry Walker batted against 10 different pitchers at least 40 times each. Some were among the most outstanding pitchers of his era. Larry batted against Tom Glavine, a future Hall of Fame lefthander, no less than 77 times and held his own, with 23 hits, including four home runs for a .299 batting average.

Walker batted against Greg Maddux and Curt Schilling more than 60 times and faced John Smoltz 59 times. In all, Larry batted 550 times against the 10 pitchers listed below and made 168 hits for a .305 average.

Larry batted .307 against the three left-handers, and .305 against seven right-handers. The following tables list the pitchers, the number of times at bat against them, the number of hits and home runs, and Larry Walker's batting average against each pitcher.

PITCHER	AB-HITS	HRS	AVERAGE
Tom Glavine	77-23	4	.299
Greg Maddux	69-19	2	.275
Curt Schilling	62-15	3	.242
John Smoltz	59-20	0	.339
Andy Benes	54-15	5	.278
John Burkett	54-21	5	.389
Denny Neagle	47-14	2	.298
Andy Ashby	46-15	3	.326
Kirk Rueter	42-14	2	.333
Doug Drabek	40-12	1	.300

Most Difficult Opposing Pitchers

PITCHER	AB-HITS	HRS	AVERAGE
Bobby Jones	39-5	0	.128
Terry Mulholland	39-8	1	.205
Frank Castillo	34-4	1	.118
Kevin Brown	31-7	0	.226

Chapter 2

The Year the Expos Would Have Won the World Series

THE 1994 MONTREAL EXPOS - *The Best Team in Baseball in 1994.*

Top row: Tim Spehr; Ken Hill, John Wetteland, Moises Alou, Cliff Floyd, Rodney Henderson, Larry Walker, Kirk Rueter, Freddy Benavides, unidentified equipment man. *Third row:* Unidentified equipment man, Gil Heredia, Jeff Shaw, Lou Frazier, Wil Cordero, Tim Scott, Butch Henry, Jeff Fassero, Randy Milligan, Pedro Martinez, unidentified equipment man. *Second row:* Equipment Manager John Silverman, Jeff Gardner, Mel Rojas, Sean Berry, Mike Lansing, Denis Boucher, Marquis Grissom, Darrin Fletcher, Lenny Webster, Travel Director Erik Ostling. *Front row:* Bat boy; Asst. Trainer Mike Kozak, Tommy Harper, Pierre Arsenault, Tim Johnson, Manager Felipe Alou, Joe Kerrigan, Luis Pujols, Jerry Manuel, Trainer Ron McLain. *In front:* Expos mascot, Youpi.

The 1994 Montreal Expos, the Best Team in Baseball

Through a combination of patient development in their own farm system, intelligent trading and effective scouting, the Montreal Expos overcame the smallest budget in baseball to put together the best team in the major leagues in 1994. Vice-President Bill Stoneman - an Expo hero as a double no-hit pitcher - along with general manager Dan Duquette and scouting director Kevin Malone had formed the nucleus of an exciting, powerful young team.

Of the nine players in the Expos 1994 opening day lineup, five were developed in the Expo farm system:

- Centre fielder Marquis Grissom
- Second baseman Mike Lansing
- Right fielder Larry Walker
- Shortstop Wil Cordero, and
- First baseman Cliff Floyd

Three players were acquired in trades:
- Left fielder Moises Alou
- Catcher Darrin Fletcher, and
- Third baseman Sean Berry.

Starting pitcher Jeff Fassero was signed as a free agent, and won 58 games over six seasons with the Expos.

Other pitchers obtained through trades included Ken Hill, John Wetteland and Pedro Martinez; while Kirk Rueter and Mel Rojas, along with outfielders Rondell White and John Vander Wal were Expo signees. Freddy Benavides, Randy Milligan and Tim Spehr, were important reserve players picked up in trades.

Blending all these different talents together was one of the most respected managers in baseball, Felipe Alou, father of Moises, and himself an outstanding player for 17 years. Felipe was acclaimed as teacher and innovator; but until 1994 he had never had a team with so much depth and balance. At last, the master manager would show the world!

The Year the Expos Would Have Won the World Series!

You could look it up but you wouldn't find it. It's not in the record book, because it never happened; but it should have happened, and if the series had been played, this is how it would have happened.

That was the tragedy of the 1994 baseball strike and lockout. Major league players began a strike August 12, and 33 days later the owners cancelled the rest of the season. For the first time since 1904, there was no World Series. When the season ended, the New York Yankees were leading the American League with 70 wins and 43 losses, three games ahead of the Chicago White Sox.

The Montreal Expos topped the National League in 1994 with the best record in baseball, 74 wins and 40 losses. Montreal was six games ahead of Atlanta and three-and-a-half games better than the Yankees.

If the Yankees had played the Expos in the World Series, it would have been a battle between David and Goliath: the richest team in baseball against the bargain basement boys from Canada - and I believe the Expos would have won decisively!

Following are my game-by-game descriptions of what would have happened in the World Series that never was.

Game One: Yankee Stadium, New York

The Yankees had home field advantage for the first two games and - if necessary - for the last two. Pitching in the fading October sunlight at Yankee Stadium, 17-game winner Jimmy Key had the Expos off balance and out in front of his slow curves. Key allowed just two hits in the first seven innings.

The Expos got a walk and a single in the fifth but Yankee catcher Mike Stanley snuffed out a potential rally when he threw out Marquis Grissom attempting to steal third base. New York built a 4-0 lead with eight hits off Ken Hill. American League batting champion Paul O'Neill hit a bases-loaded double in the fourth inning to score three runs, and Wade Boggs sliced a solo home run down the right-field line in the sixth.

With two out in the eighth, Key tried to come inside on Larry Walker, but the ball was out over the plate and Walker parked it deep into the right-field bleachers for the only Expo run. Steve Howe preserved the win by inducing three ground outs in the ninth.

GAME ONE LINESCORE

Montreal	000 000 010	1 3 1
New York	000 301 00X	4 8 0

Hill, Scott (6), Rojas (8) and Fletcher
Key, Howe (9) and Stanley
HR: Boggs (1), Walker (1)
WP: Key (1-0), LP: Hill (0-1), Save: Howe (1)

Jimmy Key would have been the first pitcher to win games in successive World Series years with different teams. (John Klein photo)

Larry Walker sends a long drive into the right field corner. (John Klein photo)

Game Two: at New York

A lead-off home run by Marquis Grissom rocked New York starter Jim Abbott and the Expos piled up 15 hits against three Yankee pitchers. Grissom, Moises Alou and Larry Walker combined for 11 hits as the Expos blitzed the Yankees 9-2. Alou had two long home runs and a double, Grissom hit a homer, a double and a triple. Walker went five for five with three doubles.

Yankee catcher Mike Stanley and manager Buck Showalter were ejected in the fourth inning for arguing too strenuously with plate umpire Jim McKean after McKean called Grissom safe on a steal of home. A front-page photo in the next day's Daily News showed Stanley tagging Grissom on the left arm as the Expo player reached for the plate.

Pedro Martinez didn't allow a hit until the fifth when he gave up a lead-off home run to replacement catcher Jim Leyritz. Pinch-hitter Randy Velardi added a sixth-inning solo blast. Pedro struck out 10 Yankees in seven innings. Expo closer John Wetteland retired six in a row and struck out the side in the ninth.

GAME TWO LINESCORE
Montreal   211 212 000   9 15 1
New York   000 011 000   2 3 0
Martinez, Wetteland (8) and Fletcher, Webster (5)
Abbott, Mulholland (4), Wickman (8) and Stanley, Leyritz (4)
HR: Alou 2, (2), Grissom (1), Leyritz (1), Velardi (1)
WP: Martinez (1-0), LP: Abbott (0-1)

Game Three: Olympic Stadium, Montreal

The first-ever World Series game at Olympic Stadium was marked by a standing ovation for Expo pitcher Kirk Rueter, a last-minute replacement for Jeff Fassero, who strained an elbow muscle in the pre-game warm-up. The tall rookie, who started the year in Ottawa, had a no-hitter until the eighth inning and combined with Mel Rojas on a two-hit shutout as Montreal beat Melido Perez and the Yankees 3-0 to grab the series lead.

Moises Alou drove in the first run with a sacrifice fly in the fourth and Larry Walker singled up the middle with the bases loaded in the sixth to score two more. Pat Kelly lined a single over second base for the first Yankee hit with one out in the eighth. Luis Polonia followed with a sharp grounder to Wil Cordero and the Expos ended the inning with 6-4-3 double play.

The Yankees threatened with one out in the ninth. Wade Boggs singled to centre field on a 3-2 pitch. After Rojas replaced Rueter, Don Mattingly was safe on a throwing error by third baseman Sean Berry. Marquis Grissom crashed into the centre-field fence after catching Jose Tartabull's line drive and fell to the ground. Cliff Floyd grabbed the ball out of Grissom's glove and threw to second baseman Freddy Benavides. His perfect relay to catcher Lenny Webster nailed Boggs for the final out.

GAME THREE LINESCORE
New York   000 000 000   0 2 0
Montreal   000 102 00X   3 6 1
Perez, Howe (8), Wickman (9) and Leyritz
Rueter, Rojas (9) and Webster
WP: Rueter (1-0), LP: Perez (0-1), Save: Rojas (1)

Kirk Rueter came from Ottawa to be a star in Montreal. (Courtesy Montreal Expos)

Game Four: in Montreal

A standing-room-only crowd of 54,343 watched Yankee sluggers O'Neill, Tartabull and Mattingly put on a home run display in batting practice. Cliff Floyd hit one off the video scoreboard in the Expos pre-game workout.

The game was a classic pitcher's duel, with great defence. Grissom ran to the fence in deep centre field to snare a drive by Mike Stanley, and Mike Gallego dove to catch a bullet off the bat of Moises Alou.

Jimmy Key pitched another gem. The former Blue Jay struck out 10 Expos but was surpassed by the Expos' 16-game winner, Ken Hill, who fanned 11 Yankees. Don Mattingly's first-inning home run with two out was the only Yankee hit.

The Expos didn't fare much better but Wil Cordero followed a fifth-inning walk to Moises Alou with a home run to left field and Montreal won 2-1. There were no other base runners for either side and the two teams set World Series records for fewest hits (2) and fewest runners left on base (0). Larry Walker struck out three times.

Don Mattingly signs autographs after batting practice. (Jim Shearon photo)

GAME FOUR LINESCORE

New York   100 000 000   1 1 0
Montreal   000 020 00X   2 1 0
Key and Stanley
Hill and Fletcher
HR: Mattingly (1), Cordero (1)
WP: Hill (1-1), LP: Key (1-1)

Game Five: in Montreal

The upstart Expos breezed to the championship behind Pedro Martinez. The turning point came in the third inning when the Yankees threatened to open the scoring with two men on and two men out.

Don Mattingly was at bat, after a walk to Wade Boggs and a single by Paul O'Neill, when Martinez picked off O'Neill at first base. Yankee manager Buck Showalter screamed interference and vainly argued that Montreal first baseman Larry Walker (a former hockey player) had body-checked O'Neill as he returned to the bag.

At the post-game news conference, Walker said, "I always stick my bum out when I reach for a throw." In the fourth, Walker tagged Scott Kamieniecki for a two-run homer. The Expos pounded two other Yankee pitchers for 12 hits to win 5-0. Martinez finished the series with 18 strike-outs and a 1.29 earned run average.

Larry Walker hit two home runs and a double in the final game. The Expos first baseman set or tied World Series records for batting average, doubles, long hits and runs batted in. Walker was named Most Valuable Player with a .524 average (11 for 21), three home runs, five doubles, two stolen bases and eight runs batted in.

GAME FIVE LINESCORE

New York   000 000 000   0 6 1
Montreal   000 210 11X 5 12 0
Martinez, Rojas (8), Wetteland (9) and Fletcher
Kamieniecki, Perez (5) Wickman (7) and Leyritz
HR: Walker 2, (3)
WP: Martinez (2-0), LP: Kamieniecki (0-1)

Pedro Martinez was at his best in the big games. (Courtesy Montreal Expos)

The Effects of the Strike

Rival managers Felipe Alou of Montreal and Buck Showalter of the Yankees were poised for great success; but the strike changed that. Neither man ever came so close to winning a pennant.

Alou was fired in 2001 and wound up in San Francisco. Showalter quit the Yankees in 1995. He was hired to help develop the expansion Arizona Diamondbacks but was fired before they won the pennant and World Series. He was also fired by the Texas Rangers.

In 2002, both men told New York Times reporter Jack Curry, they thought the strike would last a week or so and the players would be back to finish the season.

Showalter had worked his way up through the Yankee organization. Of the 1994 strike, he said, "You get near the top of the mountain and, all of a sudden, the mountain crumbles." Alou said, "That took away my only opportunity to be in the playoffs. It's frustrating. It's emptiness. That was it."

Manager Felipe Alou and his son Moises would have been the first father and son team in World Series history. (John Klein photo)

The Yankees did recover from the shock of 1994 and have since won several pennants; but the Expos unloaded many of their most promising (and expensive) players after the strike season. John Wetteland was traded to the Yankees, Marquis Grissom went to the Braves, Ken Hill to St. Louis, and Series hero Larry Walker agreed to a $22-million deal with the Colorado Rockies.

Within 10 years, the Expos were out of business and moved to Washington. The poet John Greenleaf Whittier said it best:

"For of all sad words of tongue or pen,
The saddest are these: "It might have been!"

Yankee manager Buck Showalter felt cheated. (John Klein photo)

Fifteen Canadians Have Played in the World Series

Matt Stairs was kneeling in the on-deck circle at Citizens Bank Park in Philadelphia when Eric Bruntlett scored the winning run for the Phillies in game two of the 2008 World Series. Matt never got a chance to be the hero. Carlos Ruiz, batting ahead of Stairs, dribbled a ground ball toward third base to win the game.

Matt Stairs did come to bat the following night, as a pinch-hitter for the pitcher, leading off the bottom of the eighth inning. Matt struck out swinging. That made Matt Stairs the 15th Canadian to play in the World Series.

Like Matt Stairs in 2008, John O'Neill, the first Canadian to play in the World Series, was born in Saint John, New Brunswick. O'Neill was a 26-year-old switch hitter for the 1906 Chicago White Sox. He came into play in the third game when Ed Hahn was hit in the face by a pitched ball and had to leave the game. John O'Neill took over in right field and caught one fly ball. He came to bat in the eighth inning and popped out to third base. Ed Hahn returned to the lineup the next day and O'Neill watched from the bench as the White Sox beat the Cubs. After his brief glory, John O'Neill returned to the minors. He died in 1920, at 40, of influenza.

John O'Neill, the first Canadian to play in the World Series.

Jimmy Archer, a catcher, who was born in Dublin, Ireland, but came to Canada as a baby, played one game for the Detroit Tigers in the 1907 World Series. He was hitless in three times at bat. Jimmy had slightly more success in 1910 with the Chicago Cubs. He managed two hits in 11 at bats against Connie Mack's world champion Philadelphia Athletics.

Catcher George Gibson of London, Ontario had his best year in 1909. Gibson set a record by catching 133 consecutive games for the Pittsburgh Pirates. He helped beat Ty Cobb and the Detroit Tigers. George hit a double to drive in the winning run in the first game and drove in a run in the fifth game.

Another Canadian catcher was the best hitter in the 1913 World Series between the New York Giants and the Philadelphia Athletics. Larry McLean, who was born in Fredericton, New Brunswick, hit safely in each of the four games he started and led all batters on both teams with a .500 average.

Jack Graney of St. Thomas, Ontario, was 34 years old and near the end of a 14-year career with the Cleveland Indians when he played in the 1920 World Series against the Brooklyn Dodgers. Graney was hitless in three games as a pinch-hitter. Cleveland won the World Series, five games to two. Jack Graney later had a long career as the Indians radio announcer.

No other Canadian can match the World Series success of George Selkirk, who played in six World Series with the New York Yankees and won five of them. Selkirk was born in Huntsville, Ontario, but grew up in Rochester, New York. He hit a home run off Car Hubbell, his first time at bat in the 1936 World Series.

The first Canadian to pitch in the World Series was born in Belleville, Ontario; but he didn't stay long, and he never went back. John Rutherford was six weeks old when his parents took him to England so John's father could finish post-graduate medical studies.

October 4, 1952, Rutherford replaced Brooklyn starter Joe Black against the New York Yankees. Mickey Mantle hit a line drive to deep right-centre field for a triple and scored when "Pee Wee" Reese overthrew third base. Rutherford retired the next three batters but the Yankees went on to win the series in seven games.

Ron Taylor, a right-hand pitcher from Toronto, was the next Canadian World Series pitcher with the St. Louis Cardinals in 1964. At Yankee Stadium, on October 11, Taylor pitched four scoreless and hitless innings to save a Cardinal win. Ron struck out Tom Tresh and Elston Howard and walked Mickey Mantle.

John Hiller, a left-hander from Toronto, pitched in two games of the 1968 World Series for Detroit. He worked the last two innings of game three. John allowed four hits and a walk but no runs. The next day, Hiller started the eighth inning. The first batter was safe on an error; then Hiller gave up two walks and two doubles. He didn't get a man out. After trailing three games to one, the Tigers won three in a row to take the championship.

Ron Taylor won his second World Series ring with the New York Mets against the Baltimore Orioles in 1969. Ron pitched in two games and earned his second World Series save. The Mets won three straight in New York to claim the title. Ron Taylor is the only Canadian to win the World Series with two different teams.

Reggie Cleveland, born in Swift Current, Saskatchewan, pitched in three games of the 1975 World Series against the Cincinnati Reds. In game three, October 14, at Riverfront Stadium in Cincinnati, Reggie Cleveland came in to strike out Tony Perez for the third out of the fifth inning. Cleveland also struck out Johnny Bench to end the sixth. Bernie Carbo pinch-hit for Reggie and hit a home run but Cincinnati won 6-5 in 10 innings.

Two days later, October 16, in game five at Cincinnati, Reggie Cleveland became the first Canadian starting pitcher in a World Series game. The series was tied at two games each. Boston took the lead in the first inning. Reggie Cleveland blanked the Reds through the first three innings. Tony Perez, who was 0 for 15 in the series, hit a home run to tie the score. In the sixth, Joe Morgan walked, Bench singled and Tony Perez hit another home run. Cleveland was the losing pitcher.

Rob Butler, who was born in Toronto, made baseball history October 20, 1993, when he became the first - and still the only - Canadian to play for a Canadian team in the World Series. Butler was a pinch-hitter in game four at Philadelphia. He hit a ground ball to first base. John Kruk threw to second base to force Pat Borders. The next day, Rob pinch-hit for Juan Guzman in the eighth inning of game five. Butler hit a single against Curt Schilling. Two days later, in game six at SkyDome, Rob Butler was one of the dancing Blue Jays when Joe Carter hit a home run to win the World Series.

There was an 11-year gap before the next Canadian played in a World Series. Larry Walker of Maple Ridge, British Columbia, hit two home runs and had five hits for the St. Louis Cardinals in the 2004 World Series against the Boston Red Sox.

In 2007, for the first time ever, there were two Canadians in the World Series - one on each team - and they were both pitchers. It happened October 24 at Fenway Park in Boston. Jeff Francis, a tall left-hander from Vancouver, who won 17 games for the Colorado Rockies, was chosen to pitch the first game in Boston. Left-hand pitchers often have trouble at Fenway Park, and that was true of Jeff Francis. He left after four innings with Boston leading 6-1.

Eric Gagné, a burly right-hander from Montreal, pitched the ninth inning for the Red Sox. Gagné threw 11 pitches, eight of them strikes. He retired Todd Helton and Garrett Atkins on fly balls and struck out Brad Hawpe to end the game. That was the first time two Canadians played in the same World Series game.

After 105 years, one gaping hole remains in the record of Canadian participation in the World Series. No Canadian pitcher has ever won a World Series game.

Chapter 3

Baseball in the
Early Days
1880 - 1920

A Perfect Squeeze Play by Hamilton's Wood Brothers

"If Jeffrey doesn't play, neither do we!"

Under the grandstand of Dundurn Park, Pete Wood, 18-year-old pitcher of the Hamilton Clippers, stared coldly at the team's stocky manager. Above them, a noisy crowd hooted for the game to start.

William Stroud, the besieged manager, looked from Pete to his brother Fred, the team's catcher. He met the same fixed gaze.

"When Pete pitches," said Fred, "I catch and Jeffrey plays first base. That was our agreement."

Fred Wood had played for Detroit in the National League the previous season, and Pete was already the best pitcher in the Canadian League. But Jeffrey Wood's baseball ability was summarized in his .173 batting average.

"No, no," Stroud protested, his walrus moustache twitching as he spoke. "I agreed that when Jeffrey plays, he will play first base; but I never said he would play every game."

Pete Wood replied, "It's all of us, or none of us. Which is it to be?"

William Stroud was Mister Baseball in Hamilton. For years he had outmanoeuvred some of the best men in the game. Now, as the wooden stand shook under the stamping feet of an impatient crowd, he recognized that he was the victim of a well-executed squeeze play. It was July 1885, a holiday Monday, and the biggest crowd of the season was growing restless as the Clippers waited to take the field against London. The manager had a bitter choice. He must give in to the Wood brothers or forfeit the game and give refunds to more than 1,400 people.

"All right," he growled. "Jeffrey plays first base. Now, let's get on the field."

"Just a moment." Fred, the eldest of the three, handed a sheet of paper to the manager.

"Sign this agreement. It says that when Pete Wood pitches, Fred Wood will catch and Jeffrey Wood will play first base. We don't want to go through this every game."

The manager scrawled his name and pushed the single sheet back with an angry glare. As the players took the field, Stroud went to speak with club secretary George Sterling.

"Chamberlain, pitcher of the disbanded Toledo club, is looking for work," he said. "Send him a telegram to report immediately, and ask Detroit if they will lend us a catcher."

Pete Wood, M.D., University of Western Ontario, Medical Department, 1893. (Regional Collection, D.B. Weldon Library, University of Western Ontario)

Hamilton beat London 5-4 to the delight of the partisan crowd, but there were no congratulations from manager Stroud as he addressed the Wood brothers after the game.

"Pete and Fred," he said with terse satisfaction, "you are fined $50 each and suspended one month for insubordination."

The Wood brothers were students. Baseball was their summer job. Fifty dollars was a week's pay. With less than two months left in the season, a 30-day suspension would put their studies in jeopardy. The brothers appealed their suspension to the judiciary committee and were granted a speedy hearing.

George Sterling spoke for the Clippers.

"Yes," he said, "manager Stroud did sign an agreement; but he did so under duress."

Fred Wood argued that the manager had given the same assurance verbally two days earlier.

"We only wanted him to keep his word," Fred insisted.

The judiciary committee decided both sides were right. The brothers had a signed agreement, but the manager was entitled to select the personnel for each game. Pete and Fred had acted improperly in refusing his instructions. George Sterling resolved the matter. He said the Clippers had no desire to prevent the Wood brothers from playing and would give all three an immediate and unconditional release.

Pete Wood was not unemployed for long. Not many miles from Hamilton, James "Pud" Galvin, one of baseball's legendary pitchers, was wearing out his welcome in Buffalo, New York. After seven years of brilliant success, Galvin was being blamed for the team's current misfortunes. Buffalo was in last place and Galvin had lost 19 of 32 decisions. A club director told the newspapers, "The public demands a change. We couldn't lose any more games if a pitcher were taken from the grandstand."

Galvin was given his release and manager Jack Chapman went to scour the bushes for a replacement. He found one in Hamilton.

Pete Wood had none of "Pud" Galvin's credentials, but he had a fresh face and a strong, young arm. On July 15, 1885, barely a week after his release by Hamilton, the Canadian teenager made his National League debut against first-place Chicago. **"Wood the new pitcher does well,"** proclaimed the New York Times. Chicago scored three runs in the third inning and one more in the ninth to win 4-2. Pete struck out eight batters and walked five. At Providence, five days later, the young Canadian won his first game and made two hits against Charles "Old Hoss" Radbourne, the premier pitcher of the 19th century.

Jeffrey Wood, D.D.S., University of Toronto, School of Dentistry, 1895. (University of Toronto)

When Pete returned to Buffalo, a telegram was waiting from brother Fred, now catching for London. "CONGRATULATIONS YOUR GREAT VICTORY STOP JEFFREY ACCEPTED BY TORONTO UNIVERSITY SCHOOL OF DENTISTRY."

In the next two-and-a-half months, Pete Wood pitched 24 games for the last-place Buffalo team. He won eight and lost 15. In the custom of the day, Pete also played four games in the outfield.

In September, when the Canadian season ended, Fred Wood was invited to join Buffalo as a reserve catcher. On September 30, 1885, a Wednesday afternoon, Jeffrey Wood missed classes at the University of Toronto to be in Buffalo. A telegram had informed him that brother Fred was to be catcher and younger brother Pete was to be the pitcher in the final game of the season against Boston.

For the first time in the history of the National League of Baseball (and not in 123 years since), two Canadian brothers formed the starting battery. Fred Wood hit a single his first time at bat and after seven innings the score was tied 3-3. In the eighth, Buffalo second baseman Danny Driscoll misplayed a ground ball and Boston scored twice to win the game. The great season was over.

On the first day of October 1885, a conductor collecting tickets in the smoking car of the Grand Trunk Railway train to Toronto remarked on the broad smiles of the three men wearing Buffalo baseball caps. "You fellows are mighty happy for a last-place team," he said.

Fred joined Jeffrey at the University of Toronto, where both would graduate as dentists. Pete enrolled at the University of Western Ontario and played for the London team in the Intercounty League. During the summer vacation of 1889 he pitched three games for the Philadelphia Phillies. In 1893, Pete Wood graduated as a Doctor of Medicine and returned to Hamilton to open a practice in the same house where the brothers had lived as boys.

In the following years, Fred took his dental practice to London; Jeffrey settled in Toronto, and Pete moved to Chicago. But the brothers often got together and they always remembered the day in Hamilton that changed their lives forever. That was the day some bold musketeers confronted the manager, and proclaimed, "All for one, and one for all. If Jeffrey doesn't play, neither do we!"

Manager William Stroud is top centre in this 1885 photo. Club Secretary George Sterling is in front, beside catcher W.F. Hunter. (Hamilton Public Library - Black Mount Collection)

America's Champion Batsman Really Was a Proud Canadian

James Edward "Tip" O'Neill became the greatest batter in baseball history in 1887 while playing for St. Louis of the American Association. In a year when bases on balls counted as hits, "Tip" O'Neill had the highest batting average in baseball history - .492. With bases on balls removed, it was adjusted to .435, exceeded only by Hugh Duffy's .440 for Boston in 1894.

O'Neill set records for hits, doubles, slugging average and total bases, and led the league in home runs and runs scored. The Reach Official Baseball Guide declared James E. O'Neill "America's Champion Batsman." The publisher exclaimed, "He wields his bat gracefully as well as effectively. No matter how swift or deceptive the pitching, he always scores his quota of clean hits." With glowing pride, the editor of Reach's Official American Association Base Ball Guide erroneously claimed O'Neill as an American, and assured readers "It has been given out that O'Neill was a Canadian by birth but he was born in Springfield, Mass."

The Reach editor was partly correct. "Tip" O'Neill was born in Springfield, Ontario, a village in Elgin County that now forms part of Malahide Township. Like "Babe" Ruth after him, O'Neill began his career as a pitcher. Western Ontario was his starting point but O'Neill soon moved on to Detroit and New York. He joined the Metropolitans of the National League in May 1883, three weeks before his 25th birthday. O'Neill pitched in 19 games, winning five and losing 12. The following year, he signed with St. Louis of the American Association as a pitcher-outfielder. "Tip" had the best winning percentage of the club, with 11 wins and four losses but his future course was charted when he led the team in home runs.

Over the next eight years, "Tip" O'Neill played the outfield in three different leagues, with St. Louis, Chicago and Cincinnati. He batted over .300 seven years in a row and won the batting championship two years in succession. O'Neill ended his career in 1892 as one of the greatest batters of the 19th-century game. America's champion batsman, and a proud Canadian, "Tip" O'Neill was overlooked in voting for the National Baseball Hall of Fame at Cooperstown, New York.

When his playing days ended, "Tip" O'Neill joined his mother and brothers, who were living in Montreal. He helped run the family business, a restaurant and tavern. At one time he was president of the Montreal Royals of the Eastern League, and later he became an umpire. He never married.

"America's Champion Batsman" James Edward "Tip" O'Neill. (National Baseball Hall of Fame Library, Cooperstown, NY)

On the last day of the year 1915, "Tip" O'Neill left his home on Esplanade Avenue and boarded a Park Avenue streetcar. He wore a tweed overcoat with a paisley scarf and a homburg hat.

Taking a seat beside a frosted window, O'Neill unfolded the morning Gazette. For more than a year he had been reading about conditions in the muddy trenches of France. At 57, O'Neill was too old to fight in the war and glad he had no sons to send into the trenches. When the streetcar gathered speed coming down the hill between Sherbrooke and Ontario streets, O'Neill folded the paper, put on his gloves and waited for the tram to stop at the corner of Bleury and St. Catherine. He had an appointment with the manager of the Dominion Bank.

"Mind your step," said the driver as his passenger descended. O'Neill waved over his shoulder and stepped onto the bare sidewalk. He took two steps forward then staggered and fell. In a moment the streetcar driver was at his side.

"Are you hurt?" he asked. "Can you get up?" There was no reply. A circle of onlookers quickly formed.

"Stand back," said the driver. "Give him room." Two men lifted O'Neill under the arms and carried him into Leduc's drug store, almost bumping into Doctor Morley Jackson who was waiting for a prescription to be filled.

While the men struggled to fit O'Neill into a chair against the wall, Doctor Jackson felt for the victim's pulse. There was none. Nor was there any breath, nor flicker of light in his eyes. "This man is extinct," said the doctor. An ambulance conveyed O'Neill to the Montreal General Hospital on Dorchester Street where the attending physician confirmed death by heart failure.

America's champion batsman was returned to the family homestead for burial in Woodstock, Ontario. His grave in St. Mary Cemetery is marked by a grey stone. Nearby, at the Tip O'Neill Sportsfield, a plaque dedicates the field to the "honour of James Edward "Tip" O'Neill, star of the Woodstock Actives baseball club in the year 1879, who was inducted into the Baseball Hall of Fame August 31, 1983."

1888 baseball card issued by W.S. Kimball Cigarette Company. (Library of Congress)

Mountjoy and Emslie, The First Canadian Duel

Almost half of the Canadians who have played in the major leagues were pitchers; but the list of games in which two Canadians were the opposing pitchers is remarkably small.

When Shawn Hill of Mississauga, Ontario, took the mound to pitch for the Washington Nationals against Jeff Francis of Vancouver, for the Colorado Rockies, on August 25, 2007, it was the first time in seven years that two Canadians were the starting pitchers. The Francis-Hill duel extended a baseball history that began more than 123 years earlier.

Records in the National Baseball Hall of Fame and Museum at Cooperstown, New York, reveal that the first time two Canadian-born players opposed each other as the starting pitchers in the major leagues was May 26, 1884, at Baltimore, Maryland.

Bob Emslie pitched for Baltimore against Billy Mountjoy of Cincinnati. Emslie, who was born in Guelph, Ontario, pitched in 50 games for Baltimore in 1884, winning 32 and losing 17.

Mountjoy, a native of London, Ontario, pitched 33 games for Cincinnati. He won 19 and lost 12. On that May afternoon in Baltimore, the hometown Orioles beat Cincinnati 11-3.

Emslie and Mountjoy each pitched the full game. Emslie struck out eight batters and walked two. Mountjoy struck out four and also walked two.

The two Canadian pitchers faced each other twice more in 1884 at Cincinnati and both times Mountjoy was the winner. On July 19, Cincinnati beat Baltimore 9-2, and on September 21, Mountjoy was again the winning pitcher over Emslie as Cincinnati beat Baltimore 11-10.

I am indebted to David Ball of Cincinnati for the following information.

"Cincinnati signed Mountjoy from Port Huron in mid-September, 1883. His official debut was on September 29, but on the 23rd he one-hit Baltimore in an exhibition game called due to rain after five innings.

"Billy Mountjoy pitched the first game ever played by professionals on a Sunday in Cincinnati, although the Reds had been playing Sunday games on the road for two years.

"On Sunday, October 21, Mountjoy pitched a no-hitter against Toledo in the last exhibition of the season. It was not a coincidence that he pitched both Sunday games, because Will White, the team's ace pitcher, refused to play ball on Sunday for religious reasons.

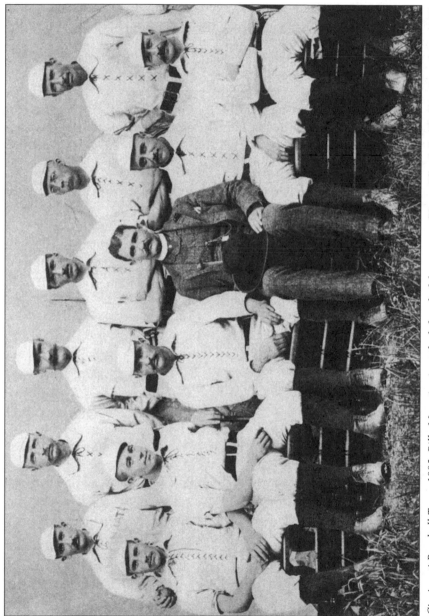

Cincinnati Baseball Team, 1885. Billy Mountjoy is at the left end of the top row (Harry Ellard, Baseball in Cincinnati, 1907)

"White was one of the last of the pure underhanded pitchers and therefore was very durable. An intelligent man of sharp and decided opinions, White was close to O.P. Caylor, the Cincinnati Commercial Gazette baseball writer and club secretary and de facto manager, and some observers felt that White used his influence to keep the rest of the pitching staff from getting a fair chance.

"On June 30, 1884, the Cincinnati Enquirer observed that it was a good thing for Mountjoy that White wouldn't play Sundays, because otherwise Mountjoy would never have pitched at all."

After his release by Cincinnati, Billy Mountjoy pitched six games for Baltimore, and then returned to Port Huron. Mountjoy died of consumption at the age of 37. His rival, Bob Emslie, went on to a long life that included a 34-year career as an umpire.

BASEBALL: DEATH OF BILLY MOUNTJOY

London, May 19 (Special) - Mr. William Mountjoy, son of the late John Mountjoy, died yesterday at his uncle's residence in London West. "Billy" Mountjoy, as the deceased was best known in his younger days, achieved considerable notoriety as a baseball pitcher and had few equals among amateur twirlers.

He subsequently joined the ranks of the professionals and afterwards settled in Port Huron where he had lived for several years. He finally fell victim to consumption and after an illness of two months passed away at the age of 37. He will be buried tomorrow.

(Toronto Globe , May 21, 1894)

Umpire from Guelph, Blind Bob Saw Plenty

It is an old baseball tradition to question the umpire's eyesight. Indeed, not many years ago, it was common practice for a stadium organist to play "Three Blind Mice" at the start of a game, as the umpires came onto the field.

"Blind Bob" was the name given to Robert Daniel Emslie, a native of Guelph, Ontario, who was a major league umpire for 34 years. John McGraw, the legendary manager of the world champion New York Giants, gave umpire Emslie that nickname.

McGraw had grounds for complaint because Bob Emslie's decision cost the Giants a game that could have clinched another championship. However, there was nothing wrong with Emslie's eyesight; he simply had to admit that he didn't see the play on which he made his fateful decision.

On September 23, 1908, with one week left in the season, the New York Giants were one game ahead of the Chicago Cubs. Playing at the Polo Grounds in New York, the teams were tied in the bottom of the ninth inning. The Giants had runners on first and third bases when Al Bridwell hit a clean single to the outfield. The runner on third scored the winning run and a large crowd swept onto the field as the New York players ran to their dressing room.

In that hasty exit, Fred Merkle, a 19-year-old rookie, who was on first base, did not touch second base. Instead, he ran to the clubhouse in right field to escape the crowd of spectators. The Chicago shortstop, Joe Tinker, called umpire Emslie's attention to the fact that Merkle had not touched second base. When home plate umpire Hank O'Day confirmed that point, Emslie declared that Merkle was "out." The inning was over and the score was still tied.

In his report to the league president, Emslie described what happened when Bridwell hit the ball:

"I had to fall to the ground to keep the ball from hitting me. When I got to my feet, I watched to see if Bridwell ran his hit out to first which he did. Just after Bridwell crossed first base, Tinker of the Chicago Club made the claim to me that Merkle, who was the baserunner on first when the hit was made, had not run the hit out to second base.

"As my back was turned to that play watching Bridwell, I did not know if Merkle had run to second or not, but as soon as my attention was called to it I looked out in right field and saw Merkle going towards the club house. I had not seen the play at second, but I went to O'Day who was watching the plate, and he said Merkle did not go near second base. I then called Merkle out and O'Day said the run did not count."

Bob Emslie umpired 4,228 games between 1890 and 1924. (National Baseball Hall of Fame Library, Cooperstown, NY)

By this point, darkness and the crowd of spectators on the field made it impossible to continue the game. It was incomplete, a game with no result. When the season ended, the Giants and the Cubs were tied for first place and the disputed tie game was replayed from the start in New York. The Cubs beat the Giants 4-2 to win the pennant.

Bob Emslie could have refused to make a decision on Merkle's failure to touch second base, on the grounds that he had not seen the play. If he had done that, McGraw's Giants would have won the original game and league championship. But Bob Emslie was used to making tough decisions and vigorously defending them. The game in New York was not the first time a crowd had flooded onto the playing field.

One afternoon, in the baseball hotbed of Brooklyn, an Emslie decision at home plate gave Boston the winning run. A swarm of angry fans crowded around the umpire. Bob Emslie flattened the leader of the charge with one punch to the jaw and the crowd quickly dispersed. The next day, Emslie was congratulated by the Brooklyn players and by an impressed spectator, James J. Corbett, the heavyweight boxing champion of the world. When action was called for, Bob Emslie was very decisive.

Elijah Pinnance, Canada's First Aboriginal Pitcher

On a wall in the Sports Hall of Fame at the Wallaceburg (Ontario) Museum, a young Canadian wearing a baseball uniform stares out from a faded photograph, with a teasing half-smile. What is that look in his eyes? It is pride, of course, and pleasure; but above all it is satisfaction.

Elijah Pinnance was a full-blooded Indian of the Chippewa band from Walpole Island, near Wallaceburg, Ontario. He was the first and only Canadian Aboriginal to pitch in the major leagues. The photograph was taken in Philadelphia in September 1903, the day after "Eddie" Pinnance, as he was known in baseball circles, pitched his first game for Connie Mack's Athletics.

Pinnance was 23 years old when he pitched against Washington, on a Sunday afternoon. At the start of the eighth inning, the public address announcer stepped in front of the grandstand to call out, "Pinnance now pitching for Philadelphia." The bleacher crowd straining to catch his name couldn't quite hear. "What's his name?" a man asked his neighbour. "Peanuts, I think," was the answer, and "Peanuts" he was called as he walked past the regulars who sat on the wooden benches beyond third base.

The Public Ledger observed, "In the eighth inning Manager Mack sent in Pinnance, his new Indian pitcher, secured from Mount Clements. In this inning the youngster performed very creditably, Coughlin, Lee and Kitteridge offering easy chances and being retired in order." The first batter in the ninth inning, pitcher Casey Patten, hit a ball off the end of the bat for a single. Robinson followed with a line drive over shortstop. Centre fielder Ollie Pickering did not move until the ball had passed him. Late afternoon shade and the 13-0 score might have affected Pickering's attention. The runner scored but Pinnance retired the next three batters to end the game.

The next morning, the former Michigan college student folded his baseball uniform into a worn Gladstone bag, added his small pitcher's glove and an almost new baseball. Then he left the boarding house, one block behind the right-field fence of the Columbia Park stadium. Walking to the corner, "Eddie" gave a newsboy two cents for a paper and asked directions to the photo studio on Broad Street.

A young couple was posing for an engagement photo when Pinnance reached the photographer's shop. He sat down, opened the paper and read this assessment of his debut. "He is only a youngster and very green but he will do to farm out next year."

Elijah Pinnance as a Philadelphia Athletic, 1903. (Sports Hall of Fame, Wallaceburg, ON)

A small man wearing a short, green smock stuck his head into the waiting room.

"Do you want to stand in front of a garden or do you prefer to sit on a bench?" he asked.

The young man put down his paper and opened the small brown leather bag.

"What I'd really like," he replied, "is to put on this baseball uniform. I'm playing for the Athletics and I want a souvenir for my family back home in Canada."

"That will be three dollars payable in advance," said the photographer. "Come in here. I don't have a change room. Put that on right away before somebody else comes along."

Despite the man's efforts to hurry him, Ed Pinnance dressed carefully in the light grey flannel and managed a dignified smile as the flash powder momentarily lit up the dark room.

"Eddie" Pinnance pitched one more game for the Athletics. He was the starting pitcher against Cleveland on the last day of the season. Pinnance pitched five innings and gave up one run on three hits. Cleveland scored two runs in the late innings to deprive the young Canadian of his first major league victory.

In the noisy dressing room after the game, teammates were saying goodbye until next year. Elijah Pinnance shook hands with Mr. Mack's other Indian pitcher. Charles Albert "Chief" Bender, a rookie from Minnesota, was just 20 years old and had already won 17 games, starting a career that would lead to the Hall of Fame.

Throughout the winter, that picture in his major league baseball uniform inspired Elijah Pinnance as he ran long miles each day on the roads of Walpole Island. In the spring, "Eddie" Pinnance reported to the Athletics training camp. When the team headed north, "Chief" Bender was the only Indian pitcher on the team.

Pinnance was assigned to Portland of the Pacific Northwest League. For the next several years, his exploits filled newspaper columns with headlines that could not be published today.

"Heap Big Chief Pinnance, the copper-skinned twirler," was the way one report described the star pitcher of the Portland team. "Second scalp of the week taken from champions by pitcher Pinnance," says another report. He was called "medicine man" and "Big Indian." In 1909, Pinnance pitched 22 scoreless innings to beat Vancouver 1-0 in a game that lasted three hours and six minutes.

Diabetes shortened his career. Ed wouldn't stay on the diet prescribed by his doctor and he had to give up baseball. Returning to Walpole Island, Pinnance worked as a blacksmith. He shod horses, repaired sled runners and sharpened saws. His son Parker recalled that his father loved log-sawing contests and often won prizes. He planted evergreens and sold Christmas trees.

Elijah Pinnance's reputation attracted many visitors. The most famous visitor was Henry Ford, who donated a threshing machine, three tractors and a plough to the Chippewa band of Walpole Island.

Pinnance struggled with diabetes for years and doctors told him frequently that he had only a short time to live, but "Eddie" was still in his workshop every day. On December 14, 1944, after supper he said he didn't feel well and lay down to rest. He never rose from his sleep. Elijah Pinnance died of a heart attack at the age of 63.

Jimmy Archer, First of the Great Canadian Catchers

In the early years of the 20th century, three of the best catchers in baseball were Canadians. All had one fatal flaw: they couldn't hit.

Jimmy Archer was first on the scene, in 1904. A native of Dublin, Ireland, Archer came to Canada as a baby and was only three years old when his family moved from Montreal to Toronto. That was where he learned to play baseball. Archer was 20 years old when he made his professional debut in North Dakota.

The following year, Archer played in Iowa and played well enough to receive a September invitation from the Pittsburgh Pirates. Jimmy caught seven games and made three hits in 20 times at bat, signalling what was to be an enduring weakness - good field; no hit. Archer spent the next two seasons in Atlanta.

In 1907, Jimmy played 18 games with the Detroit Tigers. His hitting was even worse: five hits in 42 times at bat. His redeeming grace was his quick, accurate throwing arm. Detroit turned to Archer in the fifth game of the World Series after Chicago Cubs runners ran wild on Detroit's other catchers. Jimmy threw out a Chicago baserunner; but it was too late. After the first game was called because of darkness, the Cubs won four in a row.

Archer's miserable hitting doomed him to another stretch in the minors. Jimmy was playing for Buffalo in 1908, when Chicago Cubs manager Frank Chance came to scout a pitcher. Chance was more impressed by the catcher and offered Archer a job in 1909.

The Irishman from Toronto was the Cubs' regular catcher for the next eight years. His batting average ranged from .230 to .283 but three years in a row - from 1912 to 1914 - he was named to the Baseball Magazine "All-America Team." One of Jimmy's rivals, "Chief" Meyers, the outstanding catcher of the New York Giants in the same period, paid Archer the ultimate compliment. "The best throwing catcher of them all was Jimmy Archer," said Meyers. "He didn't have an arm. He had a rifle; and perfect accuracy."

Jimmy Archer's successors, Jay Clarke and George Gibson, made their debuts in 1905. At one glorious point, in 1911, all three men were everyday catchers with their respective teams.

Jimmy Archer; born in Ireland, raised in Canada. All-star catcher for the Chicago Cubs, 1912 to 1914. (National Baseball Hall of Fame Library, Cooperstown, NY)

Jay Clarke of Amherstburg Hit Eight Home Runs in a Game

Barry Bonds hit 73 home runs in one season; Hank Aaron hit 755 in his career; but only one man ever hit eight home runs in one game. He was a bandy-legged catcher from Amherstburg, Ontario.

Justin Jay Clarke was 21 years old, just starting a professional career that would last 24 years, when he made baseball history deep in the heart of Texas.

In more than 1,500 times at bat during nine years in the major leagues, Clarke hit a total of just six home runs, and never more than two in a season. Yet, on a Sunday afternoon, June 15, 1902, in the Texas town of Ennis, Jay Clarke hit eight home runs and had 16 runs batted in as Corsicana beat Texarkana 51-3.

The box score of the game shows a total of 21 home runs. Every man in the Corsicana lineup except the pitcher hit at least one. The first baseman and the second baseman each hit three, and a pair of the outfielders had two each.

Some critics disdain Jay Clarke's record. They say the park was a bandbox. It was easy to hit home runs in that park. I ask the question, "How come nobody else hit eight in that game?"

Why not accept the fact that for one day, Jay Clarke was a "Samson of Swat," the greatest home run hitter in history. For just one day!

One report says Jay Clarke came to bat eight times; another version says he batted 10 times. All stories agree he hit eight home runs.

Years later, Clarke told an interviewer the right-field fence was only 210 feet from home plate, and he, a left-handed batter, was able to pull the ball down the line. "I got the sixth and seventh ones high in the air and the wind carried them over," he confessed. "The last one just made it over the fence."

Clarke said that after he hit his fourth home run, a cattleman stepped out of the stand and handed him a $50 bill. Following his fifth home run, another rancher did the same. When the game ended, the fans passed the hat and gave the young home run hero another $85. "That was more than a month's salary," he said.

Canada's one-day wonder, Jay Clarke, was a descendant of United Empire Loyalists who moved to Canada from Pennsylvania. Clarke was the first of half a dozen graduates of Assumption College in Windsor who went on to play baseball in the major leagues.

As a catcher with Cleveland in 1906, Clarke batted .358 in 57 games. He played 120 games the following year and batted .263. Jay Clarke was renowned as a fielder. He was the catcher for Eddie Joss when the

Jay Clarke, Cleveland Indians catcher. (National Baseball Hall of Fame Library, Cooperstown, NY)

Cleveland right-hander pitched a perfect game against the Chicago White Sox on the final day of the 1908 season.

Jay Clarke's trademark was a quick toss of his catcher's mitt toward the home dugout after he tagged a sliding runner, even before the umpire called the play. Windsor historian Tony Techko says that a fist fight nearly broke out at an old-timers' reunion when Clarke told Ty Cobb that Cobb was actually safe many times when Clarke's toss of the mitt led the umpire to call Cobb "out."

Starting at Corsicana in 1902, the catcher from Ontario travelled a baseball path that went from coast to coast. Jay Clarke played in Little Rock, Duluth, Portland, Atlanta, Cleveland, Detroit, Baltimore, St. Louis, Indianapolis, San Francisco, Houston, Memphis, Mobile, Philadelphia, Greenville, Toledo, Milwaukee, Reading, Harrisburg, and Tulsa. His last stop was Salisbury, Maryland, of the Eastern Shore League. That's where he hit his last home run at the age of 44.

When Jay Clarke died in 1949, the Windsor Star described him as "one of the last survivors of the White Wyandotte Indians, who settled generations ago in Malden Township."

George Gibson: Canadian Baseball's First Poster Boy

If George Gibson were playing today he would be making television commercials and appearing on the David Letterman Show. In 1909, when Gibson emerged as one of the stars of the World Champion Pittsburgh Pirates, the highest form of media popularity was a newspaper advertisement for Coca-Cola.

That a catcher from London, Ontario, was featured in Coca-Cola's national advertising program is a tribute to the key role that George Gibson played in defeating Ty Cobb and the Detroit Tigers in the 1909 World Series.

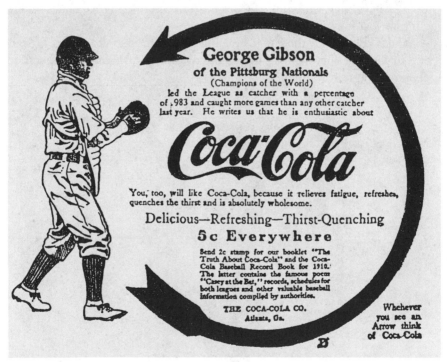

A Coca-Cola advertisement in the New York Times, 1910.

Cobb and the Tigers were the favourites to beat Pittsburgh. Ty Cobb and his teammate Donie Bush had stolen 129 bases between them. They were expected to run wild against the Pirates. Cobb stole one base in each of the first two games but no more.

In the first inning of the seventh and deciding game at Detroit, Bush tried to steal second base but Gibson made a perfect throw and Bush was

George Gibson, Pittsburgh catcher, 1915. (National Baseball Hall of Fame Library, Cooperstown, NY)

tagged for the third out. In the top of the second, Pittsburgh scored twice, and rolled to an 8-0 victory.

George Gibson matched Ty Cobb by stealing two bases himself and outhit Cobb in the series - .250 to .231. Gibson also drove in the winning run in the first game.

During the 1909 season, George Gibson set a major league record by catching 133 consecutive games. The Canadian stalwart caught all but four of the games played by the Pirates in their championship season and he was behind the plate for every Pittsburgh pitch of the World Series.

George Gibson played 12 seasons with Pittsburgh and finished his career with John McGraw's New York Giants. Gibson returned to Pittsburgh in 1920 as manager of the Pirates. When he was fired in 1934, George Gibson was the last Canadian to manage a major league baseball team and the most successful, with a record of 413 wins and 344 losses.

George Gibson was the Last Canadian Manager

Since 1876, four Canadians have managed major league teams.

Bill Watkins, an infielder from Brantford, Ontario, managed nine years in the major leagues. Watkins won the National League pennant in 1887 with Detroit.

Arthur Irwin, of Toronto, managed the Boston Reds to the American Association pennant in 1891. Irwin also managed Washington, the Phillies and the New York Giants.

Fred Lake, of Cornwallis, Nova Scotia, is the only man who managed Boston teams in both the American and the National Leagues: the Red Sox in 1909; the Doves in 1910.

George Gibson managed Pittsburgh from 1920 to 1922 and from 1932 to 1934. Gibson's Pirates finished second three times. He had the best winning percentage of any Canadian-born manager: 413 wins, 344 losses, (.546 average).

Napoleon Lajoie, Greatest Canadian Who Never Was!

Second-guessing begins with the first pitch, and "What if?" is the great question of baseball. What if the runner on second had kept running on a single to right field, instead of stopping at third base? What if the batter had taken a 3-2 pitch, instead of swinging at a sinker in the dirt?

What if Napoleon Lajoie had been born before his parents moved from Quebec to the United States? Would one of the game's greatest hitters still have made it to the Baseball Hall of Fame if he had been born in Canada?

The flow of French-Canadian families from rural Quebec to the "greener pastures" of New England is a well-documented fact of 19th-century history. More than a million residents of the northeastern United States trace their ancestors back to the farms and villages of Quebec. The most famous baseball name among those expatriate Canadians is surely Lajoie.

Napoleon Lajoie was a peerless second baseman for 21 years with the Philadelphia Athletics and the Cleveland Indians. He had career batting average of .339, and was elected to the National Baseball Hall of Fame in 1937.

James M. Murphy, author of *Napoleon Lajoie: Modern Baseball's First Superstar*, points out that Jean-Baptiste Lajoie and the former Celina Guertin raised five children on a farm near Saint-Hyacinthe, Quebec, before moving to Vermont.

The Lajoie family had four boys and one girl, all born in Quebec, when they crossed the border. Two more boys were born in Vermont before the family moved to Woonsocket, Rhode Island, where Napoleon was born September 15, 1875.

What if his parents had not moved to the United States? Would Napoleon Lajoie have been the greatest Canadian-born player in baseball history? If the Lajoie family had stayed in Quebec, would Napoleon ever have played baseball?

Another player whose parents surely came from Canada was Jean Dubuc. He was the pitching ace of the Detroit Tigers between 1912 and 1916, when he played against Napoleon Lajoie.

Dubuc pitched nine years in the major leagues and won 85 games. He won 17 games for Detroit in 1912 and won 17 again in 1915. Dubuc also pitched for Cincinnati and the New York Giants.

The handsome pitcher was born September 17, 1888, in St. Johnsbury, Vermont, where his father Napoleon was known as the

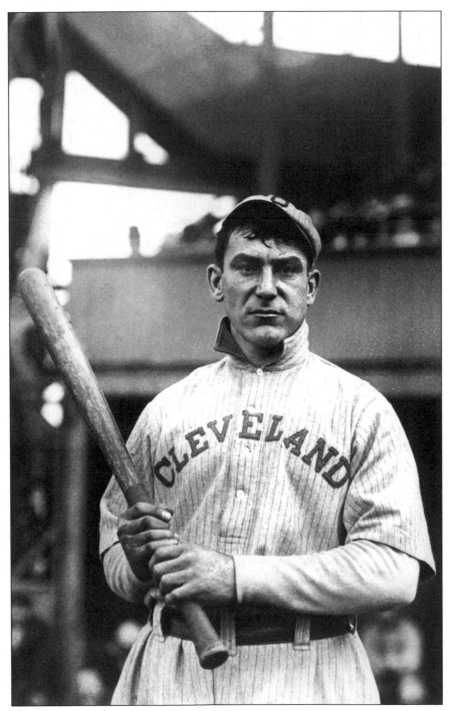

Napoleon Lajoie was one of baseball's first superstars. Five of his brothers and sisters were born in Quebec. (National Baseball Hall of Fame Library, Cooperstown, NY)

"French Canadian, who owned the Granite Construction Company." He was baptized Jean Baptiste Arthur Dubuc. When Jean was a teenager, his parents sent him to school in Montreal.

Dubuc pitched for the Montreal Royals in 1910. He opened a bowling alley and pool room on St. Catherine Street and bought shares in the Montreal Wanderers hockey team. Would it be a great surprise to learn that Jean Dubuc's parents were born in Quebec?

In 1918, Jean Dubuc was a teammate of "Babe" Ruth with the Boston Red Sox when they played the Chicago Cubs in the World Series. Dubuc pitched the last game of the regular season for the Red Sox against the Yankees in New York.

Jean Dubuc did not pitch in the World Series; but he was used as a pinch-hitter for third baseman Fred Thomas in the second game at Chicago. Dubuc, who hit four home runs during his career, struck out against "Lefty" Tyler of the Cubs in the ninth inning with two men on and one man out.

Boston used just four pitchers in the World Series: "Babe" Ruth, Carl Mays, "Bullet" Joe Bush and "Sad" Sam Jones. Ruth and Mays each won two games and the Red Sox took the championship in six games.

There were 15,238 spectators at Fenway Park for the final game. "Babe" Ruth played the last two innings in left field, and moved permanently to the outfield in 1919. In January 1920, the Red Sox sold "Babe" Ruth to the Yankees for $100,000, bringing down on Boston the "Curse of the Bambino" that would not be lifted until 2004, when the Red Sox won eight in a row against the Yankees and the Cardinals.

Jean Dubuc went to school in Montreal before starting his baseball career.
(National Baseball Hall of Fame Library, Cooperstown, NY)

Catcher Larry McLean of N.B., Shot Dead in a Boston Saloon

*"The big fellow ought to be one of the greatest
but never has been because of his careless habits."*

Hugh Fullerton, New York Times, October 4, 1913.

The careless habit that doomed Larry McLean was drink. The managers of the many teams for which he played all agreed that the big Canadian was a fine catcher and dangerous batter but none could find a way to keep him sober on a permanent basis.

Despite his drinking problem, McLean played more than 10 years in the majors and was the best hitter in the 1913 World Series. "Larry" McLean was born John Bannerman McLean in Fredericton, New Brunswick, July 18, 1881, but grew up in the Boston area. He acquired the nickname Larry because of a physical resemblance to Napoleon "Larry" Lajoie, one of the greatest players in the early years of the 20th century.

McLean stood six feet, five inches and weighed almost 230 pounds, about the size of a modern NFL linebacker. He was an imposing target for his own pitchers and a menace to any opponent. His threatening size may have contributed to his untimely death. McLean was shot dead by a frightened bartender in a Boston saloon.

Larry McLean's big league career began when he was just 19. He had a pinch-hit double on the opening day of the 1901 season for the Boston Red Sox. Larry had three more hits in 19 times at bat before being released in July and joining the Halifax Resolutes.

McLean played one game for the Chicago Cubs in 1903 and 27 games with the St. Louis Cardinals in 1904. He first attracted attention in Oregon, where he batted .355 and helped Portland to win the 1906 Pacific Coast League championship.

After his success in Portland, Larry was sold to the Cincinnati Reds and played an average of more than 100 games a year until 1912. McLean started the 1913 season with St. Louis but was traded to the New York Giants.

Larry McLean made his New York debut with two singles and three runs batted in as the Giants beat Cincinnati. On August 12, at Brooklyn, Larry helped Christy Matthewson celebrate his 33rd birthday by hitting a double as the Giants won in 11 innings. McLean played 30 games in the final two months of the regular season.

Larry helped the Giants to win their second pennant in three years, and he looked forward to a World Series against Connie Mack's Philadelphia Athletics.

Larry McLean, New York Giants catcher, 1913 World Series. (National Baseball Hall of Fame Library, Cooperstown, NY)

Hugh Fullerton of the New York Times predicted the Giants' hopes would rest on catcher "Chief" Meyers, whom he described as "the one really great hitter on the Giants." Fullerton added, "McLean, should he break in at all, is likely to make history. The big fellow ought to be one of the greatest but never has been because of his careless habits. He is a slashing, hard hitting batter, taking a terrific wallop at the ball, and is dangerous at any time."

Philadelphia won the first game 6-4 at the Polo Grounds in New York. In the second game at Philadelphia, Matthewson pitched a shutout and drove in the winning run in the 10th inning.

Larry McLean was a last-minute replacement for that game. He had two hits, including a 10th-inning single to start the winning rally. Manager John McGraw said, "Just before the game began, while Meyers was warming up the pitchers he broke his thumb on a measly little pitch and will be out for the rest of the series."

As Meyers' replacement, Larry McLean's batting was more than an adequate substitute for the injured catcher. McLean hit safely in each of the four games he started and led all batters on both teams with a .500 average.

In two of those games, Larry was lifted for a pinch-runner and his potent bat was not available in late innings. That was particularly important in game four when the Giants lost by a single run. McLean hit safely his first two times at bat but was removed in the fifth inning for a pinch-runner. His replacement struck out in the seventh inning and grounded out in the ninth.

The Giants lost all three games played in New York, and the Athletics won their third championship in four years.

When "Chief" Meyers returned as the Giants catcher in 1914, Larry McLean saw limited duty. He played even less in 1915, and was released after an argument with manager McGraw.

Six years later, the New York Times reported that Larry McLean was shot to death, March 24, 1921, in a Boston saloon. The saloon manager, John J. Connor, said he shot in self-defence when McLean started to climb over the counter to attack him.

According to Connor, McLean had been drinking. When the saloon manager refused to give him some cigarettes, McLean took offence and threatened to beat him up. As McLean started to climb over the counter, Connor reached for his gun and shot him. Larry McLean staggered to the sidewalk, where he collapsed and died. He was 39 years old.

Chapter 4

The
1930s and 40s

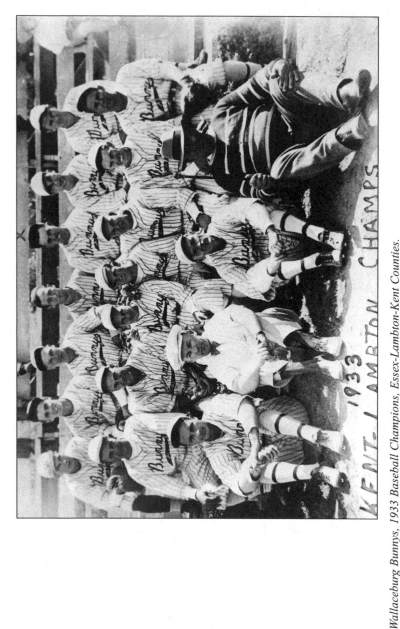

Wallaceburg Bunnys, 1933 Baseball Champions, Essex-Lambton-Kent Counties.
Front row: Walter Conway, Clare "Bunny" Sutherland, sponsor; Carl Young, Herb "Casey" Doan, manager:
Middle row: Lester "Boney" Shepley, Ernie McFadden, Bill Conway, Lorne Goodman, Harry "Bucky" Hystead, Charlie Gormely, Don Pettifer:
Top row: Vaughan "Mud" Judson, Al Foster, Joe Butterman, Red McFadden, Bill McIntyre, John "Goose Egg" Rankin, Donald Fish.
(Photo courtesy Bill McIntyre, via Mann Historical Files)

Spring Training in Florida
With Casey's Dodgers in 1935

It's impossible to imagine in today's big-business baseball world but in March 1935, two young lads from Wallaceburg, Ontario, shared spring training with the Brooklyn Dodgers. Bill McIntyre and Charlie Gormely, members of the Wallaceburg Bunnys, champions of the Essex-Lambton-Kent Intercounty League, decided to get a head start on the baseball season.

Crossing the border at Windsor, they made their way to Orlando, Florida, and Tinker Field, off-season home of the Brooklyn Dodgers. Bill McIntyre described it as "a modest, perhaps even decrepit, facility for a big league ball team. An old frame building served as dressing room, shower room and equipment rooms. The plumbing and lighting were archaic." There was a covered wooden grandstand behind home plate and uncovered wooden bleachers behind third base and first base.

"Charlie and I got to Orlando a few days before the pitchers and catchers were due to report and about a week ahead of the rest of the players. We were hoping to find the park open so we could do some running and throwing," says Bill. "We were surprised to find half-a-dozen Dodger players in a game of 'Pepper.' Third baseman Joe Stripp was hitting golf balls in the outfield."

The two Canadians put on their baseball spikes and gloves, intending to run and throw on the sidelines, but were soon invited to join the Dodgers. Spring training consisted of morning and afternoon workouts that stressed conditioning and repeated execution of technical aspects of the game, such as fielding a sacrifice bunt or taking a relay throw from the outfield.

Charlie and Bill chose a shade tree near the left-field fence for the two-hour lunch break. "Soon after," Bill recalls, "Casey Stengel and his assistant, Otto Miller, sat down under a nearby tree. 'Come on over, fellows,' Casey hollered, 'there's more shade over here.'" Those lunch breaks became an "inside baseball" clinic for the young Canadians.

While Charlie worked with the infielders, Bill was shagging flies in the outfield where the pitchers ran sprints after batting practice. "Les Munns, a big right-hander from New York, and I became friends," McIntyre says. "Once, I made a running catch of a line drive. Les ran over, 'Great catch,' he said, 'but if you want to make this club, you better let a fly ball land on your head. All the others do!'"

When exhibition games began, only Dodger players were allowed in the clubhouse or on the field. "For the first game against the Phillies, the bleachers behind third base were almost full so Charlie and I sat back of first base, where the bleacher was nearly empty," Bill recalls. "At the end of the inning, one of the Phillies passed about three feet from us. 'Hey fellas, that stand is for the colored folk' he said out of the side of his mouth. We moved to the other stand."

Spring training is a time for experiment. Bill McIntyre remembers a game against Detroit. In the fifth inning, the first Dodger batter, Harry Eisenstadt, led off with a triple. The next batter hit a fly ball to centre field. "Before the catch, 'Jo-Jo' White, the Detroit fielder, realized there was no way to prevent the runner from scoring, unless..."

With the ball still in the air, White pretended to catch the ball and simulated a throw to the infield. Eisenstadt took off for home. The third-base coach realized they had been tricked and called Eisenstadt back, just in time to avoid being tagged for a double play.

Another incident involved Brooklyn catcher Al Lopez, later a successful manager and member of the Baseball Hall of Fame. The Dodgers were protecting a one-run lead, McIntyre recalls. "The other team had runners on first and second with nobody out. It was a perfect situation for a sacrifice bunt or a double steal.

"Lopez called for a pitch-out but the runners held their bases. The batter was now set up for a sacrifice bunt. Lopez called for a fastball. As the pitcher released the ball, Lopez dashed from behind the plate to a spot just inside the third-base line. He fielded the bunt on one hop and threw to third base for the force out. The relay to second pulled the fielder off the bag; but the second baseman's throw to first was in time for a double play that was almost a triple play."

One of the most-talked about players in spring training was a man who batted .320 for the Dodgers in 1934, and set a record for outfielders with a fielding average of .994.

He was strong and fast, and the newspapers praised his extraordinary upper-body strength, developed by shovelling coal as a locomotive fireman in Pennsylvania.

Charlie Gormely asked Danny Taylor, the left fielder, "What kind of guy is [the player]?" The answer was brief and pointed. "He's a screwball," said Taylor. Gormely and McIntyre kept a close watch on that player. Their conclusion: "He was a maladjusted individual, an introvert to the point of being a 'loner' who rebuffed friendly overtures from his teammates," said McIntyre.

The two Canadians returned to Wallaceburg, enriched forever by their experience at a major league training camp. Six months later, Bill McIntyre and Charlie Gormely remembered Danny Taylor's description of the player when they read the following headline in the daily newspaper:

BALLPLAYER IS KILLED
IN PLANE AS HE ATTACKS THE CREW
Hit over Head by Pilot with Fire Extinguisher
After 15-Minute Mid-Air Battle with
Ship Out of Control over Toronto

It happened September 17, 1935, two weeks before the end of the season. Following a series against the Cubs in Chicago, the player, Les Munns and pitcher Bobby Barr were sent home by the Dodgers. They boarded an American Airlines flight from Chicago to Newark. The man, who had a bottle, started drinking. He got into an argument with another passenger. He knocked down a stewardess who tried to intervene and was finally returned to his seat by the co-pilot, with the help of his Dodger teammates.

When the flight stopped at Detroit, the player was ordered off the plane. The airport manager testified the player was drunk and quarrelsome. While Munns and Barr continued on to Newark, the man tried to book passage on another flight but was refused. Undaunted, he chartered a small plane to take him to Buffalo. The only passengers were the player, pilot William Joseph Mulqueeny of Detroit, and the co-pilot, Irwin Davis.

The two men said the player sat quietly at first but soon began bumping the pilot on the shoulder. Then he got into a fight with the co-pilot. Mulqueeny later testified that the plane was rocking dangerously and he lost all sense of direction during that fight, which lasted 10 to 15 minutes.

"I had to come to a decision," he said. "It was a case of three of us crashing, or doing something to the player." The pilot reached for a small fire extinguisher. "I watched my chance," he said, "and walloped him over the head." Mulqueeny had to hit the man two or three times to stop the fight.

When the plane made an emergency landing at Toronto, the ballplayer was dead. The pilot and co-pilot were charged with manslaughter and held in jail. Three days later a coroner's court ruled the killing was self-defence.

Perth Was a Good Baseball Town, Emil Graff Just Couldn't Leave It!

Emil Graff spent most of his youth around Baker Field in Philadelphia, where Connie Mack's Athletics were the toast of the town. He loved baseball from the moment he was old enough to swing a bat.

Baseball brought Emil to the Ottawa Valley in 1935, to be the catcher for the Perth Royals. He was 25 years old. "I thought it was just a summer job," Emil told me; but he stayed for life.

Emil lived in the same boarding house with pitcher Oscar Judd, who would go on to a major league career. "Oscar had a curve that broke low and away," Emil remembered. "You felt like a coal miner after a game with Oscar Judd. You were always in the dirt." Oscar chewed tobacco all the time.

When a 3 and 2 pitch got away from Graff with the bases loaded, Judd spat out a black stream and muttered, "If I had a catcher..." Graff replied, "You don't need a catcher. You need a brick wall."

In 1936, a new league was formed: the Canadian-American League, with three teams from Ontario and three from New York. Ottawa, Perth and Brockville were the Canadian teams and the American clubs were Ogdensburg, Watertown and Oswego.

The Perth Royals played their games at the Perth Collegiate athletic field. Opposing players said it was impossible to hit a ball out of the park in left field because of a row of tall maple trees. "You might be able to roll it out if you hit a ground ball down third base," said Emil, "but you certainly couldn't hit a ball over those trees."

The Royals were a good hitting team. Seven players batted over .300, and Perth finished in first place with 50 wins and 30 losses. Mike Sperrick, the Perth second baseman, was the batting champion with an average of .360. Sperrick and left fielder Joe Gunn were named to the all-star team. Norman Hibbs was the Royals' best pitcher, and "Hiker" Moran later pitched for the Boston Red Sox.

Emil Graff had two job offers in 1937. Connie Mack, the most famous manager in baseball, wanted him to work in the Philadelphia farm system. The Perth Royals asked him to succeed Steve Yerkes as playing-manager.

Emil had met Isabel Ennis of Perth and he didn't want to leave town. Emil stayed in Perth, married Isabel and the newlyweds borrowed $1,000 from the bank to start a chicken farm.

Soon after, Emil Graff was flat on his back, confined to bed. "The doctor found a hole in my heart," he said. "I was off for nearly a year. Isabel had to do everything. She fed the chickens, ran the farm and looked after me."

Emil recovered. He never had serious health problems again and spent the rest of his life in Perth. "I loved baseball," said Emil, "but Perth is a town that is just too good to leave."

PERTH ROYALS, 1936 CANADIAN-AMERICAN LEAGUE CHAMPIONS:
Top row (left to right) Emil Graff, catcher; Joe Mooney, shortstop; Frank Marinette, first base; Mike Sperrick, second base; Hugh Grabowski, pitcher; Eddie Howard, centre field; Steve Yerkes, manager.
Front row: Al Tarlecki, third base; Joe Gunn, right field; Norman Hibbs, pitcher; Fred Barnes, left field; Charles Oliver Thomas, pitcher; Ross Barkwell, pitcher.
(Hollington Photo; courtesy Emil Graff)

Oscar Judd, Good Hitter,
Was Injured Trying to Bunt

Who was the first Canadian-born pitcher to win 20 games in both the American League and the National League? Ferguson Jenkins won 20 or more games in a season six years in a row for the Chicago Cubs of the National League between 1967 and 1971, and he won 25 games for the Texas Rangers of the American League in 1974.

However, the first Canadian to win 20 games in each league was Oscar Judd, a left-hand pitcher from an Ontario town that doesn't exist any more. Oscar won 20 games for the Boston Red Sox between 1941 and 1945, and 20 games for the Philadelphia Phillies between 1945 and 1948. Judd won a total of 40 games in his big league career and he split those wins 20-20 between the two leagues.

Other people talked about his hitting - and he was good enough to be used as a pinch-hitter - but Oscar insisted he was first a pitcher, and a better pitcher than most people gave him credit for. He was already 33 years old when he made his major league debut in Boston. Two years later, Oscar was selected for the American League all-star team, and at age 40 he was still good enough to pitch a no-hit game for the Toronto Maple Leafs of the International League in 1948.

Thomas William Oscar Judd was born February 14, 1908, in Rebecca, Ontario, a town of less than 200 people that now lies buried beneath the asphalt runways of the London (Ontario) airport.

After playing amateur baseball in Ingersoll and Guelph, Oscar pitched for seven teams in seven different leagues from the Ottawa Valley to Georgia, and the Pacific Coast. He won 22 games for Sacramento in 1940 to earn his chance at the big leagues.

Oscar Judd faced just one batter in his debut with the Boston Red Sox. It was April 16, 1941, against Washington. Starting pitcher Charlie Wagner had blown a four-run lead in the eighth inning and Oscar came in to retire Ben Chapman for the third out. Ted Williams pinch-hit for Judd in the Boston half of the inning and flied out to right field. The Red Sox eventually won in 12 innings.

"Tom" Judd, as the Boston newspapers referred to him, made his next appearance at Cleveland on May 1. Fellow-Canadian Jeff Heath had just cleared the bases with a fifth-inning triple to give the Indians a 6-3 lead. Judd allowed one hit over the rest of the game. Oscar marked his first time at bat by hitting a double off the centre-field wall.

In 1942, Oscar Judd was the Red Sox's opening-day pitcher at Yankee Stadium in New York. He gave up five singles and struck out

Oscar Judd, all-star pitcher for the 1943 Boston Red Sox. (National Baseball Hall of Fame Library, Cooperstown, NY)

Oscar Judd (left), ace of the 1946 Phillies, with team-mates "Schoolboy" Rowe (centre) and Ken Raffensberger. (Philadelphia Athletics Historical Society)

five but lost 1-0. The only run followed a two-base throwing error by the third baseman.

For the season, Judd started 19 games and went the distance in 11. He won eight and lost 10, and confirmed his hitting reputation with a pair of home runs. Boston finished in second place, nine games behind the Yankees. Ted Williams won the triple crown with 36 home runs, 137 runs batted in and a .356 average.

The 1943 season was a disaster for the Red Sox, who lost Williams, Dom DiMaggio and Johnny Pesky to military service. Boston tumbled from second place to seventh. Judd and relief pitcher Mike Ryba were the only Boston pitchers who won more games than they lost.

Oscar Judd made a splendid start, with seven wins and three losses in the first three months. Oscar was chosen to the American League team for the all-star game at Shibe Park in Philadelphia. "Dutch" Leonard, Hal Newhouser and Tex Hughson each pitched three innings for the Americans. Judd was not called on to pitch and he watched his teammate Bobby Doerr hit a home run with two men on base as the American League beat the Nationals 5-3.

In the next month, Oscar won four more games: at Washington, in Boston against St. Louis and Detroit, and in St. Louis where the Red Sox swept a doubleheader on August 15.

Judd was the ace of the staff, with a record of 11 wins and six losses. Oscar was one of the best pitchers in the league but he didn't pitch another game in the final six weeks of the season. Why didn't Boston's best pitcher pitch even one inning after August 15?

I found the answer in the microfilm collection of the Boston Public Library. A day-by-day search of the Boston Globe and the Herald-Traveller revealed that Oscar Judd missed a scheduled appearance because of "a sore arm."

Judd couldn't pitch for the final six weeks because he was injured when manager Joe Cronin asked him to bunt in a game against Detroit on July 28. Oscar badly bruised a shoulder muscle when a high, inside pitch by Virgil Trucks drove the top end of the bat into his shoulder with such great force that it left Judd's upper arm sore and discoloured.

Oscar started against Cleveland four days later but lasted just one-third of an inning. Judd didn't pitch for another two weeks, and he made his final appearance of the year in St. Louis, August 15. He pitched five innings and won 3-2. That was Oscar's 11th and final victory of the year.

For the last month-and-a-half of the 1943 season, Oscar Judd's shoulder was too sore for him to pitch. It was still sore the next year, and Oscar pitched only 30 innings in 1944. The following year, Judd made two brief appearances with the Red Sox.

On May 31, 1945, Oscar was claimed on waivers by the Philadelphia Phillies. In the next three years, he pitched almost 30 games a season. When he won 11 games in 1946, the Associated Press called Oscar Judd, "The Phillies one-man pitching staff."

How ironic it is that Oscar Judd, Boston's best-hitting pitcher - and best-pitching pitcher - was injured because he was told to bunt instead of being allowed to hit away!

George Selkirk of Huntsville, Good Enough to Be a Yankee

Of all the Canadian-born players in the first half of the 20th century, George Selkirk was clearly the best. He had to be very good to play for nine years with the best team in baseball, as a teammate of "Babe" Ruth, Lou Gehrig, Joe DiMaggio and six other players who wound up in the Baseball Hall of Fame.

Selkirk was born in the Georgian Bay area at Huntsville, Ontario, but his family moved to Rochester, New York, when George was five years old. That's where he developed his baseball ability and first attracted attention as a high-school catcher.

George Selkirk made his debut with the Yankees on the day "Babe" Ruth said goodbye. It was August 12, 1934, in a Sunday doubleheader that was advertised as Ruth's farewell to Boston, the city where his career began.

The biggest crowd ever to see a baseball game in Boston spilled out of the stands and stood behind ropes in the outfield. The official attendance was 40,000 and another 15,000 people were turned away.

"Babe" Ruth played left field, Ben Chapman was in centre field and George Selkirk played right field. Ruth had a double and a single in the first game, and he walked twice in the second game. George Selkirk had a single in each game. George played in 46 of the Yankees' final 49 games that year, and finished with 55 hits and a .313 batting average.

The next year, Selkirk not only replaced "Babe" Ruth in the Yankee outfield, he even wore Ruth's number three uniform. George told manager Joe McCarthy, "If I'm going to take his place, I'll take his number too." Selkirk made 153 hits in 128 games, and batted .312 with 11 home runs and 94 runs batted in.

Joe DiMaggio made his debut as the Yankee left fielder in 1936. George Selkirk played right field. He batted over .300 for the third year in a row, and had 18 home runs and 107 runs batted in.

In the spring of 1937, George Selkirk switched to left field and DiMaggio moved to centre field. For the next dozen years, "Joltin' Joe" was the symbol of effortless grace in the field and unbridled power with the bat.

Playing in DiMaggio's glow, Selkirk rose to new heights. George was batting .344 and was tied with Hank Greenberg for the lead in home runs when disaster struck on Canada Day.

July 1 was then known as Dominion Day, and it was on that day in 1937 that George Selkirk broke his collarbone, diving for a fly ball in

George Selkirk, New York Yankees. (National Baseball Hall of Fame Library, Cooperstown, NY)

Philadelphia. He missed two-and-a-half months and did not play again until mid-September. Even though he missed half a season, George hit 18 home runs and drove in 68 runs in 78 games.

Selkirk's best year was 1939, when he batted .306, hit 21 home runs and had 101 runs batted in. In May, George hit four consecutive home runs against the same Philadelphia relief pitcher over two consecutive games.

Between 1936 and 1942, the Yankees won the American League pennant six times in seven years and they won the World Series five times. George Selkirk had a hand in all that glory.

The slugger from Huntsville hit a home run off Carl Hubbell his first time at bat in the 1936 series. Selkirk hit safely in nine consecutive World Series games. No other Canadian ever drank champagne from the championship cup as many times as George Selkirk.

From 1943 to 1945, Selkirk served in the U.S. Navy. After the war, he became the playing-manager of the Yankees' top farm team, the Newark Bears.

At the age of 38, George Selkirk returned to his native province, and to the city of Toronto where he briefly played for the Maple Leafs in 1932. George came back to the stadium on the lakeshore. He stood once again on the field from where, in 1934, he left to join the Yankees at "Babe" Ruth's Boston farewell.

Don Errey Made a Wooden Leg and Bert Shepard Pitched Again

Lance Corporal Donovan Errey of Wallaceburg, Ontario, couldn't speak a word of German but he didn't need an interpreter to tell him that the doctors in a prisoner-of-war camp wanted to amputate his left foot.

"What are they saying?" the young Canadian asked a New Zealand medical officer making the rounds with two German doctors. "It's badly infected. They want to amputate," said the New Zealander. "I think I can save it. They're going to let me try."

The young man facing the loss of his foot had grown up quickly in the three years since joining the Essex Scottish Regiment at the age of 17 with his older brother, Victor, in Windsor. He landed at Dieppe, France, in the summer of 1942. Within hours, thousands of Canadians were evacuated from the beaches.

Like other soldiers, Don Errey helped carry wounded comrades to the rescue boats. When all the boats were filled, he was left in the Channel for about three hours holding onto anything that would float. Don crawled ashore to find that he was wounded.

"As soon as I stood, my foot swelled up like a balloon," he said. "I had been hit by a bullet but didn't feel it in the cold water." Two German soldiers who captured him couldn't help laughing.

"All I had on was my undershorts. They carried me on their rifles and put me in a big barn with other prisoners." Don wound up in hospital at Obermanfeld. Gangrene had set in and the Germans were ready to amputate his foot. The doctor from New Zealand cleaned it every day, and saved Don Errey's foot.

Once he was mobile, Don went looking for his brother Victor. "We both went ashore at Dieppe but I never saw him after the landing," he said. "I thought he might be a prisoner in another area, so I volunteered for work duty." Don became quite a pest trying to get from camp to camp but he never did find his brother.

Errey was a nuisance to the Germans but a godsend to prisoners who had lost a limb. A despondent British soldier, crying that he would never walk again, stirred the Canadian to a rash promise. "I'll make you a leg," said the young corporal who had the reputation of being good with his hands. "The shoemaker gave me a wooden foot last to use as a model. It was clumsy but we improved as we went along."

Don made artificial limbs out of any scrap material he could find, including old chair legs. "I used jam pails to make arms for a soldier who lost both arms so he could hold a cigarette or read a book," he recalled.

Geneva Convention inspectors visiting the camp saw what Don was doing and sent him steel bars through the Red Cross. He gave chocolate and cocoa out of food packages from Canada to a German mechanic who shaped the flat pieces of steel. Don also recruited two other prisoners. "One was good with leather; the other was handy with wood," Don recounted. "I did all the metal work." Together, they fashioned about 300 legs, arms and splints.

In 1944, Don Errey met Lieutenant Bert Shepard, an American pilot who lost part of his right leg when his plane was shot down near Berlin.

Before enlisting, Shepard had been a pitcher for Bisbee, Arizona, in the Class C Arizona-Texas League. In the prison camp, the American and the Canadian became good friends. When Bert's stump healed, Don made an artificial leg.

"It had a bending toe and a bending ankle," he said. "The knee joint also bent and locked at a certain point." Lieutenant Shepard was soon running on his wooden leg.

"Thanks to Don Errey, I was able to maintain muscle tone and develop good mobility," Bert told me. Shepard was freed in a prisoner exchange, and in March 1945 he was fitted with a new leg at Walter Reed Hospital in Washington, D.C.

Four days later, Bert Shepard reported to the Washington Senators training camp and was hired as an assistant coach and pitcher. Once the season began, Bert was not getting any playing time so he asked to be sent to the Senators' farm team at Chattanooga. He won two games and lost two and also played first base before being recalled to Washington.

When the Senators visited Detroit in July, Lance Corporal Don Errey was a special guest of the Washington Baseball Club. "My dad, myself, another man from Dominion Glass and his son, who was about 13, had lunch with Bert at his hotel," Errey said.

"Then we went to the ballpark. We met all the players in the dressing room and Bert gave me an autographed baseball." A frown wrinkled Don Errey's forehead as he remembered. "The whole team signed that ball for me. This kid kept asking to hold it." Don never saw the ball again.

Bert Shepard, with his artificial leg, pitched only one game in the major leagues. It was the second game of a doubleheader at Washington, August 4, 1945, against Boston. The Red Sox won the first game and they had scored 12 runs before Bert entered the game in the fourth inning.

With the bases loaded and two out, Shepard struck out Eddie Lake, and pitched five more innings to finish the game. He allowed one run on three hits, walked one batter and struck out two.

In September, Bert had another operation on his leg. "I was on crutches for two-and-a-half years," he said. "That ended my baseball career."

Washington pitcher Bert Shepard presented an autographed baseball to Lance Corporal Don Errey in July 1945. (Photo courtesy of Don Errey)

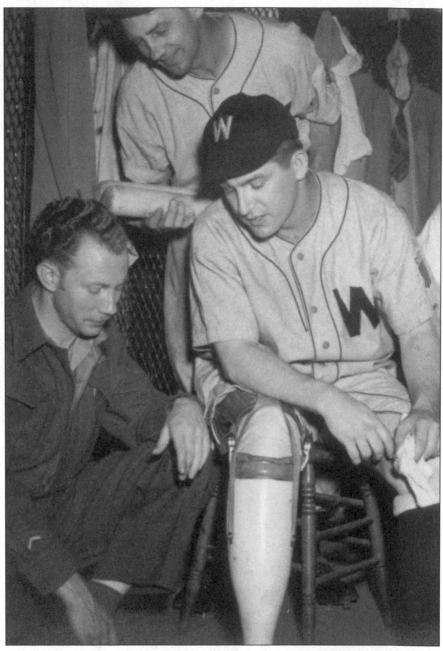

Don Errey examined the artificial leg of Bert Shepard in the Washington Senators dressing room. (Photo courtesy of Don Errey)

Bert Shepard moved to California and worked as a safety engineer for Hughes Aircraft. He took up golf and won two national championships for golfers with disabilities.

After his discharge from the Canadian Army, Don Errey made an arm for a rural mailman. "He put the mail into the mail boxes with his right hand," Don said, "but his left hand was gone. I made him a hand to steer the car. That was the end of it."

A hospital near Detroit offered Don a job. "But I didn't want to go to the States," he said. Don worked seven years as warehouse manager for H.J. Heinz, until the Wallaceburg plant was closed. "They moved me to Leamington to deal with complaints.

"Every morning there was a stack of complaints on my desk. That started to get to me; so I quit and moved to London." Don worked as a travelling salesman for Harding Carpets for the next 30 years until he retired. In his London apartment, Don Errey showed his scrapbooks and photos to a visitor from Ottawa.

NOTE: Victor Errey was killed at Dieppe on August 19, 1942. He was 24 years old. Victor is buried in Brockwood Military Cemetery, the largest Commonwealth war cemetery in the United Kingdom.

Pitcher Joe Krakauskas,
Great Potential; Never Realized

Joe Krakauskas could throw a baseball through a wall. That's not speculation. It's a reported fact. It happened in September 1936, at Trenton, New Jersey. Krakauskas was 21 years old, and had just finished the regular season in Brockville, Ontario. Joe had pitched a no-hit, no-run game, and struck out more than 200 batters over the season.

Impressed by Joe's performance in Canada, the Washington Senators invited him to try out for their farm team in the New York-Pennsylvania League. Melvin Murphy, business manager of the Trenton team, went to meet Joe at the hotel. On his way, Murphy picked up a dozen baseballs, and had the box under his arm when he shook hands with Krakauskas.

"How's your arm, Joe?" Murphy asked.

"Let me see one of those balls," Krakauskas answered.

Joe grabbed one of the balls, went into his wind-up motion, and fired the ball right at the wall. A woman's scream pierced the air, as the astonished Murphy stared at a hole in the wall.

Krakauskas signed a contract to pitch for the 1937 season, and went home to Hamilton, Ontario. Joe returned to Trenton in April, and won 14 games in the minors. In September, Joe jumped straight from New Jersey to the Washington Senators.

Joe Krakauskas made his major league debut in what looked like a hopeless situation, on a Thursday afternoon in Philadelphia. Washington was down six runs after two innings. Joe was sent out to start the third inning. "Let's see what the kid can do," said manager Bucky Harris.

The "kid" from Canada allowed only one hit and no runs over the next seven innings. Joe's pitching inspired the Senators to erupt for seven runs in the fifth inning. They won the game 13-6.

In the closing weeks of the 1937 season, Krakauskas pitched complete games to beat St. Louis, Cleveland and the Yankees.

On September 28, the tall left-hander beat the Yankees 2-1. Joe DiMaggio singled to score "Red" Rolfe in the first inning. After that, Krakauskas struck out nine batters and shut out the Yankees over the last eight innings.

In less than three weeks, the graduate of Hamilton's Cathedral High School pitched five games and won four of them.

The following spring, Joe Krakauskas expected to be one of the Senators' starting pitchers but manager Harris had other plans. Joe didn't throw his first pitch until April 29, and he faced only one batter in that game.

Joe Krakauskas, Washington Senators, 1939. (National Baseball Hall of Fame Library, Cooperstown, NY)

Joe came in to start the ninth inning at Philadelphia, with the score tied. He walked the first batter, Bill Werber, and then was replaced by Bill Phebus, who walked two more batters to load the bases. Werber, the runner on third, stole home with the winning run, and Joe was the losing pitcher.

Krakauskas did not make his first start until June 16; and when he did, it was at Cleveland against the American League strikeout king, Bob Feller, and the first-place Indians.

Joe pitched five innings, and allowed three runs on eight hits. A two-run home run by Ken Keltner was the big blow for Cleveland. Krakauskas struck out three batters and walked two.

For almost two months, Joe did not start another game. Then he pitched twice within five days against the Yankees' best pitchers. At New York, August 11, Joe gave up four hits and six walks in five innings. He lost to "Lefty" Gomez 9-6. Five days later, Krakauskas struck out 10 Yankees in seven innings; but he gave up a two-run home run to DiMaggio, and lost to "Red" Ruffing 6-2.

After escaping from the bullpen, and going head-to-head against three of the best pitchers in the league, Joe Krakauskas was ready to finish the season with a spectacular flourish. In the final 30 days, Joe started seven games, and went the distance five times.

Krakauskas beat New York twice in that stretch. In Washington, Joe struck out eight Yankees on September 11, and had two hits himself against "Spud" Chandler. On September 28 in Yankee Stadium, Joe gave up a triple to Joe DiMaggio for the only New York run in a 4-1 victory.

During that final month, the Canadian left-hander was virtually unbeatable. Washington won 13 games and lost 13 in September; but in the games that Joe Krakauskas pitched, the Senators won six and lost only one.

So far in his career, Joe Krakauskas had pitched the equivalent of six months of major league baseball. He had started 34 games and had won 11 and lost six. If there was one warning signal, it was the number of bases on balls Krakauskas allowed. While striking out 122 batters, Joe walked 110.

Washington manager Bucky Harris tried to be optimistic. "Krakky will be a number one pitcher one of these days," Harris said. "He's wild right now, and wildness destroys his effectiveness. As soon as he finds the plate with every second pitch, he's bound to be good."

By 1939, Joe Krakauskas was the number three man in the Washington pitching rotation, behind "Dutch" Leonard, who won 20 games, and Ken Chase, a left-hander, who won 10 and lost 19.

That was the year wildness caught up with Joe Krakauskas. For the first time, he walked more batters than he struck out in 1939. Joe had always been successful with his fastball; but when batters stopped swinging at the first pitch, he was in deep trouble.

Krakauskas started 29 times for the Senators and pitched 12 complete games. He won 11 and lost 17. Joe's earned run average jumped to 4.60 from 3.12, and opposing batters averaged almost 10 hits per nine innings.

In 1940, Joe Krakauskas was back in the bullpen. He started 10 games and relieved 22 times. Once again, Joe walked more batters than he struck out, and it showed in the results: one win and six losses, with an ERA of 6.44.

Washington Times-Herald reporter Vincent X. Flaherty lamented the decline of the young pitcher. When Krakauskas came to Washington three years before, Flaherty said, "The big, blond and bow-legged kid had everything; speed, endurance, a modicum of intelligence, and the muscular and mental co-ordination of a natural athlete."

On Christmas Eve 1940, Washington traded Krakauskas to the Cleveland Indians for outfielder Ben Chapman. Joe never again approached the brilliance of his first days with Washington. He pitched 41 innings for Cleveland but spent most of the next two years in the International League.

From 1942 to 1945, Joe Krakauskas served in the Royal Canadian Air Force.

Joe got his last chance with Cleveland in 1946. He pitched in 29 games but averaged less than two innings a game and finished with two wins and five losses. That was the end of Joe's big league career: an endless promise that was never fulfilled.

He lived in Detroit for many years, and then returned to Hamilton in 1959. Joe Krakauskas contracted encephalitis, a brain disease, and died July 8, 1960, at the age of 45.

Don Newcombe Saw Heath's World Series Dream Shattered

"That was the worst thing I ever saw in baseball," Don Newcombe said, pointing to the cover of my book, *Canada's Baseball Legends*. The photo shows Newcombe's teammate Roy Campanella tagging Jeff Heath on the right leg, while Heath's left foot is bending backwards behind him.

Between 1945 and 1952, the Montreal Royals were the top farm team of the Brooklyn Dodgers. Some of the greatest players of that era played in Montreal. Jackie Robinson, "Duke" Snider, Roy Campanella and Don Newcombe were among the future Brooklyn heroes I watched as a 12-year-old fan at Delorimier Stadium.

Exactly 50 years after it happened, I spoke with Don Newcombe at a baseball banquet about the August night in 1948 when he pitched a no-hitter against the Toronto Maple Leafs.

I was standing behind home plate when the last batter, Vic Barnhart, drilled a line drive off Newcombe's chest. The six-foot, four-inch pitcher staggered backwards. He turned in a circle, looking for the ball that had fallen at his feet. Everybody in the stadium was shouting and pointing while Barnhart ran towards first base. Finally, Newcombe saw the ball, picked it up and threw to first, just in time to get the final out.

Just a month later, Don Newcombe was in Brooklyn, watching from the Dodger dugout as the greatest Canadian-born player of his era, Jeff Heath, began the final games of the regular season at Ebbets Field.

Heath was an outfielder with the Boston Braves, who were playing the Dodgers before facing the Cleveland Indians in the World Series. Rex Barney was pitching for the Dodgers and another rookie from Montreal, "Duke" Snider, was playing centre field. The Braves were already leading in the sixth inning when Jeff hit a long double over Snider's head. When the next batter singled to right field, Heath headed for home.

The Braves had clinched the pennant but manager Billy Southworth urged them not to let up. Jeff Heath came sliding into home plate as though the season hung in the balance. Catcher Roy Campanella was on the outside of the foul line waiting for the throw. Heath slid to the inside of the plate. As Campanella tagged Heath on the right leg, Jeff's left foot bent backwards behind him.

"You could hear the bone break all the way to the dugout," Newcombe remembered. "The umpire yelled for a stretcher right away." As his team-mates rushed to the plate, Jeff Heath lay on his back, his head in his hands, and screamed with pain.

Jeff Heath's left foot bends backwards as Roy Campanella tags him out; Ebbets Field, Brooklyn, 1948. (National Baseball Hall of Fame Library, Cooperstown, NY)

After 13 years in the majors, the best Canadian player of his era was going to the World Series for the first time until he broke his ankle trying to score a run that didn't matter.

When the Series began, Jeff Heath had a cast on his ankle and a pair of crutches as he took the elevator up to the press box for the opening game at Braves Field in Boston.

Heath's former team-mate, Bob Feller, was pitching for Cleveland in the bottom of the eighth inning of a scoreless game. Boston catcher Phil Masi was leading off second base when the Indians' shortstop Lou Boudreau sneaked behind him just as Feller made a perfect throw to the bag.

The picture sequence in the newspaper showed Boudreau with the ball in his glove tagging Masi before he got back to the base, but the umpire called him safe. The Indians argued in vain, and when play resumed, Tommy Holmes singled to drive in Masi with the only run. Feller allowed just two hits but the Braves won the game one to nothing.

In the end, Cleveland prevailed over Boston in six games but for Bob Feller and his former team-mate, Jeff Heath, the 1948 series was a personal disappointment. Feller was beaten twice by the Braves in the only World Series he ever played, and Heath could only lean on his crutches and watch.

Jeff Heath never got that close to the World Series again. He retired after the 1949 season with a total of 1,447 hits, including 194 home runs, and a lifetime batting average of .293. Until Larry Walker came along 40 years later and rewrote the record book, Jeff Heath was the greatest Canadian-born batter in baseball history.

Dick Fowler Pitched Longest Game and the Only Canadian No-Hitter

Imagine you have bursitis and you feel pain every time you raise your arm. Now, imagine you are a baseball pitcher and you have to raise your arm and fling it forward as hard as you can more than 100 times in a two-hour period.

That was the kind of pain Dick Fowler often felt when he was pitching late in his career. Gordon Goldsberry, one of his team-mates, said, "I talked to Dick on the mound many times when he had tears in his eyes from the pain."

Fowler's wife Joyce believed the bursitis resulted from a marathon game Dick pitched in his first major league season. It was June 5, 1942, at Shibe Park in Philadelphia against the St. Louis Browns. Fowler was a gangling 21-year-old rookie. Johnny Niggeling, a 38-year-old veteran, was the opposing pitcher.

For three hours the two men took turns setting down the opposition. There was no score after nine innings, and still no score after 12, when George Caster replaced Niggeling.

Joyce Fowler said, "I was there that night and I thought it would never end. St. Louis used everybody but the bat boy and Connie Mack kept sending Dick back out. I always believed that game caused the bursitis that gave him so much pain and eventually ended his career."

After 15 innings, there was still no score. In the 16th, Walt Judnich led off with a triple; Chet Laabs followed with a sacrifice fly, and St. Louis scored the only run of the game.

Dick Fowler pitched against St. Louis three more times that summer and lost all three games. When the season ended, he joined the 48th Light Highlanders and spent the next three years in the Canadian Army. Dick didn't pitch again until he was discharged and rejoined the last-place Athletics in September 1945. In the first five days, he pitched three times in relief and was awful. He gave up 11 runs in 11 innings.

On September 9, 1945, in the second game of a doubleheader in Philadelphia, Dick Fowler made his first start since 1942. He struck out six batters and pitched a no-hitter against the St. Louis Browns. Still, he wasn't sure of winning.

St. Louis pitcher John Miller had allowed only three hits and there was still no score. In the bottom of the ninth, Philadelphia right fielder Hal Peck led off with a triple that rolled to the fence in centre field. Irvin Hall came to the plate expecting to see the sign for a bunt. "I was looking for the squeeze play," said Hall, "but the third base coach Al Simmons

Dick Fowler at Yankee Stadium, New York, 1947. (National Baseball Hall of Fame Library, Cooperstown, NY)

came down to me. 'Irv,' he said, 'the old man [Connie Mack] didn't give the squeeze sign, so look for a ball above your belt to hit to the outfield and let's get the hell out of here.'

"At that moment," said Hall, "I had no idea Fowler had a no-hitter. The St. Louis outfield was drawn in. The first pitch to me was above the waist. I swung and hit a line drive over the second baseman's head. The ball rolled to the wall and the game was over.

"In the clubhouse everybody was yelling. I said to the shortstop, Eddie Joost, 'What's all the noise about? We win a game once in a while.' He answered, 'Dick pitched a no-hitter.'" Irvin Hall said, "There were 16,000 people in the stands that day; and I'll bet that everyone except me was aware of the situation. Maybe it was better I didn't know when I came to bat."

After being mobbed by his teammates, Dick Fowler went to a phone booth under the grandstand to telephone his wife, Joyce, who had been living with relatives in Toronto while he was in the army. Fowler told reporters, "I threw every pitch that [catcher] Buddy Rosar called. I had been away for three years and I figured he knew the hitters better than I did."

Dick Fowler played 10 years in the major leagues, all with the Philadelphia Athletics. He won 15 games in 1948, and again in 1949, but his greatest glory in baseball came in September 1945, when Dick stepped right out of the Canadian Army into a special niche at the Baseball Hall of Fame in Cooperstown, New York.

Until Ferguson Jenkins was voted into the Hall of Fame in 1991, the only Canadian content at Cooperstown was a picture of Dick Fowler in a display honouring the men who have pitched no-hit games in the major leagues.

Pitcher Khalid Ballouli
Is Dick Fowler's Grandson

Dick Fowler had two children, a son and a daughter. Tom never took much interest in baseball. He had other things on his mind. Tom was born with a benign tumour, a deformity that affected the left side of his face. When Tom was just three years old, doctors told his parents he had only five months to live.

Tom recovered but underwent surgery after surgery for many years. He still managed to attend college, to marry and raise a family of his own before he died in his early 40s.

Tom's sister, Candice, loved baseball and used to throw a ball with her father. Her favourite memories are of Sunday mornings, talking with her dad while she prepared the breakfast they ate together.

Candice Fowler met her husband, Walid Ballouli, while attending university. Candice and Walid have a son, Dick Fowler's grandson, who also loves baseball. When he was 12 years old, Candice told me "My son Khalid breathes, eats and lives baseball. He is on a Pony League all-star team that has advanced to the state tournament. Our lives revolve around baseball schedules."

Canadian parents who juggle game and practice times for hockey and soccer will understand the situation. Khalid Ballouli was also an "A" student in high school. His marks helped him get a college education at Texas A&M University.

Khalid began as a shortstop but as he grew older and taller, he concentrated on pitching. Dick's widow, Joyce Fowler, said Khalid's delivery was just like his grandfather's.

He is six feet, two inches tall; Dick was six feet, four. Khalid began his professional career in 2002 at the age of 22 with Ogden, Utah, of the Rookie League. He appeared in 15 games, 12 of them as the starting pitcher.

Khalid averaged slightly less than five innings per game but he had a remarkable record of striking out 65 of the 262 batters he faced. That is one out of every four batters.

Ballouli walked only 10 batters, a very impressive strikeouts-to-walks ratio of 6.5 to 1. Khalid won four games without a loss.

Beloit, Wisconsin, of the Class A Midwest League was the next step up the ladder in 2003. Prince Fielder, who now plays for the Milwaukee Brewers, was a teammate. Khalid started eight games for Beloit but also pitched in relief. He earned two saves, while recording five wins and four losses.

A move to High Desert in the California League was a real test for Khalid in 2004. He started 25 games and wound up with six wins and 14 losses for a last-place team. Khalid's strikeouts-to-walks ratio was almost 4 to 1, with 128 strikeouts and 34 walks.

Ballouli's impressive strikeout total earned him a promotion to Huntsville, Alabama, of the Southern League in 2005. Khalid pitched five shutout innings in his debut but was increasingly used in relief. He was the closer in five games and earned two saves.

Until Huntsville, Khalid had encountered no problems other than opposing batters. Now, for the first time, Ballouli had to deal with injuries. Khalid hurt his shoulder in July and could not pitch again that season.

Ballouli was anxious to start well in 2006, but in May his shoulder was sore again and in late July he was on the disabled list with a shoulder strain. Khalid had to think about his future.

He would be 27 when the next baseball season began, and advancing to the major leagues was a question mark. In the end, Khalid says, his recurring shoulder problems and his desire for postgraduate education led him to give up his pitching career.

Khalid Ballouli said goodbye to teammates at spring training in March 2007. If he had not been injured, he said, he would have continued for at least two more seasons. His new plan for the future was to enter the M.A. program at Texas A&M University, focusing on sports management, and a Ph.D. degree.

Khalid Ballouli, Huntsville Stars, 2006. (Courtesy of Huntsville Stars)

Marchildon and Fowler,
Double Trouble from Canada

Phil Marchildon, who was born in Penetanguishene, Ontario, and Dick Fowler, born in Toronto, both pitched for the Toronto Maple Leafs of the International League and became formidable teammates with the Philadelphia Athletics between 1941 and 1949.

In their prime, Phil and Dick were among the best pitchers in baseball. Marchildon won 17 games in 1942 for a last-place team, and he lifted the Athletics into fifth place when he won 19 games in 1947. Fowler won 15 games in 1948, and again in 1949.

Phil was seven years older than Dick but the two men were great friends and roomed together on road trips. Each man missed three years because of military service between November 1942 and September 1945. Marchildon, a tail gunner whose plane was shot down, spent nine months as a prisoner of war and lost 40 pounds. Phil also suffered post-combat stress that affected his health.

The two Canadians spent four complete seasons together with Philadelphia, in 1942, and from 1946 to 1948. During that period, they appeared in fully one-third of all games for the Athletics and made a big contribution to the team's modest success. Marchildon started 125 games; Fowler, 102.

I was surprised that the Canadian combo pitched so few doubleheaders together. Philadelphia played a total of 118 doubleheaders in those four seasons.

Marchildon or Fowler pitched in 82 doubleheaders, but seldom on the same day. In fact, the two Canadians pitched on the same day just 10 times in those four seasons: once each in 1942 and 1946; four times in 1947; and four times again in 1948.

The Athletics record when Phil Marchildon and Dick Fowler pitched the two games of a doubleheader was 11 wins and nine losses. The two Canadian pitchers produced a .550 winning percentage, compared to the team's .432 record for those four seasons.

Fowler was a rookie in 1942 when Marchildon started 31 times and won 17 games. Dick started 17 games; he won six and lost 11. Although the Athletics played 33 doubleheaders in 1942, the two Canadians pitched on the same day only once.

On Sunday, September 13, in St. Louis, Phil Marchildon pitched the first game, and gave up a three-run home run to Chet Laabs in the sixth inning. The As lost the opener 6-0.

Dick Fowler pitched the second game and had a no-hitter through five innings. In the sixth, the first batter singled, the second man doubled and

Phil Marchildon, Philadelphia As, 1946. (National Baseball Hall of Fame Library, Cooperstown, NY)

the third batter drove in a run with a ground ball. Fowler was replaced by Roger Wolff, who gave up two runs late in the game and took a 3-2 loss

When Marchildon and Fowler resumed their careers after the war, the two pitchers established a rhythm as the lead pair for Philadelphia. In 1946, Fowler followed Marchildon in pitching the next game nine times. Dick and Phil started only one doubleheader that year. It was against

Cleveland June 3. Marchildon lost the first game 6-5 to "Red" Embree. Fowler pitched a complete game to win the second game 3-2 against Bob Lemon, who was making his major league pitching debut.

The fortunes of the former Maple Leafs grew closer together in 1947. Dick followed Phil 14 times that year, while Marchildon pitched the next game after Fowler five times.

The two men started four doubleheaders, and the As swept three of them. Phil pitched the first game and Dick the second when they beat St. Louis in May, and Boston in June.

On August 17, at Washington, Dick Fowler beat Early Wynn 2-1 in the first game. Phil Marchildon won the second game 5-2. Two weeks later, the Senators took revenge in Philadelphia, beating Marchildon 4-0, and Fowler 7-4 on September 1.

The sequence changed in 1948. Fowler followed Marchildon seven times. Phil pitched the next game after Dick six times. The two men started four doubleheaders.

Against Cleveland, June 6, Phil lost the first game 5-3 and Dick lost the second game 11-1. Dick and Phil lost another doubleheader to Cleveland on July 15. Fowler was the loser in the second game, and the winning pitcher was the legendary Satchel Paige. The great Negro League star signed a contract with the Indians on his 42nd birthday, and won his first game in the major leagues eight days later against Dick Fowler.

On July 19 against Chicago, Dick pitched a shutout for his league-leading ninth win in the first game of a twi-night doubleheader. Phil also pitched a complete game to win 6-4.

The two Canadians pitched together in a doubleheader for the last time, September 10, 1948, at Washington. Dick Fowler won the first game 9-6, and Marchildon pitched a three-hit shutout to win the second game 3-0.

That game was called after eight innings to allow the Athletics to catch a train for Boston. Climbing into the Pullman car in Washington that night, Phil Marchildon had no idea he would never win another game.

Marchildon had a difficult year in 1948. Phil pitched more innings and lost more games than any other Philadelphia pitcher. He said simply, "I think that was the year the war caught up with me."

Dick Fowler pitched the opening game of the 1949 season in Washington. President Harry Truman threw out the first pitch. Dick lost to the Senators 3-2.

Marchildon made his first start three days later against Boston. Phil and Mel Parnell were matched in a scoreless duel after eight innings. In the ninth, Phil gave up four walks and two hits and Boston won 4-0.

Dick Fowler, Philadelphia As, 1947. (National Baseball Hall of Fame Library, Cooperstown, NY)

Five days later, at Yankee Stadium, Marchildon made two pitches to the lead-off batter and had to leave the game with a sore shoulder. He started four more games but never lasted more than three innings.

In March 1950, Phil Marchildon was sold to Buffalo of the International League. He was released after a month; then attempted a comeback with Boston. Phil pitched one inning in relief but admitted, "There was nothing left."

Phil Marchildon went back home to a job in Toronto. Dick Fowler remained with the Athletics until 1952. He pitched two more years in Charleston, West Virginia, many times fighting back tears because of bursitis pain.

A Woman's Place is at Home, and First, Second and Third!

Extract from remarks by William Rayner of St. Thomas, Ontario, Canadian Baseball Hall of Fame Induction Ceremony, June 4, 1998.

"If you look at the picture at the right, it's hard to imagine that those sweet, innocent-looking ladies, some, doting grandmothers, were once the terror of women's baseball and they have the scars to prove it!

"One such person was the late Olive Bend Little, small in stature, mild-mannered in later life but in her day a powerhouse pitcher. Never afraid to pitch inside, she once broke an opposing batter's wrist. The All-American Girls Professional Baseball League was as unique as the era in which it was formed.

"As war raged a world away, somewhere on the Prairies an anxious mother and father stood with their teenage daughter, cloth suitcase and baseball glove in hand, waiting for a train to take her to a tryout in Chicago. Far from the safety of home and family, she dreamed of playing professional baseball - for money. At a time when the average salary in the United States was about $40 a week, the AAGPBL players earned from $50 to $125 a week.

"Night after night, in cities in the American Midwest, those girls played before thousands of fans while an ocean away war continued unabated. More than 10 percent of the players were Canadian women, drawn from sandlots, church leagues and cities in five different provinces.

"The Canadians proved they could play with the best Americans. Some 15 Canadians were ranked as all-stars. Two Canadians were batting champions: Gladys "Terry" Davis from Toronto was the 1943 batting Queen with a .332 average, and Helen Callaghan of Vancouver won the title in 1945, batting .300.

"The women inducted into the Canadian Baseball Hall of Fame were a well-kept secret for nearly 50 years. It took a movie, *A League of Their Own*, to provide the recognition they so richly deserved. In 1988, the National Baseball Hall of Fame and Museum at Cooperstown, New York, dedicated a room to the women's league.

"The Canadian Baseball Hall of Fame had the foresight to create the category of honorary member. Jackie Robinson and former prime minister Lester Pearson were the best-known members in that category until 64 Canadian women who played in the All-American Girls Professional Baseball League were inducted as honorary members."

William Rayner of St. Thomas, Ontario, traced the records of the 64 Canadian-born players, and submitted a nomination for honorary membership to the Canadian Baseball Hall of Fame. The nomination was accepted and unanimously approved by the selection committee. Rayner was asked to introduce the women at the induction ceremony.

The names of the 64 Canadian women who played in the AAGPBL, along with their maiden names and home towns, are listed on the following pages.

Fifteen Canadian women players are seen in this photo at their induction into the Canadian Baseball Hall of Fame. Top row, left to right: Jeanne Gilchrist, Lee Surkowski Delmonico, Martha Rommelaere Manning, Lucella MacLean Ross, Audrey Haine Daniels, Janet Anderson Perkin. Middle row: Margaret Callaghan Maxwell, Mildred Warwick McAuley, Penny O'Brian Cooke, Kay Heim McDaniel. Front row: Elsie Wingrove Earl, Anne Surkowski Deyotte, Betty Carveth Dunn, Terry Donahue, Ruth Middleton Gentry. Missing from photo: Colleen Smith McCulloch, Arleene Johnson Noga. (Canadian Baseball Hall of Fame)

Canadian-born Players,
All-American Girls
Professional Baseball League

NAME *(maiden name in brackets)*	HOMETOWN
Abbott, Velma	Regina, SK
Allen, (Petryna) Doreen	Regina, SK
Baker, Mary "Bonnie"	Regina, SK
Barbaze, Barbara	Toronto, ON
Barr, Doris	Winnipeg, MB
Beckett, (Jewitt) Christine	Regina, SK
Bennett, Catherine	Regina, SK
Boyce, Ethel	Vancouver, BC
Callow, Eleanor	Winnipeg, MB
Coben, Muriel	Saskatoon, SK
Cook, Dorothy	St. Catharines, ON
Cooke, (O'Brian) Penny	Edmonton, AB
Daniels, (Haine) Audrey	Winnipeg, MB
Davis, Gladys	Toronto, ON
Davis, (Jones) Marguerite	Regina, SK
Delmonico, (Surkowski) Lee	Moose Jaw, SK
Deyotte, (Surkowski) Anne	Moose Jaw, SK
Donahue, Terry	Melaval, SK
Dunn, (Carveth) Betty	Edmonton, AB
Dusanko, (Sabo) Julie	Regina, SK
Earl, (Wingrove) Elsie	Saskatoon, SK
Emerson, June	Moose Jaw, SK
Fox, (Nicol) Helen	Ardley, AB
Gentry, (Middleton) Ruth	Winnipeg, MB
Gilchrist, Jeanne	New Westminster, BC
Golden, Thelma	Toronto, ON
Grant, Olga	Calgary, AB
Hanna, Marjorie	Calgary, AB
Hickey, Lillian	Vancouver, BC
Holmes, (Zurkowski) Agnes	Regina, SK
Hundeby, (Grambo) Thelma	Domremy, SK
Hunter, Dorothy	Winnipeg, MB
Janowski, Alice	Sherbrooke, QC
Junor, Daisy	Regina, SK

Key, (Ferguson) Dorothy . . . . Winnipeg, MB
Kustra, (Shastal) Mary . . . . Winnipeg, MB
Little, Olive . . . . Poplar Point, MB
Manning, (Rommelaere) Martha . . . . Edmonton, AB
Martz, (Knezovich) Ruby . . . . Regina, SK
Mason, Ruth . . . . Moose Jaw, SK
Maxwell, (Callaghan) Margaret . . . . Vancouver, BC
McAuley, (Warwick) Mildred . . . . Regina, SK
McCreary, Ethel . . . . Regina, SK
McCulloch, (Smith) Colleen . . . . Vancouver, BC
McDaniel, (Heim) Kay . . . . Edmonton, AB
McFaul, (George) Gene . . . . Regina, SK
Moroz, (Wawryshyn) Evelyn . . . . Tyndall, MB
Noga, (Johnson) Arleene . . . . Ogema, SK
Panos, Vickie . . . . Edmonton, AB
Perkin, (Anderson) Janet . . . . Bethune, SK
Ross, (MacLean) Lucella . . . . Lloydminster, AB
Sandiford, (Nelson) Helen . . . . Toronto, ON
Schatz, Joan . . . . Winnipeg, MB
Schick, (Teillet) Yolande . . . . St. Vital, MB
Schofield, June . . . . Toronto, ON
Smith, Shirley . . . . Toronto, ON
St. Aubin, (Callaghan) Helen . . . . Vancouver, BC
Stanton, (Watson) Marion . . . . Chatham, ON
Stark, Mae . . . . Hamilton, ON
Thompson, Anne Jane . . . . Edmonton, AB
Walmsley, Thelma . . . . Sudbury, ON
Wicken, (Berthiaume) Elizabeth . . . . Regina, SK
Wildfong, (Measner) Hazel . . . . Holdfast, SK
Witiuk, (Shero) Doris . . . . Winnipeg, MB

Total of 64 women: 25 from Saskatchewan, 12 from Manitoba, 10 from Ontario, 10 from Alberta, 6 from British Columbia, and one from Quebec.

Roland Gladu Was Suspended For Playing in Mexican League

You won't find a plaque for Jorge or Bernardo Pasquale in the National Baseball Hall of Fame; but if the players union ever created its own hall of honour, the two Mexicans would be legitimate candidates for admission. The Mexican brothers helped to raise players' salaries to their current multi-million dollar levels.

Just after World War Two, when major league baseball players earned an average of between $5,000 and $10,000 a year, the brothers from Mexico City started a salary spiral by offering as much as three times the going rate.

More than a dozen big leaguers made the jump south of the border but most beat a hurried retreat when the new Commissioner, A.B. "Happy" Chandler, threatened a life suspension for anyone who failed to return. St. Louis Browns shortstop Vernon Stephens hit a home run his first time at bat in Mexico but came home when Chandler issued his ultimatum.

At least two Canadians were among the players who did go to Mexico. Pitcher Jean-Pierre Roy, who won 25 games for the Montreal Royals in 1945, accepted an offer of $15,000 a year. Outfielder Roland Gladu, who batted .338 as Roy's teammate, signed a three-year contract for $10,000 a year. Jean-Pierre Roy was disillusioned by poor playing fields and shabby hotels. He returned to Canada without playing in any games.

On May 9, 1946, Commissioner Chandler announced the suspension of 13 players for five years. The list included Roland Gladu, Brooklyn Dodgers catcher Mickey Owen and New York Giants pitcher Sal Maglie. Two weeks later, Max Lanier, the St. Louis Cardinals' best pitcher, with six wins and no losses, defied the Commissioner. Lanier jumped to Mexico for a reported $20,000 a year.

Roland Gladu stayed in Mexico for two years. "Fields in some cities were not good," Gladu said, "but compared with the money they were paying in the National League, playing in Mexico was all right."

Gladu's only complaint was about playing at night. "The lights were terrible," he said. "Batting against Maglie or Lanier was no joke. You could hardly see the ball."

Roland Gladu returned to Canada in 1948 as a player-manager in the outlaw Quebec Provincial League. Sal Maglie and Max Lanier also came to Quebec when the Mexican League went out of business.

Sal Maglie's suspension was lifted in 1950, and he rejoined the New York Giants. Maglie won 23 games in 1951, and he helped the Giants overcome the Dodgers' 10-game lead to win the pennant.

When Roland Gladu died in Montreal in 1994, at the age of 81, he remained the only Canadian ever suspended by major league baseball.

Roland Gladu hit home runs in five countries: Canada, U.S.A., Cuba, Mexico and England. (Montreal Gazette photo)

Was Doug Harvey Canada's Greatest Athlete of All Time?

Doug Harvey was a man who lived life to the full. In the field of sports, Doug touched all the bases. He was called the greatest hockey defence-man of all time. But Doug Harvey was also a boxing champion, as well as a top-notch football and baseball player.

Harvey was born in Montreal the week before Christmas, December 19, 1924, and died 65 years later, the day after Christmas, in 1989. Doug didn't live long enough to receive his first old age pension cheque. The cause of death was cirrhosis of the liver.

A member of the Hockey Hall of Fame and the Canada's Sports Hall of Fame, Doug was a natural athlete who excelled at many sports. He was the heavyweight boxing champion of the Canadian Navy. Doug won a baseball batting championship and he was named the most valuable play-er for the HMCS Donnacona football team that later won the Grey Cup.

Doug Harvey may have been Canada's greatest athlete ever. Yet, when Doug entered West Hill High School in 1938, he was considered too small for contact sports. He was assigned to the soccer team. In time, Doug moved up to the senior football team, which played for the city championship.

Doug also played hockey for West Hill. In 1942, coach Jack Black converted Harvey from centre to defence. West Hill won the city championship the next year, and Doug Harvey found the position that he was born to play.

How good a hockey player was Doug Harvey? When he died in 1989, Bob Morrissey, writing in the Montreal Gazette, described him as "Doug Harvey, who used the ice the way an international grandmaster uses a chessboard."

Red Fisher, a columnist who watched NHL stars for more than 50 years, wrote, "Doug Harvey was a free spirit. He enjoyed the game of life perhaps too well, but that is not for us to judge. What he left for all of us, though, was judged a long time ago: the sweep of his stride, the deadly accuracy of his passes, the speed of his shot and his total dedication to winning. He was the best."

Within the hockey community there has been, if not a conspiracy of silence, at least an unwillingness to acknowledge Doug Harvey as a sports champion. Some deplore Doug's alcohol problems after he stopped playing. But there is no shame in remembering his greatness, the joy with which he played the game and the level to which he raised everyone who played with him.

Bernie Geoffrion (left) and Doug Harvey (right) were stalwarts of the Montreal Canadiens team that won the Stanley Cup five years in a row, 1955-56 to 1959-60. (Molson photo)

Howard Riopelle, who played with Doug for the Canadiens and the Montreal Royals, recalls how calm and relaxed Harvey was. "After the pre-game meal, players would be anxious and fidgeting. Doug would fall asleep in a chair. One guy asked him, 'How can you be so calm?' Doug told him, 'There's no point in worrying. I can't do anything about the game until we get on the ice.'"

This chapter describes Harvey's baseball skills by looking at some highlights of his days with the Ottawa Nationals of the Border League. Doug played from 1947, when he was 21 years old, just starting a sports career, until 1950 when he had to choose between baseball and hockey.

Doug Harvey began his professional baseball career with the Ottawa Nationals in 1947. Ottawa and Kingston, along with four teams from New York - Watertown, Auburn, Geneva and Ogdensburg - formed the Border League. The Nationals played their home games at Lansdowne Park, which was more famous as the home of the Rough Riders football team. The third base line ran parallel to the north side stand. There was almost no room in foul territory but between the lines, the fielders had to cover a lot of ground. The outfield ran halfway to the Rideau Canal.

Harvey played right field for Ottawa. He appeared in just 10 games in 1947; but in 1948 Doug played in 109 of the team's 127 games and finished fourth in the batting race with an average of .340, including 22 doubles, 16 triples, 4 home runs and 73 runs batted in. The following year, Harvey was late joining the baseball team because of an extended hockey season that saw Doug and the Canadiens lose a seven-game playoff to the Detroit Red Wings.

Doug Harvey played his first game of the 1949 season June 1 against Kingston at Lansdowne Park in Ottawa. The Kingston pitcher had a no-hitter through six innings. Harvey led off the seventh inning with a single and went on to score the first run as Ottawa beat Kingston 3-0.

Doug Harvey hit safely in each of his first 15 games with the Nationals. His hitting streak was interrupted June 14 against Auburn, but he still managed two walks and a sacrifice. Doug started another streak in the next game and hit safely in 10 more games before being held hitless on June 25 in the second game of a doubleheader against Watertown.

In his first month with the Ottawa Nationals, Doug Harvey played 33 games and made 47 hits in 126 times at bat for a .373 batting average. He hit five home runs, batted in 33 runs and stole six bases. Through July and August, Harvey was the sparkplug with timely hitting and aggressive base running as the Ottawa Nationals moved from fourth place to finish second, behind Geneva.

Although he missed the first 20 games of the season, Doug Harvey led the league in runs scored and runs batted in, and won the Border League batting championship with an average of .351. Doug hit 27 doubles, 10 triples and 14 home runs and had 109 runs batted in. Harvey struck out only 28 times in 422 times at bat, and he also stole 30 bases.

Doug Harvey's contribution to the Ottawa Nationals was summed up in the deciding play of the first game of the Border League playoffs at Lansdowne Park. The Nationals and Auburn were tied heading to the bottom of the ninth inning. Harvey was up first, with second baseman Bill Metzig to follow.

Gordon Ryan of the Ottawa Journal Sports staff described the scene as Doug Harvey led off the inning with a long hit and made a mad dash for home:

"The game was deadlocked. Ottawa hadn't collected a hit since the second inning. Then Harvey connected, sending the ball into deep centre field. The Auburn left fielder tried to pick it up and fumbled just as Harvey rounded second base.

"Metzig said, 'I was sitting on the bench hoping when Doug lit into that pitch. I watched the ball roll and Doug dig for second. Being next at bat I thought to myself: it's up to you to bring that run in. Then Doug rounded second and Erickson fumbled the ball out in the field. That miscue decided the issue.

"'Boy, I thought we were beat for a minute but you have to give it to Harvey. He's a great competitor and he played it out right to the last. He really roared in on home plate.'

"Catcher Sam Brusa tagged Harvey a good two feet from home plate but dropped the ball. Umpire Bell had no sooner called Harvey out than

Ottawa Nationals, 1948 Border League pennant winners. Doug Harvey is at the extreme right of the top row. Manager Bill Metzig (with glasses) is in the middle of the front row. Shortstop Peter Karpuk, who also played for the Ottawa Rough Riders football team, is standing at left end of top row. (Library and Archives Canada: PA 139689)

he had to wave the safe signal when the charging runner brushed the ball out of the catcher's outstretched hand."

That victory in the opening game was the highlight of the Ottawa Nationals' season. Auburn won the second game 5-4 and then won the next two at home, 11-4 and 3-1.

Ottawa won games five and six to force a deciding game. The final game was played in Ottawa, on a Friday night, September 16. A crowd of 3,500 cheered in vain for the Nationals. Ottawa had runners in every inning and left 10 men on base. Auburn scored two unearned runs in the second inning and held on for the victory.

The following year, Doug Harvey played 10 games for the Ottawa baseball team but by then he was on his way to stardom with the Montreal Canadiens. In future, his batting exploits were limited to goodwill appearances with the Canadiens softball team that toured Montreal playgrounds during the summer.

How good an athlete was Doug Harvey? Look at Harvey's record with the Ottawa Nationals baseball team. Measure his success as the heavy-weight boxing champion of the Canadian Navy. Consider his football playing with West Hill High School, HMCS Donnacona, and the Montreal Winged Wheelers.

Finally, look at his Hall of Fame credentials as a hockey player, and I believe Doug Harvey should be recognized as Canada's greatest athlete of all time.

Doug Harvey was the 1949 Border League batting champion, with a .351 average. (Library and Archives Canada: PA 139689)

Chapter 5

The
1950s and 60s

Vern Handrahan, P.E.I. Pitcher, Struck Out 19 Batters in Game

In 12 years as a professional pitcher, Charlottetown native Vern Handrahan handled thousands of baseballs. Most are long forgotten; but one ball remains a treasured possession. It is a souvenir of a remarkable pitching record: the day he struck out 19 batters in Boise, Idaho. Umpire George Sosnak, who did drawings and script lettering as a hobby, hand-lettered details of the historic game on an official Pioneer League baseball and presented it to Vern.

"Here are the names of the players on both teams and the box-score of the game." Handrahan shows the lacquered baseball with justifiable pride. One surface of the ball has a drawing of a Brave's head, the symbol still used today by the Atlanta Braves organization. Another surface has a drawing of Vern, the date, August 29, 1962, and the final score, Boise 11 Great Falls 5.

Handrahan was 24 years old, in his third year of professional baseball. "When we were warming up before the game, the catcher, Glenn Clark, said to me, 'Why don't you try the slider.' Well, I did and that's how I got all those strikeouts. They were just waving at it. The ball was moving all over. I made three wild pitches and the catcher had four passed balls." After the game, umpire Sosnak told Vern, "If I had known you were so close to the record, I

Vern Handrahan holds a ball from the game in which he struck out 19 batters for the Boise Braves of the Pioneer League, August 29, 1962. (Charlottetown Guardian photo by Heather Taweel)

would have called more strikes in the ninth inning. There were a few pitches that could have gone either way."

Like most Canadian boys, Vern Handrahan began his athletic career as a hockey player. "I like hockey well enough," says Vern; "but I was kind of injury-prone. When I was 16, I collided with a guy at centre ice and landed on the blade of another player's skate. I had a deep cut inside the upper leg. So, I decided to give up on hockey."

Vern's career as a professional ball player was launched in Stellarton, Nova Scotia. "They had a pretty good league and there were lots of American college boys playing in Nova Scotia every summer. I was 19 years old and had come over from Charlottetown with Donnie MacLeod to try out for the Stellarton Albions. Donnie was a pitcher too and a very good hitter.

"At the end of August, we were driving to Kentville to play the last game of the playoffs. We had three cars with five players in each. On the way, the coach got a flat tire; so we had to start the game with only 10 players. I was the pitcher and we were ahead 6-0 in the fifth inning when the coach showed up with the other players. When the inning was over, the coach took me and three other guys out of the game and put in the fellows who were in the car with the flat tire. Kentville came back to beat us 10-8.

"As I walked back to the bench, Jeff Jones, one of the scouts sitting behind us, told me he wanted to talk to me after the game. I thought he was going to give me some tips about pitching, so I was really surprised when he asked me if I wanted to play professional baseball for the Milwaukee Braves. Donnie MacLeod and I both signed contracts and we headed off together to the Braves minor league training camp at Waycross, Georgia, in March 1959."

The Braves training camp was like a baseball factory. "There were about 400 of us trying out and everybody had a big white number on his cap so the coaches could tell who you were. I was about number 340 and every day a few fellows were told to go home, but I stuck around and in April I was sent to the bottom of the baseball ladder at Wellsville, New York, in Class D." Vern remembers all the details of his first season. "We had four guys who hit over .300 and we finished in first place, seven games ahead of Geneva. We beat Corning and Elmira in the playoffs to win the championship." Handrahan pitched in a total of 30 games, including 10 starts. Vern won eight and lost eight and had three complete games and one shutout.

The next year, Vern started at Eau Claire, Wisconsin, in the Northern League. "Joe Torre was our catcher. In June, they sent me back to Wellsville." In 1961, Handrahan was back at Eau Claire. Vern pitched well enough to get a promotion to the Pioneer League in 1962. He won 13 games for Boise and led the league in strikeouts, including the single game record of 19. On the strength of his strikeout performance, Vern was drafted by the Kansas City

Athletics of the American League. "A week before spring training in 1963, I was opening a can of cat food and I got a deep cut on my pitching hand that took 12 stitches to close." Handrahan missed most of spring training and was sent to Lewiston, Maine.

"The next year, I started an exhibition game in spring training and gave up one run in six innings. That put me on the A's roster." Vern Handrahan made his major league debut, April 14, 1964, in Detroit. "Billy Bruton hit a three-run homer off me just inside the foul pole." In June, he was sent to Rochester, New York. "I pitched in Toronto against Claude Raymond," Vern remembers. "A fan yelled out, 'We're going to have a Canadian winning pitcher tonight.'"

August 1, 1966, Vern Handrahan was recalled to the majors and a place in the American League record book. Vern says, "We were in Cleveland. Jim 'Catfish' Hunter started for us. He pitched six shutout innings. We used five other pitchers and there was still no score after 10 innings." Kansas City scored the first run of the game in the top of the 11th. In the bottom of the inning, Handrahan came in with a man on first and one out. "I retired Leon Wagner for the second out. The next batter hit a single to put runners on first and third." Jim Landis hit a bouncer right back to the mound and Vern threw him out to end the game. "I got the save and it still is a record for most pitchers used in a 1-0 shutout."

That save against Cleveland was as close as Vern Handrahan came to winning a game in the major leagues. He pitched in 16 games for Kansas City in 1966, and struck out 18 batters in 20 innings. In 1967, Vern was sent to Birmingham of the Southern League. He recalls the names of teammates who went on to star in the World Series with the Oakland A's, "Reggie Jackson, Rollie Fingers, Joe Rudi and Dave Duncan. We had a great team; finished first and won the playoffs."

After Birmingham, Vern played the next three years one step away from the majors, Vancouver in 1968, Des Moines in 1969, and Toledo in 1970. The end of the line came in March 1971, at the Detroit Tigers training camp in Lakeland, Florida. "I worked hard all winter and was in really good shape," Vern recalls. "I had a pretty good spring; but Detroit had some young pitchers and I got caught in the squeeze. I didn't want to go back to the minors, so I came home."

The ending was sad, but the memories are good for the tall man who returned to Charlottetown to walk the city streets as a letter carrier for Canada Post. "I had 12 years as a pro and I have no regrets." His wife, Ann Bradley, who went to school with Vern in Charlottetown, says with a smile, "I loved it. The places we went, the people we met, the friends we made. It was great, every minute."

*Vern Handrahan at Boise. Four years later, Vern shared a shutout record with Jim
"Catfish" Hunter as a member of the Kansas City A's. (Courtesy of Vern Handrahan)*

Lester Pearson
Loved Baseball

Lester Pearson won the Nobel Peace Prize as a diplomat working for peace in the Middle East. He became Canada's 14th Prime Minister, and all his life Pearson loved baseball. He played the game as a boy and followed the sport as an adult. Pearson was born April 23, 1897, at Newtonbrook, Ontario, in what is now the North York area of Toronto. Lester was the second of three sons. His father was a Methodist minister who also played first base.

Lester Pearson told of going as a boy of 14 to a holiday game at Toronto's Hanlon Point Stadium, and giving a play-by-play description to his nearly blind grandfather. Lester and his brother Vaughan played baseball for the Guelph Maple Leafs of the Inter-County League. Pearson insisted Vaughan was good enough to have played professionally.

While studying at Oxford University, Lester Pearson played with a Canadian hockey team that toured Europe. The Swiss called Pearson "Mister Zig-Zag." He enjoyed all sports, but baseball was his lifelong passion. As an adult, he was never happier than when throwing a baseball to open an amateur tournament or to launch a new season as honorary president of the Montreal Expos.

In the fall of 1963, the National Film Board began shooting a candid film, to reveal the human side of the Prime Minister's job. While the film was being made, a longshoremen's strike began. The ports of Montreal, Quebec City and Trois-Rivières were shut down; grain shipments by western farmers were halted.

A scene in the film shows Prime Minister Pearson in his office, leaning back in his chair, watching the Yankees and the Dodgers in a World Series game on television.

Allan MacEachan, the Minister of Labour, comes into the office. He starts to give Mr. Pearson some news about the strike. The Prime Minister tries to listen, but in the middle of MacEachan's sentence, we see Pearson's attention shift to the television screen. The announcer says, "Koufax winds up; here's the pitch!" After the pitch, Lester Pearson turns to his Labour minister and says, "Pardon me, Allan, would you tell me that again."

Lester Pearson throws out the first pitch for a Little League tournament at Lansdowne Park in Ottawa. (Library and Archives Canada: PA127430)

Miracle on Adelaide Street, Two Boys from Chatham

The odds of a Canadian boy playing in baseball's major leagues are about one in a million. The odds of two boys from the same city reaching the majors in the same year are hard to imagine. So it must have been some kind of miracle that four years in a row, from 1976 to 1979, two boys who grew up on the same street in Chatham, Ontario, were both pitching in the major leagues.

A little boy cries in a tree. "Ferguson, bring him down this minute." A mother runs out of her house to chastise her teenaged son who had put the little boy in the tree. "I was only teasing, Mom. He's not hurt," Ferguson Jenkins explained to his mother as she consoled little Billy Atkinson.

Six-year-old Billy lived in the house across the street. He had to pass Fergie Jenkins on his way to school. This morning, Billy said something bold and the 16-year-old boy, who was more than six feet tall, lifted the curly-haired youngster into the air and planted him on the lowest branch of an elm tree.

Too scared to climb down, Billy cried as loud as he could until Mrs. Jenkins came to his rescue. Now, sitting in his living room with his wife and his own teenaged son, Atkinson laughs as he recalls an early encounter with his famous childhood neighbour.

A small white frame house with a high-pitched roof, 213 Adelaide Street in Chatham's east end, is where Ferguson Jenkins was born and lived most of his early life. Right across the street at 206 Adelaide is the house where Bill Atkinson lived.

Two blocks farther down, there's a wide path between houses and big shade trees at the entrance to Stirling Park, where Ferguson Jenkins and Bill Atkinson played as boys. "Even when he was a professional, Fergie came down to the field to play with us kids," Atkinson says.

The year Bill Atkinson turned 16, Fergie Jenkins took him to Chicago for a couple of days to see the ball field, the place he lived and some of the sights of the big city. "The season was over but he showed me around. We talked about how he pitched to certain batters. What kind of pitch you throw when there is a man on base. I was just getting started and Fergie was sharing his secrets."

Fergie doesn't live there any more but the sign on the highway still says, "Welcome to Chatham, Home of Ferguson Jenkins, Baseball Hall-of-Famer."

Bill Atkinson couldn't wait to follow in Fergie's footsteps. "Cleveland and Philadelphia were interested but they couldn't sign me until I was 18.

The bullpen gets loose while Ferguson Jenkins pitches at Connie Mack Stadium in Philadelphia, 1969. (National Baseball Hall of Fame Library, Cooperstown, NY)

Bill Atkinson made his major league debut at Jarry Park in September 1976. (Courtesy of Bill Atkinson)

OVER THE FENCE IS OUT!

Because Montreal was a Canadian club they could sign me so long as someone else signed as my guardian. I was 17 and I couldn't wait, so I signed with Montreal for $1,000."

Atkinson started his climb to the majors at Jamestown, New York, in 1972. En route to Montreal he stopped in West Palm Beach, Quebec City, Memphis and Denver. The call to join the Expos came in September 1976. He pitched four times in the last two weeks of the season and did not allow a run.

Bill remembers pitching at Wrigley Field in Chicago on the last day of the 1976 season, "I stood on the same mound where Fergie pitched for so many years." Atkinson struck out the first batter he faced. He retired the next batter on a fly ball; then was lifted for a pinch-hitter. In four years with the Expos, Bill appeared in 98 games as a relief pitcher. He won 11 and lost four.

On the mound, Bill yields to Jenkins. "He was one of the greatest pitchers of all time. I was an honest worker," says Atkinson. Bill has only one regret: "I never pitched against Fergie. He was in the National League for many years with the Chicago Cubs but when I got to the Expos, Fergie was over in the American League with Texas and Boston."

Ferguson Jenkins was a fair hitter when he was young and once hit two home runs in a game against the Expos. Bill Atkinson started his baseball career as a catcher and says, "I could always hit!" Relief pitchers don't get to bat very often but Bill proudly points out that his lifetime batting average of .300 is the highest for any big league player born in Chatham.

Doug Melvin Took Longer; But He is Still in the Majors

Believe it or not, there was a third pitcher living in Chatham. Doug Melvin didn't live on Adelaide Street. He lived across town on Kingsway Drive; but Doug played baseball at the same Stirling Park where Ferguson Jenkins and Bill Atkinson played. In the winter Doug joined Fergie and Bill in workouts at John McGregor Secondary School.

Doug's father, Art Melvin, recalls, "If anyone was fooling around, Fergie would snap his glove and say, 'I'm not wasting my time with people who don't want to work.' That was usually enough to bring everybody into line." Art Melvin says, "Fergie was a great influence for all the boys in Chatham."

Fergie is tall. Bill Atkinson is small, compared to Fergie; but Doug Melvin is just right; about medium height. Doug is nine years younger than Fergie and two years older than Bill. It took him longer to get to the big leagues but he is still there. In 2008, Doug Melvin celebrated his 30th anniversary as a major league executive. He has been general manager of the Milwaukee Brewers since 2003, and his contract was extended through 2012.

"As a teenager, I enjoyed baseball," Doug says, "but I was a better basketball player." He set a school basketball record by scoring 55 points in one game. He also played hockey and played football against Bill Atkinson. They were at rival high schools. Ferguson Jenkins inspired Doug's decision to play baseball.

"Everybody in Chatham knew who Fergie was and even when he was a professional he would come to the ball field." Melvin signed a professional contract with the Pittsburgh Pirates when he was 19 and began his baseball career at Bradenton, Florida, in 1972. He pitched in eight games, including two starts, and had a record of three losses with an earned run average of 5.14.

The following year, Doug was strictly a relief pitcher with Niagara Falls. He had one win, one loss and one save in 15 games. In January 1974, Melvin was released by the Pirates. He broke his ankle playing basketball and sat out the baseball season.

When his ankle healed, Doug decided to give it one more shot. "I got in a little Chevy Vega and drove to the southernmost camp in Florida. I told myself I would knock on all the doors on my way north and if nobody hired me, I would come home to Canada. My first stop was the Yankees camp at Hollywood, Florida. Pat Gillick gave me a 10-day tryout, and I made the team."

Doug Melvin as a Pittsburgh Pirates rookie pitcher in 1972. (Courtesy of Murray King)

Doug spent four years in the Yankee farm system. He won 12 and lost 11 in two years at Fort Lauderdale. He was promoted to New Haven where he won 16 and lost only four in two seasons.

Melvin was 26 years old and had a good record but no future. Recognizing that he was not going to get to the majors, Doug spoke to Jack Butterfield, the Yankees' director of player development, in 1979. "Before I get out of baseball," said Melvin, "I want to be sure I'm doing the right thing. In my eyes, I don't think I am a prospect." Butterfield replied, "I can confirm that."

Doug Melvin went home to Canada, married, and had just started a new job at the Superior Machine Tool and Die factory in Chatham when he had to make a career decision. "The Yankees phoned, and asked if I would be interested in pitching batting practice and pulling together scouting reports from men in the field," he says. Doug jumped at the chance. When his own work was done, Melvin says, "I just hung around and listened to the veteran coaches on the Yankee staff, "Yogi" Berra, Jim Hegan, Bob Lemon, Mickey Vernon and Clyde King." King, as the general manager in 1985, gave Doug Melvin his big chance.

"I was travelling with the team and still pitching batting practice," Doug recalls. "We were playing in Chicago. Clyde King phoned and said he would like me to come back to New York and be the scouting director." Melvin spent eight years in the Yankees front office; then moved to Baltimore for nine years as assistant general manager and director of player development.

Doug was hired as general manager of the Texas Rangers in 1994 and was fired after the 2001 season. He worked as a consultant for the Boston Red Sox, and in October 2002, Doug took over a Milwaukee team that was in last place, 50 games under .500.

According to Doug Melvin, "The prime role of the general manager is to make sure that everybody in the organization is working together, with the same positive focus and the same approach to drafting, evaluating and developing players. We have 24 amateur scouts looking at high school and college players to find the next Prince Fielder. We have a medical staff, a conditioning staff and minor league coaches and managers whose job is to groom those young players for a career in baseball."

The emphasis is on building the team from within: knowing each player's strengths and weaknesses and how he can contribute at every level, from the rookie league to the majors. "It also means being aware of which players are released by other teams because they don't match that team's requirements but who might be able to help your team."

Big trades are the glamour part of the general manager's job, and Melvin was ready to deal when C.C. Sabathia was made available by Cleveland in July 2008. Neither Sabathia's $11-million salary nor the fact he would

Yankee batting practice pitcher Doug Melvin (middle), with "Yogi" Berra (left) and Clyde King. (Courtesy of Murray King)

become a free agent after the season stopped Melvin from trading three minor league prospects to get the left-hand pitcher. Sabathia won his first nine decisions with Milwaukee and in September he consistently pitched on three days' rest to get the Brewers into the playoffs.

Firing the manager is the painful part of the job, but Doug Melvin has done that too. Ned Yost was fired with 12 games left in the 2008 season, after losing 11 of 14 games in September and dropping into a tie with Philadelphia in the wild card race. Melvin said, "It's tough when you have someone who has done what Ned has done. He built the organization back where it hasn't been in 15 years. I feel I quit on Ned a little bit by not allowing him to do it for the last two weeks. But in the end, the decision was made."

Gene Dziadura, a former scout for the Phillies, and a History teacher in Chatham when Doug was growing up, is not surprised at Doug Melvin's success. "I first saw him when he was about 15 years old, in baseball and in football. He had a very strong work ethic and leadership qualities. He had poise and spoke well. In fact, he was just like his father, a nice person; modest but very capable."

Looking back on his pitching career and everything that has happened since, Doug Melvin admires the achievements of Ferguson Jenkins and Bill Atkinson. The third man from Chatham has shown there is more than one way to make it to the big leagues; and, in the end, his way is more enduring.

Ferguson Jenkins Against His Hall of Fame Contemporaries

Ferguson Jenkins is now old enough to receive the old age pension. Canada's greatest pitcher, and the first Canadian to be elected to the National Baseball Hall of Fame, turned 65 in December 2008. There are days when Fergie feels his age, but he never looks it. Tall and slim, at six feet, five inches and 210 pounds, Jenkins was a picture of fluid grace as a pitcher, and he still moves like an athlete. His home backs on a golf course and he can be standing at the tee anytime he wants to. Fergie travels across North America speaking at dinners and special events, mainly for charitable causes. Baseball was good to him and Jenkins is happy to give back to the game.

Everyone knows that Ferguson Jenkins is in the Baseball Hall of Fame but not everybody appreciates just how good he was. Jenkins is the only pitcher in major league history to strike out more than 3,000 batters while walking fewer than 1,000. Fergie averaged 16 wins per season for 18 years. He won 20 games or more six years in a row with the Chicago Cubs, and in 1971, when he won 24 games, Ferguson Jenkins won the Cy Young Award as the best pitcher in the National League. Two years later, he was traded to the Texas Rangers of the American League.

Fergie was traded to a Texas team that had finished dead last in the major leagues. With Ferguson Jenkins pitching, Texas jumped from 57 wins and 105 losses in 1973, to 84 wins and 76 losses in 1974: a net gain of 27 games. Fergie won 25 games and Texas finished in second place. Jenkins should have won the Cy Young Award in 1974; but he lost out to Jim "Catfish" Hunter of the Oakland A's, who also won 25 games for the first-place team.

In terms of performance, Jenkins and Hunter were almost identical in 1974. Both pitchers won 25 and lost 12. Hunter started 41 games and completed 23. He pitched 318 innings and had six shutouts. Jenkins started 41 games and completed 29. Fergie pitched 328 innings and had six shutouts. Jenkins had more strikeouts, 225 to Hunter's 143; but Hunter's earned run average of 2.49 was better than Fergie's 2.83.

Oakland won the pennant and World Series for the third year in a row in 1974, and Jim Hunter was a significant factor in that success. Hunter won 242 games during a 15-year career and is a member of the Hall of Fame; but I still believe Ferguson Jenkins' achievement of helping a last-place team rise to second place was deserving of the Cy Young Award in 1974.

Ferguson Jenkins displays his Cy Young Award at the Canadian Baseball Hall of Fame. (Canadian Baseball Hall of Fame)

Ferguson Jenkins was inducted into the National Baseball Hall of Fame in 1991, along with Gaylord Perry, a winner of 314 games with eight different teams. During his career, Fergie pitched against 12 pitchers who were inducted into the Hall of Fame: Perry, Tom Seaver, Steve Carlton, Bob Gibson, Phil Niekro, Nolan Ryan, Jim Hunter, Jim Bunning, Juan Marichal, Don Drysdale, Don Sutton, and Jim Palmer.

Pitchers don't win games by themselves; hitters have to hit and fielders have to make plays. The match-up of two ace pitchers is a great crowd favourite but managers prefer not to send their best pitcher against the other team's best pitcher. As a result, Ferguson Jenkins did not often pitch against a competitor of equal rank. Between 1966 and

1982, Jenkins pitched a total of 58 games against his 12 Hall of Fame contemporaries. Fergie won 27, lost 24 and had seven no-decisions. He pitched six shutouts, won eight games by one run and lost seven times by a single run, including four games where the final score was 1-0. Here are the details of those match-ups of Hall of Famers:

American League Opponents

Jim Palmer	Five times from 1974 to 1980, 4 wins, 1 loss.
Jim Hunter	Four times from 1974 to 1979, 2 wins, 2 losses.
Nolan Ryan	Twice in 1979, 1 win, 1 loss.
Gaylord Perry	Once in 1976, no decision (ND).

National League Opponents

Bob Gibson	Nine times from 1967 to 1972, 5 wins, 3 losses, 1 ND.
Steve Carlton	Seven times from 1969 to 1982, 4 wins, 2 losses, 1 ND.
Phil Niekro	Seven times from 1967 to 1982, 2 wins, 4 losses, 1 ND.
Juan Marichal	Six times from 1967 to 1973, 1 win, 4 losses, 1 ND.
Gaylord Perry	Four times from 1967 to 1969, 2 wins, 2 losses.
Jim Bunning	Four times from 1966 to 1970, 4 wins, no losses.
Tom Seaver	Three times from 1969 to 1973, 1 win, 1 loss, 1 ND.
Don Drysdale	Three times from 1967 to 1969, no wins, 3 losses.
Don Sutton	Three times from 1967 to 1982, 1 win, 1 loss, 1 ND.

One Hall of Fame member against whom Fergie did not pitch is Sandy Koufax, the great left-hander of the Los Angeles Dodgers. Koufax retired after the 1966 season, which was Jenkins' first season as a starting pitcher. Sandy and Fergie almost pitched against each other in the last week of the season.

The Dodgers won a doubleheader Friday, September 23, with Don Drysdale and Don Sutton as the starting pitchers. Koufax had pitched the day following Drysdale in his three previous September starts, and should have pitched the next game against Ferguson Jenkins of the Cubs. However, September 24 was Yom Kippur, the most solemn Jewish holiday. Both Sandy Koufax and Ken Holtzman of the Cubs, as devout Jews, were absent that day.

Joe Moeller started for Los Angeles. Ferguson Jenkins pitched his first major league shutout. He beat the Dodgers 4-0. Koufax and Holtzman did pitch in the Sunday game. Sandy, age 30, was winding up a career cut short by arthritis. Holtzman, a 20-year-old rookie, would pitch 14 years and win more games than Koufax. Ken Holtzman pitched a no-hitter through eight innings. Ken gave up two singles and a walk in the ninth, but he held on to beat Koufax and the Dodgers 2-1. It was a weekend to remember for Jenkins and Holtzman, who were friends, as well as teammates, for six years in Chicago.

The Great Canadian Duel:
Jenkins vs. Reggie Cleveland

Ferguson Jenkins and Reggie Cleveland are the two greatest Canadian-born pitchers of all time. Jenkins, from Chatham, Ontario, had remarkable success with the Chicago Cubs and the Texas Rangers. Reggie Cleveland, who was born in Swift Current, Saskatchewan, won 105 games with St. Louis, Boston, Texas and Milwaukee and was the first Canadian starting pitcher in a World Series game. There was only one Canadian pitcher better than Reggie Cleveland and he (Jenkins) is in the Hall of Fame.

Both pitchers began their careers in the National League and each also pitched in the American League. Jenkins, who is four years older than Cleveland, joined the Philadelphia Phillies in September 1965. He won two games for the Phillies and was traded to the Chicago Cubs at the start of the 1966 season. In 1974 he was traded to the Texas Rangers; to Boston in 1976; back to Texas in 1978; and finally back to Chicago to end his career.

Reggie Cleveland made a four-inning debut with the St. Louis Cardinals in 1969 but didn't become a starting pitcher until 1971. Reggie won 12 games in 1971, 14 games in 1972 and 14 in 1973. He was traded to Boston in 1974, and in 1976 Cleveland and Jenkins were Red Sox teammates.

Ferguson Jenkins and Reggie Cleveland pitched against each other only four times over eight seasons: twice in the National League and twice in the American League. Each time, Reggie Cleveland was pitching for the visiting team.

Their first meeting was July 31, 1972, at Wrigley Field in Chicago before a sell-out crowd. Reggie Cleveland was the Cardinals' top pitcher with a record of 12 wins and five losses; Jenkins had 13 wins and nine losses. In the fourth inning, Jenkins came to bat with runners on second and third and two men out. Fergie hit a single off Reggie to drive in both runners. Cleveland was lifted for a pinch-hitter after five innings; Jenkins scattered six hits in a complete game shutout.

One year later, July 28, 1973, the two Canadians met again in Chicago. This time, Reggie Cleveland earned the win as the Cardinals scored three runs in the first inning and won 7-2. Jenkins gave up seven hits in five innings and left trailing 5-1. Cleveland pitched six innings. He hit a single off the Cubs relief pitcher and won his 11th game against five losses.

Ferguson Jenkins won 25 games for the Texas Rangers in 1974. (National Baseball Hall of Fame Library, Cooperstown, NY)

Reggie Cleveland pitched more than 200 innings, four years in a row, for the St. Louis Cardinals. (National Baseball Hall of Fame Library, Cooperstown, NY)

The two pitchers had been traded to new teams the next time Jenkins and Cleveland faced each other. April 24, 1974, at Arlington Stadium, Jenkins was pitching for the Texas Rangers and Cleveland was pitching for the Boston Red Sox. Both men pitched a complete game and each allowed six hits. Texas scored an unearned run in the first inning. Boston tied the score in the top of the seventh. In the bottom half, Cleveland retired the first two batters but Jim Spencer doubled, Joe Lovitto was walked intentionally and Lenny Randle doubled to drive in both runners. The final score was 3-1 for Texas; win to Jenkins.

The final meeting between the two great Canadians took place six years later in Texas, August 22, 1980. Reggie Cleveland was the starting pitcher for the Milwaukee Brewers and Fergie was pitching for the Rangers in the first game of a doubleheader. Milwaukee scored three runs in the second inning. Boston tied the score in the third inning. Jenkins had to leave the game in the fifth inning with two on and one out and the score still tied 3-3.

Dave Rajisch relieved Fergie and faced just one batter. Ben Oglivie hit into a double play to end the inning. In the Texas fifth, Al Oliver hit a two-run home run off Reggie Cleveland and Texas won 12-6. Reggie Cleveland was the losing pitcher but Ferguson Jenkins did not get the win because he failed to complete five innings. Dave Rajisch was the winning pitcher.

Jenkins and Cleveland
Take Two From the Yankees

As the two best Canadian pitchers of all time, Ferguson Jenkins and Reggie Cleveland were potentially a powerful force in doubleheaders for the Boston Red Sox. Jenkins and Cleveland combined to sweep the New York Yankees in the only doubleheader they pitched in 1976 on July 31 at Fenway Park. Ferguson Jenkins allowed just one earned run and scattered six singles to beat the Yankees 4-2 in the afternoon game. Fergie pitched a complete game in two hours and 23 minutes.

In the night game, Reggie Cleveland took five minutes longer but was equally successful. He allowed two earned runs in seven-and-a-third innings and did not give up an extra-base hit as the Red Sox won 6-4, sweeping a pair from the pennant-bound Yankees. It was the first time two Canadian pitchers had won a doubleheader since July 19, 1948, when Dick Fowler and Phil Marchildon of the Philadelphia Athletics shut out the White Sox in 17 of 18 innings.

The two Red Sox Canadians pitched in the same game twice in 1976. On May 23, Cleveland bailed out Jenkins at New York. Fergie gave up five runs in five innings but Reggie held the Yankees to one run the rest of the way and he got the win as Boston came from behind to beat New York 7-6. Cleveland was used 27 times in relief in 1976 and 14 times as a starter.

Ferguson Jenkins pitched in relief of Reggie Cleveland June 28, and was the winning pitcher as Boston beat Baltimore 12-8. Rick Jones started for Boston but Cleveland replaced Jones in the fourth inning with Baltimore leading 5-4. Reggie gave up two more runs. Jenkins started the sixth inning and gave up a home run to the first batter he faced. Fergie allowed only one more hit over the last four innings. Meanwhile, Boston rallied with eight runs, proving once again that no lead is safe at Fenway Park. That was the only time Jenkins pitched in relief for the Red Sox.

At the beginning of September, Jenkins injured his right Achilles tendon in a game against Texas and did not pitch again that year. Reggie Cleveland took Fergie's place in the rotation and won his last three starts, allowing only one earned run in 25 innings.

On October 2, the second-last day of the season, Reggie Cleveland beat Baltimore 1-0. He defeated Dennis Martinez, a rookie making just the fourth start of a career that would stretch over 22 years and include a perfect game for the Montreal Expos against the Los Angeles Dodgers in 1991.

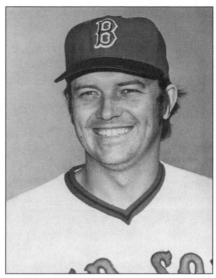

Ferguson Jenkins was traded to Boston for three players in November 1975. (National Baseball Hall of Fame Library, Cooperstown, NY)

Reggie Cleveland was the first Canadian starting pitcher in a World Series game for Boston in 1975. (National Baseball Hall of Fame Library, Cooperstown, NY)

In 1977, Jenkins and Cleveland combined to start one-third of all Red Sox games. Fergie started 28 times and Reggie 27. Jenkins had 11 complete games and Cleveland had nine. Jenkins had 10 wins and 10 losses; Cleveland won 11 and lost eight. Each pitched one shutout. The two Canadians followed one another in the rotation on several occasions in 1977.

Reggie Cleveland pitched eight-plus innings May 4, to beat Seattle 5-2. The next day, Ferguson Jenkins pitched the full nine innings against the Mariners to win by the same score. One week later, Reggie and Fergie lost successive games at Oakland.

Cleveland and Jenkins started only one doubleheader in 1977. At Milwaukee, May 22, Reggie Cleveland started the first game and was leading 4-0 after three innings. In the fifth inning, Reggie gave up five runs. Boston came back to score seven runs in the eighth inning and won the game 14-10. Ferguson Jenkins started the second game for Boston but gave up six runs on 13 hits and the Red Sox lost 6-0.

Reggie Cleveland teamed up with Don Aase for an unusual Labour Day doubleheader sweep against the Blue Jays in Toronto. Aase pitched a three-hitter in the first game to win 8-0. Cleveland gave up five hits to win 6-0. Ron Fairly of the Blue Jays hit a triple to lead off an inning in each game but couldn't score. In the first game, Aase struck out Sam Ewing and Doug Ault and retired Rick Cerone on a ground ball to keep Fairly at third. In the second game, Fairly tripled to start the ninth inning. Cleveland struck out Otto Velez and Doug Ault; then he retired Steve Bowling on a grounder to second base to end the game.

Boston finished 1977 in a tie for second place with Baltimore, and in December the disappointed Red Sox traded Ferguson Jenkins back to the Texas Rangers. The two Canadians were reunited for one more season when Boston sold Reggie Cleveland to Texas in April 1978.

Jenkins won 18 and lost eight for Texas in 1978. He started 30 games, completed 16, and pitched four shutouts. Reggie Cleveland did not start a single game. He was the Texas closer. He pitched 53 times and finished 41 games, earning 12 saves with an earned run average of 3.09. Reggie saved a win for Fergie May 15 against Milwaukee by retiring Robin Yount for the third out.

July 14, 1978, was sweet revenge for both Canadians. Jenkins beat the Red Sox 4-3 at Fenway Park and Cleveland retired the side in the ninth inning to get the save. Reggie Cleveland also saved a win for Jenkins September 1 at Milwaukee. Fergie gave up back-to-back singles to start the ninth. Reggie came in to retire three in a row on ground balls.

That was the last time that Jenkins and Cleveland played on the same team. In December, Reggie Cleveland was traded to Milwaukee.

Doctor Ron Taylor Beat
Ferguson Jenkins, Once

Ron Taylor, who is now a doctor in Toronto, was one of the unheralded relief pitchers of the 1960s and '70s. He wasn't a closer so he didn't accumulate the saves that made Rollie Fingers and others famous; but he did win two World Series championships with the St. Louis Cardinals and the New York Mets. In four World Series games, Ron Taylor pitched seven innings and did not allow either a hit or a run.

As a relief pitcher, Taylor did not often have a chance to go head-to-head with the likes of Hall of Fame starting pitchers, but Ron Taylor pitched against Ferguson Jenkins once and he won the game. Ron didn't start the game but he and Fergie were both in the game at the moment of decision. It was June 22, 1970, at Wrigley Field in Chicago.

Jenkins was the starting pitcher for the Cubs against Gary Gentry of the New York Mets. Chicago was leading 3-0 when Gentry left after four innings; but the Mets scored four times in the fifth to take the lead. "Tug" McGraw worked two-and-a-third innings and gave way to Ron Taylor in the bottom of the seventh with the bases loaded and one out. The Mets were leading 5-4. Taylor retired pinch-hitter Willie Smith on a ground ball to second base but the runner on third scored to tie the game. Ernie Banks ended the inning with a fly ball.

Fergie Jenkins started the eighth inning but gave up singles to the first two batters and was replaced by Hank Agguire. The next batter, Donn Clendenon, hit a three-run home run and the Mets won the game 9-5. Ron Taylor retired the Cubs over the last two innings, and he was the winning pitcher. Jenkins was the losing pitcher. That was the only time Ron Taylor pitched against Ferguson Jenkins. Taylor was the winning pitcher again the very next day. Ron set down six batters in a row in the eighth and ninth innings, and Duffy Dyer hit a pinch-hit home run in the 10th inning.

When baseball has been your life for 15 to 20 years, retirement can be a shock for a lot of players. Ron Taylor had a university degree in electrical engineering and had worked as an engineer during the winter. "I was 35 when my baseball career ended," he says. "The only jobs in engineering were in sales and I didn't think I would be a very good salesman. I had three choices: get a business degree and go into administration; take a Ph.D. in engineering and become a designer; or I could do something I always wanted to do - study medicine."

Ron Taylor pitched 11 shutout innings in his major league debut at Fenway Park in Boston. He lost on a 12th-inning home run. (National Baseball Hall of Fame Library, Cooperstown, NY)

OVER THE FENCE IS OUT!

The associate dean of medicine at the University of Toronto agreed Ron would have no trouble getting into medical school if he were 23 years old. "But," he told Ron, "you haven't been in a classroom for more than 10 years and we don't know if you can take the course load." Ron wasn't ready to give up.

The university agreed that if Ron took an honours science program and got good marks his application would be considered. "What are the odds I will be accepted?" Ron asked. "If you get high marks, it's 50-50 you'll be admitted," he was told. Ron passed with distinction and was accepted into medical school, where he repeated his success.

Doctor Ron Taylor opened a general medical practice in a two-storey house just a block east of Yonge Street, north of St. Clair. The doctor examined patients with colds, stiff knees and the normal illnesses a family doctor sees. He also served as team physician for the Toronto Blue Jays, prescribing treatment for aches and sprains at home games in Toronto and weekends in Florida during spring training. He was sometimes seen pitching batting practice or jogging in the outfield. A little exercise and some fresh air is just what the doctor ordered.

Scotty Bowman Helped Me
Through the Longest Game

Jack Reed played three years for the New York Yankees and hit only one home run. I saw it sail high and deep into the bleachers in left centre field at Tiger Stadium in Detroit on Sunday night June 24, 1962. Reed's home run came in the 22nd inning and it won what was then the longest game in baseball history.

I was broadcasting the game for listeners of CFRA in Ottawa and the Valley. It lasted exactly seven hours; the longest game in history by time - and it seemed to go on forever. The Tigers had a chance to win it hours earlier when Rocky Colavito led off the bottom of the 12th inning with a triple. "Man on third, with nobody out," I said. "Things look good for the Tigers."

Yankee manager Ralph Houk threw up the only defence possible. He walked the next two batters intentionally and drew in his outfield. Chico Fernandez came to bat with the bases loaded. Any hit would win the game; a decent fly ball would do as well. Chico smashed a line drive over the shortstop that would have been a hit but left fielder Tom Tresh, playing shallow, didn't have to move to catch the first out.

Now it was time for some strategy by Detroit manager Bob Scheffing. "Red" Wilson was the next batter and Scheffing gave the sign for a suicide squeeze. As the pitcher threw the ball, Colavito came charging in from third base. Wilson bunted the ball straight up in the air. Catcher "Yogi" Berra dropped to his knees to catch the ball in front of home plate and, without moving, tagged the sliding Colavito for a double play to end the inning.

I could hear Yankee broadcaster Mel Allen exclaim, "How about that!" For the next two hours, the team took turns hitting ground balls and pop flies with no serious threats to score. As the time neared eight o'clock, Dizzy Dean and Pee Wee Reese said good night on CBS Television and made way for the "Ed Sullivan Show." With me in the booth hanging to the left of home plate was Russ Betz, an engineer from radio station WJBK in Detroit, who set up the microphones, kept time for commercial breaks, and gave me the signal when it was time for me to talk again.

For this occasion only, we were joined by Scott Bowman, assistant coach of the Hull-Ottawa Canadiens hockey team, who had made the trip to Detroit and was sitting beside me. Scotty was to play an important role in maintaining my ability to talk. Seven hours is a long time to sit in a booth; a long time to talk. On a summer afternoon, a few soft drinks will help to keep the voice fluid but what goes in must come out. The nearest

Jim Shearon at Tiger Stadium, Detroit, 1962. (CFRA photo by Norman Kert)

washroom was up a ladder and underneath the grandstand - almost a five-minute trip. We had two-minute commercial breaks at the end of each inning.

After the Colavito episode, I told the listeners, "When we come back Scotty Bowman will bring you the out-of-town scores." "Talk slowly," I whispered to Scotty, and dashed up the ladder. As the game dragged on, all other games had ended and there were no further out-of-town scores to report; no chance for me to climb the ladder. Scotty came to the rescue. He went up the ladder, bought a large soft drink, drank it and passed me the empty container.

As nine o'clock approached, the Yankees came up for the 22nd time. Roger Maris, who hit 61 home runs the year before, was walked intentionally to start the inning. He was followed by Jack Reed, who entered the game in the eighth inning to give Mickey Mantle's knees a rest. Phil Regan was the Detroit pitcher.

"A tall, right-handed batter, Reed is still looking for his first run batted in," I said. "The first pitch is down low." The next pitch was over the plate and Jack Reed parked it deep in the upper deck to give the Yankees the lead 9-7. But the drama wasn't over. In the bottom of the inning, the Tigers got a man on base and Norm Cash, who hit 41 home runs the year before, came to bat.

"Here's the pitch. Cash swings and hits one deep to right field. It's heading for the roof ... and it curves FOUL!" Thank goodness, I thought. If that ball had been fair, we'd never get out of here. Cash struck out and the game was over.

Back in Ottawa the next day, I had a phone call from Dr. Clint Whyte, an obstetrician, who told me how he heard every word of the broadcast. "I was listening at my cottage in the Gatineau when an expectant mother phoned to say she was ready to go into labour. I drove to the Civic Hospital, listening on the car radio. In the parking lot, I put a transistor radio in my pocket and stuck the plug in my ear. I delivered the baby, listening to the ballgame. I continued to listen in the car going home and I enjoyed a cool glass of beer back at the cottage as I listened to the last inning."

The Little League Team
Had a Left-Handed Shortstop

It was tryout day for the Little League baseball team; the first day for a new manager. A suntanned, blond-haired 11-year-old boy insisted he wanted to play shortstop. His name was Floyd. The manager suggested he might try the outfield or first base.

"I've never heard of a left-handed shortstop," he told the boy.
"That doesn't mean there couldn't be one," was his reply.

The man had to agree the boy was right. "O.K., Floyd, you're the shortstop. Let's see what you can do."

During the next two months, Floyd proved that there could be a left-handed shortstop. He caught pop flies and line drives with one hand and chased any ground balls that came near. Floyd managed to grab most of them and he had a strong - if not always accurate - throwing arm. The first baseman, Gordon, a tall 12-year-old who could jump and stretch, got a good workout that summer.

Robert was the team captain, best hitter and number one pitcher. Myron was the catcher, Doug played third base and David played second base. The second pitcher, Richard, was a 10-year-old left-hander. He threw a very slow ball that opposing batters couldn't wait to hit. Most of the time they swung before the ball reached the plate. Richard would replace Robert in the last inning of a game if the team had the lead. His slow pitches were a big change from Robert's fastballs and Richard helped to win a lot of games.

The team finished second in a four-team league and got to play the first-place team in a best-of-five playoff. The night before the first game, the manager had two phone calls. The first was from assistant coach Jack Mandeville, who informed him that the third baseman's parents had just left for the cottage and Doug would not be available for any more games.

The second call was from Richard's father. "If Richard isn't the starting pitcher tomorrow," he said, "he's not playing."

Even a rookie manager knew the first rule of Little League survival: parents can suggest but they cannot dictate.

"I guarantee that Richard will be our starting pitcher in one of the games," he said as diplomatically as possible, "but the other coach and I haven't decided yet who will be the starting pitcher tomorrow."

The father's answer made it clear diplomacy wasn't going to work.

"If you don't tell me right now that Richard will start tomorrow, he won't be at the game."

That meant the team would be short two players, but the manager was never tempted to concede.

"It would be a shame if you kept Richard out of the game," he said, trying to make the father feel some remorse. It was no use.

"I'm not keeping him out of the playoffs; you are," he said and hung up.

The team lost three straight but it wasn't a disgrace. The winners were the first-place team. They played well all season and none of their boys went to the cottage or stayed at home. Robert pitched all three games and pitched well. It might have been a close series if all the players had been present; but the manager had no chance to be disappointed.

He and Jack Mandeville shook hands with all the boys after the final game and thanked them for their effort. The last boy was Floyd. His blond hair covered one eye as he looked up at the manager.

"Thanks for letting me play shortstop," he said. "Maybe next year I'll try out for pitcher."

Chapter 6

The Modern Era

Kevin Reimer's Perfect Game, Seven for Seven in Milwaukee

The brightest lights sometimes shine in the darkest settings. It was a Tuesday night in Milwaukee, August 24, 1993. The Brewers were in last place in the American League East and playing against the Oakland Athletics, who were in last place in the American League West.

Despite the lowly position of the two teams, three future Hall of Fame members played in the game: Robin Yount, the Milwaukee centre fielder, and two Oakland pitchers, "Goose" Gossage and Dennis Eckersley.

But, if you had to vote on the basis of that one game, the most likely candidate for the Hall of Fame would have been Kevin Reimer, the designated hitter for Milwaukee, and the only Canadian in the starting lineup.

Reimer, from Enderby, British Columbia, was a powerful hitter who played for Canada's Olympic team before turning professional with the Texas Rangers. He is one of the few Canadians to hit 20 home runs in a major league season.

On that late August evening, in the second game of a doubleheader, Kevin Reimer came to bat seven times and got on base seven times. He had six hits and an intentional walk.

Kevin scored four runs, including the winning run, and he got extra base hits off two Hall of Fame pitchers. As the designated hitter, Reimer singled in the second, fourth and fifth innings against Bob Welch. He doubled in the seventh against "Goose" Gossage and doubled in the ninth against Dennis Eckersley.

Kevin went in to play right field in the 11th inning, and was walked intentionally by Kelly Downs when he came to bat. He also singled in the 13th inning and scored the winning run.

"I had some good games against Oakland over the years," said Kevin Reimer. "It gives you some inner confidence. Their pitchers were aggressive and I was a free swinger so I was able to make good contact. The year I hit 20 home runs, 'Goose' Gossage and I were good friends when we played together in Texas. Goose was yelling at me after I hit the double off him. I couldn't hear what he was saying but he was grumbling in his big voice."

After the season, Milwaukee wanted Kevin to take a big cut in pay. There was also the threat of a lockout in 1994, so Reimer accepted an offer to play in Japan. "I figured if they were sitting out in the States, I would still be drawing a paycheque."

Playing in Japan turned out to be a strange but exciting experience. "We had interpreters all the time," Kevin said. "They coached us in the proper thing to do." There were some things that Kevin didn't have to be told.

Kevin Reimer began his career with the Texas Rangers. (Courtesy of Texas Rangers)

Reimer wasn't the only Canadian playing in Japan. Rob Ducey, a former Toronto Blue Jay, had also come to the Japanese league. There were just two Canadians playing in the whole country and they got into a shoving match at home plate.

Kevin smiles as he remembers. "Ducey was struggling that day and our catcher, who was just a little guy, was mouthing off to him at the plate. I could see Ducey was getting hot. I told the guys in the dugout, 'Be careful. If he gets mad, he could hurt somebody.'

"Sure enough the catcher kept it up. Ducey got on base and after a couple of plays he was at third base. The next batter hit the ball on the infield and Ducey is running home.

"He comes in standing up because he's pretty fast but he doesn't even try to touch home plate. The catcher is over on the first base side and Ducey runs into him pretty hard.

"I ran from the dugout and grabbed Ducey. If it had been somebody else I might have thrown a punch but I just wanted to let him know I thought that was a cheap shot."

The Japanese players were surprised but pleased that Kevin stood up for them against another Canadian. After the game, Ducey called Reimer on the phone and asked, "What were you doing?"

Kevin's answer was, "When you put on a team uniform, you stick up for your team and you defend your players. You could have hurt that guy and I wanted to let you know I don't like that. I'm not mad any more. I'll buy you a beer and we can talk about it."

Kevin Reimer grew up in Enderby, which is in the Okanagan Valley, halfway between Vancouver and Calgary. The Reimers don't head for the city very often. They have always enjoyed an outdoor life. The Shuswap River and Okanagan Lake are nearby; so are the mountains and several provincial parks.

Kevin and his family are keen about archery, and take part in competitive shoots. He now runs a taxidermy business. "Do you hire people to do the work for you?" I asked. "No, I do it all myself. I have taken courses with some of the best professionals and I attend seminars." Reimer also coaches his daughter's volleyball team.

Kevin inherited his baseball skills from his father, Gerry, who played against Ferguson Jenkins in the minor leagues and ended his career in the Pacific Coast League.

"My dad spends the winter in Arizona playing golf and softball," he says. Kevin prefers his mountain home. Only occasionally does he recall the glory of a baseball career and a magical night when he went seven-for-seven against the best pitchers in baseball. British Columbia is his home. This is where Kevin Reimer belongs.

Kevin Reimer played 200 games as a designated hitter. (Courtesy of Salt Lake Buzz)

Pitcher Matt Maysey
Was Perfect Too!

Kevin Reimer wasn't the only Canadian with a perfect batting record in that 1993 game. The sixth Milwaukee pitcher, Matt Maysey, a tall right-handed pitcher who was born in Hamilton, Ontario, came out to pitch the 13th inning.

Maysey gave up a lead-off single to Mike Bordick but Brent Gates hit into a double play. After another single, Dave Henderson popped to second base to end the inning. Since the designated hitter had taken a fielder's position, the Milwaukee pitcher was now required to bat.

In the bottom of the 13th, with the score tied 6-6, Kevin Reimer singled to right field. Pitcher Matt Maysey was the next batter and he stroked a single to centre field. After Pat Listach bunted to load the bases, catcher Dave Nillson, an Australian, singled to left. Kevin Reimer scored the winning run, and the winning pitcher was Matt Maysey.

Matt Maysey played for the Montreal Expos in 1992. (Score baseball card, 1993)

That extra-inning victory against Oakland was the only game Matt Maysey won in the major leagues, and his overtime single was the only time he ever came to bat. Kevin Reimer remembers that Matt Maysey was jumping up and down. "He was very excited as they brought his jacket out to him."

If you look at www.retrosheet.org and search under Players, you will find that Matt Maysey has a batting average, an on-base percentage and a slugging average of 1.000. Eat your heart out, Larry Walker!

Rheal Cormier, Relief Pitcher, "Frenchy" Lasted a Long Time

American players and coaches don't mean it as an insult when they call a French-speaking Canadian "Frenchy." Since there is rarely more than one French-Canadian on any American team it is an easy form of identification. Nearly every Francophone who plays in the United States is called by that nickname, and Rheal Cormier was no exception. A former lumberjack from New Brunswick's Acadian peninsula, Rheal pitched his first game in the major leagues for the St. Louis Cardinals in 1991 and pitched in nearly 700 games for five different teams until 2007.

Rheal Cormier was originally a starting pitcher. His highest win total was in his second year, 1992. Rheal won seven games in a row in the last month-and-a-half to finish with 10 wins and 10 losses for the Cardinals. Cormier failed to match that success in the next two years and was traded to the Boston Red Sox in April 1995. Rheal appeared in 48 games for Boston, including 12 starts. He had seven wins and five losses with an earned run average of 4.07.

In January 1996, Cormier was traded to the Montreal Expos. He made 27 starts for the Expos, won seven and lost 10. His best performance was an 8-0 shutout of the St. Louis Cardinals at the Olympic Stadium on April 22 when he allowed just three singles and struck out nine batters. It was Cormier's first win as an Expo, his first major league shutout and only complete game of the year.

In 1997, Rheal Cormier pitched just one game for the Expos, against the Colorado Rockies April 5 in Montreal. He retired the first three batters; but in the second inning Rheal gave up a walk, a home run and three singles before leaving the game. That was the final start of his career. He was diagnosed with tendonitis of the left elbow and placed on the disabled list. On May 21, he had surgery, a tendon transplant, and was transferred to the 60-day disabled list. There was doubt that he would ever pitch again.

Cormier was released by the Expos in October 1997 and signed soon after with the Cleveland Indians. Rheal started three games for the Indians' Akron farm team in the Class AA Eastern League. He pitched a total of 10 innings in 1998 and had an earned run average of 6.52 with no decisions. Uncertain that he could pitch any more, the Indians made Cormier a free agent.

Rheal was not ready to retire. He felt there was still a job for a left-hand pitcher who can throw strikes. In January 1999, Rheal signed with the Boston Red Sox and became exclusively a relief pitcher. From that point on, Cormier pitched 508 times without starting a game.

Baseball's law of averages maintains that a left-handed pitcher has a better chance of retiring a left-handed batter, and a right-handed pitcher is more likely to retire a right-handed batter. If the batter is a switch hitter, which means he can bat from either side of the plate, the law of averages holds that you might as well stay with the pitcher in the game unless your records show that batter has had previous success against that pitcher. Managers pay close attention to pitcher-batter match-ups late in a game if the score is close.

Of course, observing these rules does not guarantee success. To illustrate, April 10, 2004, at Florida, Cormier started the seventh inning with the score tied 3-3. Juan Pierre, a left-handed batter, was leading off for the Marlins, followed by Luis Castillo, a switch hitter, and Miguel Cabrera, a right-handed batter. Cormier retired Pierre on a ground ball to second base. Since the next batter was a switch hitter, Cormier remained in the game. Castillo singled to centre field. With the right-handed batter Cabrera coming to bat, manager Larry Bowa removed Cormier and brought in Roberto Hernandez, a right-handed pitcher. Cabrera hit a home run to win the game 5-3 and Rheal Cormier was the losing pitcher because he put the lead run on base.

Two weeks later, at St. Louis, the Phillies were leading 2-1 in the eighth inning. Todd Worrell retired the first batter on a ground ball but then gave up a single and a double. Cormier was called in with runners on second and third and one out to pitch to the left-handed batter Jim Edmonds. Rheal struck him out. Scott Rolen, a right-handed batter, was up next with Colin Porter, a left-handed batter, to follow. The law of averages was clear. Rolen was walked intentionally to load the bases with two out so that Cormier could pitch to the left-handed batter. However, Tony LaRussa, the St. Louis manager, replaced Porter with Reggie Sanders, a right-handed batter. In reply, Bowa called for Roberto Hernandez to replace Cormier. Sanders hit the first pitch for a triple to score three runs and the Cardinals won the game 5-2.

Sometimes, a relief pitcher will lose even when he does his job the way it should be done. At the Olympic Stadium in Montreal, the Dodgers were leading the Expos by one run in the ninth inning. Montreal had a man on second with two out. Steve Wilson, a left-handed pitcher from Victoria, British Columbia, came in to pitch for the Dodgers. Wilson's job was to induce a ground ball or a pop-up. The batter, Delino DeShields, hit a ground ball right through the legs of the first baseman. The ball rolled into the right field corner. The runner scored and DeShields wound up on second.

The next batter hit a high pop fly behind first base. The second baseman, the right fielder and the first baseman circled under the ball

Rheal Cormier began his career in 1991 with the St. Louis Cardinals. He pitched in nearly 700 games before retiring in 2007. (Courtesy of St. Louis Cardinals)

while DeShields ran for home. Three Dodgers raised their gloves to the ball but none of them caught it. The ball dropped to the ground as DeShields touched home plate with the winning run. Both batters were credited with doubles; Steve Wilson was charged with the loss.

Between 1999 and 2006, Rheal Cormier pitched 504 innings in 508 games. That was an average of 63 games and 63 innings per year. In other words, he rarely pitched more than one inning; sometimes, he faced only one batter. Cormier had a remarkable run in 2003 pitching for the Philadelphia Phillies. Rheal worked in 65 games and struck out 67 batters in 84 innings. He won eight games without a loss and had an ERA of 1.70. Cormier's very solid work was eclipsed by the brilliance of Eric Gagné's 55 consecutive saves and an ERA of 1.20, which earned Gagné the Cy Young Award as best National League pitcher of 2003.

Cormier's busiest year was 2004 when he pitched in 84 games, more than half the Phillies games. His career total was 71 wins and 64 losses. A relief pitcher needs good control. He can't afford to walk a batter or hit a batter, although he does have to be able to pitch inside to keep the batter from leaning over the plate. Rheal Cormier did a good job of keeping the ball around the plate. From 1999 through 2006, Cormier struck out 334 batters and gave up 143 unintentional walks in 504 innings.

Middle-inning relief pitchers don't get the recognition they deserve, but fortunately for Rheal Cormier those who do good work are well paid. During his 16 years as a major league pitcher, the former lumberjack from New Brunswick earned a total of just over $24 million, including a personal best of $3 million from the Phillies in 2004. For a man who worked about three days a week for six months a year, that was pretty good money for part-time work.

The Zimmerman Brothers
Made History in Texas

Only once in major league history have two Canadian brothers pitched for opposing teams in the same game. It happened the day after Canada Day, July 2, 1999, at the Ballpark in Arlington, Texas. The Zimmerman brothers, Jeff and Jordan, from Kelowna, British Columbia, were the pitching rivals.

Jeff, soon to be 27, and almost three years older than Jordan, was off to a spectacular start as a rookie relief pitcher for the Texas Rangers. He had appeared in 31 games and had allowed only three earned runs in 51 innings. Jeff had won seven games without a loss and was chosen to play in the 1999 All-Star game at Fenway Park in Boston.

Jordan, a left-hander, promoted to the Seattle Mariners in May, had pitched a total of eight innings in 11 games and had an earned run average of 7.88. Jordan couldn't know that this was his last chance to pitch in the major leagues.

The score was tied 5-5 when Jeff Zimmerman came out to pitch the top of the eighth inning for Texas. He faced four batters; gave up a single and struck out one batter. In the bottom of the eighth, Roberto Kelly hit a

Jeff Zimmerman.
(Texas Rangers photo)

Jordan Zimmerman.
(Seattle Mariners photo)

Jeff Zimmerman won his first nine decisions in 1999 and pitched in the All-Star Game at Fenway Park in Boston. (Courtesy of Texas Rangers)

home run to give Texas the lead, but Seattle tied the score in the top of the ninth against John Wetteland.

Jeff's brother, Jordan Zimmerman, came into the game in the bottom of the ninth inning to pitch for Seattle, with two men on base and the score tied 6-6. Jordan pitched to just one batter. Left fielder Rusty Greer hit a single to drive in the winning run. Two days later, Jordan Zimmerman was optioned to the minors. He never pitched in the major leagues again.

Jeff became the Texas Rangers' closer. In October 2001, he was rewarded with a three-year contract worth $10 million. Less than five months later, in March 2002, Jeff injured his elbow in spring training. Despite many attempts over the next few years, Jeff Zimmerman never pitched another game for the Texas Rangers.

Matt Stairs, Professional Hitter

Matt Stairs hits the game-winning home run that beat the Dodgers in Los Angeles. Catcher Russell Martin reaches in vain for the ball that landed deep in the bleachers. (AP photo by Chris Carlson)

Matt Stairs likes to say he is "just an ordinary Joe." It's not true. His real identity was revealed in the 2008 National League Championship Series when Matt's pinch-hit home run beat the Los Angeles Dodgers. "They don't call him a professional hitter for no reason," said his Philadelphia teammate Shane Victorino. Double negative aside, Victorino was right on the money. Matt Stairs is a professional hitter, and has been for more than 20 years.

Talking to reporters after his game-winning hit, Matt Stairs said, "I'm not going to lie - I try to hit home runs and that's it. I'm not going to hit a single and steal second base, God knows that. So I think the biggest thing is get up there, swing hard and elevate."

Matt Stairs' ability to elevate is the reason the five-foot, nine-inch batter from New Brunswick has enjoyed a 20-year career, and is still playing at the age of 40.

When he started out, as a 20-year-old member of Canada's Olympic team in 1988, Matt was a shortstop and third baseman and he was easy to recognize. "Just look for the guy with the dirtiest uniform," Bernie Beckman, executive director of Baseball Canada, told me. Stairs spent a lot of time in the dirt, diving for balls hit near third base. Matt clearly believed that "a man's reach should exceed his grasp."

Stairs signed with the Expos in January 1989, and played three years as a shortstop, or second or third baseman, at West Palm Beach, Jamestown, Rockford, Jacksonville and Harrisburg before converting to the outfield at Indianapolis in 1992.

Matt made his major league debut at Cincinnati, May 29, 1992, as a pinch-hitter in the 10th inning of a tie game. He struck out against Rob Dibble. Two days later, Matt got his first major league hit. It was a single in the second inning with the bases loaded and two out. Two runs scored and the Expos beat Cincinnati 6-2.

When Stairs was starting out, the Expos outfield consisted of Moises Alou, Marquis Grissom and Larry Walker, with Rondell White, Lou Frazier, John Vander Wal and Curtis Pride also competing for playing time. It was not a good place for him to be.

In June 1993, the Expos sold Matt's contract to the Chunchi Dragons of the Japanese league. Stairs batted .309 in Japan, and was re-signed by the Expos, who promptly traded him to Boston. Matt played 1994 and 1995 in the minors.

Stairs was called up to Boston late in June 1995, and he hit his first major league home run in Kansas City, July 5. He stayed with the Red Sox for the last three months of the season but had only 88 times at bat and was released in October.

Stairs signed with Oakland for the 1996 season. He started the year with a pinch-hit home run against Detroit, but was sent to Edmonton of the Pacific Coast League.

Two months later, Matt was recalled to Oakland and made a spectacular return against the California Angels. On July 5, Matt hit a grand-slam home run in the first inning. He came up again in the same inning with runners on second and third, and hit a single to drive in two more runs.

Oakland set a record by scoring 13 times in the first inning, and Matt Stairs batted in six of those runs. Stairs had an eight-game hit streak in July, and delivered four consecutive pinch hits. Matt finished with a .277 batting average and 10 home runs in 61 games.

In 1997, Matt Stairs finally got a chance to play every day. He responded with a personal best performance: a .298 batting average, 27 home runs and 73 runs batted in. Among Canadian players, only Larry Walker had ever hit more home runs than Matt.

That was the start of four wonderful years in Oakland. Matt loved playing every day and the fans in the Bay area admired his hustle and free-swinging style. In 1998, Stairs hit 26 home runs, the first Canadian to hit 25 home runs or more in consecutive seasons. He also tied a record, hitting home runs in five consecutive games.

Recognizing his contribution, the A's gave Matt a contract that raised his salary from $325,000 to $1.9 million in 1999, then to $3 million in 2000, with a third year at $3.2 million. In 1999, Stairs hit 38 home runs, and 21 more in 2000. In November 2000, Oakland traded Stairs to the Chicago Cubs, beginning a series of moves that took Matt to seven different teams in seven years.

Baseball is a wonderful game but it is also a business. Loyalty is in short supply. Teams drop players every year as their needs change, and players go where they can make the most money. After Oakland, Stairs played with Chicago, Milwaukee, Pittsburgh, Kansas City, Texas, and Detroit before coming back to Canada for two years with the Toronto Blue Jays.

On August 31, 2008, Matt was traded to the Philadelphia Phillies, his 11th major league team. He was the last player added to the post-season roster and his rocket-like blast against Dodger closer Jonathan Broxton justified the Phillies' late-season move.

In 12 years, Matt Stairs has averaged more than 20 home runs per year. He leads all Canadians in bases-loaded home runs, with 10, and pinch-hit home runs, with 15. The slugger from New Brunswick has produced timely hits that earned him the respect and admiration of his teammates. Shane Victorino summed it up when he said, "To do what he does at the age of 40, I'm smiling two times bigger because I feel so good for him."

When he retires as a "professional hitter," Matt Stairs' next job title could be coach or manager. Allan Baird, former general manager of the Kansas City Royals, told Tyler Kepner of the New York Times that Stairs could be an ideal manager some day. "The people who are respected in this game are consistent in their character," said Baird, "and that's the way he is. He's all about substance; he's not about style. He gives you an honest day's work every single day."

Matt Stairs Leads Canadians in Bases-Loaded Home Runs

As of January 1, 2009, Matt Stairs is the all-time Canadian leader in bases-loaded home runs. The free-swinger from New Brunswick hit 10 bases-loaded home runs against 10 different teams, and 10 different pitchers. Larry Walker is second on the list with seven grand slams,

Matt Stairs hit 38 home runs for the Oakland Athletics in 1999. (Courtesy of Oakland Athletics)

Matt Stairs began his career with the Montreal Expos. (Courtesy of Montreal Expos)

followed by Jeff Heath, who hit five. Among active players, Justin Morneau is next with three and Jason Bay has two.

Matt Stairs hit seven bases-loaded home runs against right-handed pitchers (RHP) and three against left-handers (LHP). Matt hit seven of his grand-slam home runs in American League parks, and three in the National League. Matt's team won every game in which he hit a home run with the bases loaded.

Here are the details of Matt Stairs' bases-loaded home runs:

While playing for the Oakland Athletics:

1. July 5, 1996, vs. California, 1st inning, Ryan Hancock, RHP.
2. September 28, 1997, at Seattle, 7th inning, Norm Charlton, LHP.
3. April 16, 1998, vs. Kansas City, 4th inning, Tim Belcher, RHP.
4. June 24, 1998, at San Francisco, 8th inning, Steve Reed, RHP.
5. April 30, 1999, vs. Boston, 1st inning, Kip Gross, RHP.
6. August 13, 1999, at Toronto, 5th inning, Paul Spoljaric, LHP.
7. June 6, 2000, vs. San Diego, 1st inning, Rodrigo Lopez, RHP.

With the Kansas City Royals:

8. April 20, 2004, at Cleveland, 6th inning, Jeriome Robertson, LHP.
9. July 14, 2005, at Detroit, 8th inning, Franklyn German, RHP.

As a member of the Toronto Blue Jays:

10. May 19, 2007, at Philadelphia, Clay Condrey, 8th inning, RHP.

Matt Stairs has played for six American League and five National League teams. Stairs has never hit a bases-loaded home run while playing for a National League team.

Innuendo Cannot Diminish
Eric Gagné's Achievement

A shadow was thrown over one of the most brilliant achievements in Canadian sports history when former U.S. Senator George Mitchell mentioned Eric Gagné in his report on illegal use of steroids by major league baseball players.

Big, strong and overpowering, Eric Gagné blew away batters as the closing pitcher for the Los Angeles Dodgers from 2002 to 2004. Over three seasons, Gagné preserved 152 Dodger victories in 158 opportunities - a success rate of 96 percent. One year, 2003, he was absolutely perfect: 55 saves in 55 chances!

Gagné struck out 137 batters in 82 innings and limited opposing batters to a combined batting average of .133. No wonder the Baseball Writers' Association of America gave him the Cy Young Award as the outstanding National League pitcher of 2003.

No other pitcher had ever been so dominant in his assigned role, and the voting for the Cy Young Award reflected that supremacy. Eric Gagné was the first choice of 28 of 32 voters. He was the second choice of two others, and Gagné's total of 146 points was double that of the runner-up, Jason Schmidt of San Francisco.

Eric Gagné wasn't always a high-profile relief pitcher. He began his career as a starting pitcher in 1999, and made 48 starts over three years. Gagné won 11 and lost 14, with an earned run average of 4.61. Overshadowing that mediocre record was a very impressive average of 7.5 strikeouts per game.

From 2002 on, Eric Gagné was strictly a relief pitcher, and almost exclusively the closer, the man who finished the game. He earned his first save April 7, 2002, against the Colorado Rockies. Eric pitched to four batters in saving a 6-4 Dodgers victory. Gagné kept doing the same thing for the next three years.

Between 2002 and 2004, Eric pitched exactly 82.1 innings each year. Gagné struck out 365 batters in 247 innings and he set a National League record of 85 consecutive saves. Eric Gagné's dominating role also led to record salaries.

After winning the Cy Young Award in 2003, Gagné asked for a salary of $8 million but an arbitration panel decided he would get $5 million. In January 2005, there was no need for arbitration. Eric and the Dodgers agreed to a contract that guaranteed him $19 million for two years: $8 million in 2005 and $10 million in 2006. The deal also included a $12 million option for 2007, with a $1-million buyout if the Dodgers decided not to pick up the option.

Los Angeles Dodgers pitcher Eric Gagné celebrates another save, against the St. Louis Cardinals. (AP photo by Danny Moloshok)

Eric Gagné was the highest-paid Canadian pitcher in baseball history. It is an illustration of just how much baseball salaries have increased in the modern era, that Ferguson Jenkins, the only other Canadian to win the Cy Young Award, said his highest salary was $275,000 with the Texas Rangers.

From 2002 to 2004, Gagné was like an indestructible machine. But after signing his new deal, the machine started to malfunction. Eric Gagné was on the disabled list at the start of the 2005 season because of pain in his right elbow.

Eric made his 2005 debut on May 14 against the Atlanta Braves. Gagné came out to pitch the ninth inning with the Braves leading 3-1. Chipper Jones led off with a home run to right field; Andruw Jones followed with a home run to left field and Julio Franco singled to centre. Gagné struck out the next three batters to end the inning. He pitched 13 more times in the next month and recorded eight saves in eight opportunities. On June 15, Gagné went back on the disabled list and underwent surgery on his right elbow. He missed the rest of the season.

Eric Gagné's eight saves in 2005 cost the Dodgers $1 million each. The next year was even worse. His right elbow was still sore and Eric again started the season on the disabled list after additional elbow surgery. He made his 2006 debut against the Phillies June 2. Eric faced five batters and did not allow a hit. On June 6, against the Mets, Gagné pitched the ninth inning. He struck out the first two batters and got a fly ball for the third out.

That was Eric Gagné's last game as a Dodger. In July, he complained of back pain and underwent surgery for two herniated discs. He was on the disabled list for the rest of the year. The Dodgers declined their $12-million option. They paid the $1-million buyout, and made Eric a free agent. Gagné signed a contract for the 2007 season with the Texas Rangers that guaranteed him $6 million. He pitched in 34 games for Texas, and recorded 16 saves in 17 opportunities. Eric struck out 29 batters in 33 innings and had an earned run average of 2.16 when he was traded to the Boston Red Sox on July 31.

Testimony in the Mitchell Report showed that the Red Sox discussed possible steroid use when considering a trade to obtain Gagné. At no time has there been any proof that Gagné used steroids. Mitchell's report stated that a witness claimed to have sent a shipment of steroids to Eric Gagné in August 2004, the year after Gagné won the Cy Young Award.

Texas was in last place and going nowhere; Boston was in first place and looking to stay in front of the Yankees. On the theory that you can never have too much pitching, Gagné was a short-term investment. Eric pitched in 20 games for Boston. He finished 11 games and did not have any saves. Gagné allowed 26 hits in 18.2 innings and had an earned run average of 6.75.

Eric pitched in four playoff games for the Red Sox; then worked a perfect ninth inning of the first game of the World Series. With Boston leading 13-1, Gagné retired Todd Helton and Garrett Atkins on fly balls, and then struck out Brad Hawpe to end the game. Eric Gagné accepted his World Series championship ring with justified pride. In Los Angeles his success had been personal; in Boston, Eric contributed to a team championship.

Despite three years of less than sparkling success, Eric Gagné had no trouble finding work for the 2008 season. The Milwaukee Brewers needed a closer and Gagné was the best man available in the free agent market. Two weeks before Christmas, Eric signed a contract for $10 million and started preparing for a new beginning with his fourth team in three years.

In February 2008, Gagné told reporters at the Milwaukee Brewers' spring training camp that he was sorry for "the distraction" caused by the mention of his name in the Mitchell Report. "I feel bad for my family and what they had to go through, and all my friends, and especially my teammates here in Milwaukee," said Gagné. That was all he would say.

Eric Gagné had trouble in the early part of the season and lost his job as the Brewers' closer; but he came back to play a role in helping the Brewers to make the playoffs for the first time since 1982. Eric appeared in 50 games. He won four and lost three, and he recorded 10 saves in 17 opportunities. Gagné pitched twice in the playoffs against Philadelphia and did not allow a run

When Brad Lidge recorded 46 saves in 46 opportunities for the 2008 Phillies, it again brought into sharp focus the magnificence of Eric Gagné's 55 saves in 55 chances for the 2003 Dodgers, and his record of 85 consecutive saves. Despite the Mitchell Report, whenever great seasons by relief pitchers are remembered, the name of Eric Gagné will still lead the list. No innuendo can diminish his achievement.

Russell Martin, Finally
a Catcher Who Can Hit!

Now that he is recognized as the best catcher in the National League, it is surprising that Russell Martin resisted his manager's advice to switch from third base to catcher. "At first, he didn't want to move because he was a very good third baseman," says Dann Bilardello, former Montreal Expos catcher, who was manager of the Los Angeles Dodgers' farm team at Columbus, Georgia, in 2003.

There have been more than a dozen Canadian catchers in the major leagues but it has been almost a hundred years since there was a Canadian catcher who could hit with power. Since 1911 no Canadian catcher had played 100 games and batted over .275, until Russell Martin came along. The fluently bilingual Martin, who was born in Toronto but grew up in Montreal, broke the mould of good-field, no-hit Canadian catchers in 2007 and 2008 when he was chosen to the National League all-star team with the Los Angeles Dodgers.

Russell Martin played 151 games in 2007 - a new single-season record for a Canadian catcher - and batted .293. He hit 19 home runs, drove in 87 runs with 158 hits and stole 21 bases. It was Martin's second full season as the Dodgers' everyday catcher. He batted .282 in 117 games in 2006.

The 24-year-old Canadian was the starting catcher for the National League in the 2007 All-Star Game and he earned the rare double distinction of winning a Golden Glove and a Silver Slugger Award in the same season. Major league managers and coaches vote to select the best defensive players (Golden Glove) and best hitters (Silver Slugger) at each position. Larry Walker is the only other Canadian ever to win a Golden Glove; Walker and Justin Morneau are the only previous Canadians to win a Silver Slugger.

Russell Martin was originally drafted by the Montreal Expos when he graduated from high school in 2000; but he did not sign a contract. He chose instead to go to junior college in Florida. Two years later, Martin was selected by the Dodgers in the 17th round of the 2002 draft, and reported to the Gulf Coast Dodgers at Fort Myers, Florida, as a third baseman.

In 2003, Russell moved up a level to Columbus, Georgia, in the South Atlantic League, and stepped into a brand-new position. His manager was a former catcher for the Montreal Expos, Dann Bilardello. "Good catchers are hard to find," said Bilardello. "Russell Martin was athletic, had good feet and soft hands; plus he was strong, and showed leadership

Like a warrior dressed for battle, Russell Martin of the Los Angeles Dodgers surveys the field. (AP Photo by Ben Margot)

qualities." John Debus, the Dodgers' catching coordinator, and Bilardello persuaded Martin that he could get to the majors quicker as a catcher.

"After the first workout, I knew right away he would be really good," said Bilardello. "At first, he was frustrated because he knew he was a good third baseman. I just kept telling him he was outstanding and had the tools and toughness to be a great catcher."

Martin was sent to Ogden of the Pioneer League where he could play every day. Russell became a full-time catcher the hard way; he led the league in passed balls with 27, almost twice as many as any other catcher in the league. Bruised knees, broken fingernails and the dirtiest uniform on the team were all signs of his learning experience.

By 2004, the hard work paid off; Russell was named to the Florida State all-star team. He played 101 games at Vero Beach and committed only nine errors, with a fielding average of .990.

Russell took his hitting to another level in 2005 with Jacksonville of the Southern League. He caught 129 games and batted .311. That earned him a promotion to the Dodgers' top farm team at Las Vegas of the Pacific Coast League in 2006. After just 23 games, Russell was called up to Los Angeles to replace an injured catcher and immediately became the number one catcher, not just for the Dodgers, but for the whole National League.

For his achievements as the All-Star catcher, the Canadian Baseball Hall of Fame named Russell Martin winner of the 2007 Tip O'Neill Award as the outstanding Canadian baseball player of the year. Former Dodger manager Tommy Lasorda said, "No one is more deserving of this honour. I saw all the hard work, effort, desire and sacrifice he put into learning the new position and now Russell Martin is the best."

Dann Bilardello, the former Expo, who saw the potential in Russell Martin, says simply, "He was a great kid to coach and I'm glad for his success. He put in the work and he deserves the recognition he is getting."

The 2008 season underlined Russell Martin's value to the Dodgers. New manager Joe Torre moved Martin up and down the batting order; from sixth to fourth or fifth, and even into the lead-off spot. Wherever the manager put him, Russell did the job.

Martin showed his maturity as a hitter. As a lead-off batter, he learned to take a walk. In the September overtaking of Arizona, Russell walked three times in one game and scored the winning run after drawing a base on balls. For the first time in his career, Russell walked more often than he struck out. During the season, he walked 90 times and scored 87 runs.

In the playoffs, Russell Martin had four hits and drove in five runs in the Dodgers' sweep of the Cubs. Against Philadelphia, Russell had two hits and two walks in the first two games. Then, like the rest of the

Dodgers, Martin stopped hitting. In the last three games, Russell went 0 for 10 and struck out three times. Russell's frustration at losing was evident in his angry complaint to umpire Mike Winters after a called third strike in the final game.

Losing to the Phillies left a bitter taste; but as Russell Martin prepared for the 2009 season, he had so much to look forward to. In just three short years, he has become the best catcher in the league, and he is only 26 years old. The future looks bright!

Jason Bay Comes to Boston

Jason Bay was happy to play in Pittsburgh, but he was very glad to be traded to the Boston Red Sox. Approaching his 30th birthday, the native of Trail, British Columbia, had quietly gone about his business for five years with only modest recognition.

Bay was the first Canadian to be chosen Rookie of the Year in 2004, and he was voted to the National League all-star team in 2006; but playing for a last-place team with a limited payroll is not a recipe for happiness. So, when the Red Sox decided to trade Manny Ramirez July 31, 2008, the door to full media exposure opened and Jason Bay stepped forward with a flourish.

The fans at Fenway Park gave Jason a standing ovation when he came to bat for the first time with the Red Sox, and his new teammates swarmed him in congratulation when Bay tripled and scored the winning run to beat Oakland 2-1 in 12 innings.

"I felt like I had been here all year," Jason told reporters.

In the final two months of the season, Jason Bay hit nine home runs and batted in 37 runs for the Red Sox. In the playoffs, Jason kept on hitting. He hit a home run to win the first game in Anaheim, and he hit a three-run home run to win the next game. Bay also doubled and scored the winning run in the final game.

Jason Bay's success with Boston is the high point in a career that started when he was drafted by the Montreal Expos. He played two years in the Montreal farm system, and then was traded to the New York Mets, who in turn traded him to San Diego. Jason played exactly three games for the Padres and made two hits, including a home run. August 27, 2003, Jason was on the move again when San Diego traded him to Pittsburgh.

Bay played 27 games with the Pirates in 2003 and batted .291. The following year, Jason hit 26 home runs in 120 games and was named the National League Rookie of the Year. That was the start of a solid run of personal success that was diminished by the team's failure to progress beyond fifth place in a six-team division.

Once he got a chance to play every day, Jason rarely missed a game. He played all 162 games in 2005, and 159 games the following year. In 2008, Bay played in 155 games with Pittsburgh and Boston.

Durability and consistency have been hallmarks for Jason Bay. He has averaged 30 home runs and 100 runs batted in. Like many power hitters before him, Bay does strike out a lot. In 2006, he set a new record of 156 strikeouts in a season by a Canadian player, and during his first five years in the major leagues, Jason averaged 141 strikeouts a season.

Jason was stepping into big shoes when he moved to Boston. Manny Ramirez is one of the best hitters in baseball. But the quiet man from British Columbia did his share to get Boston into the playoffs, and he kept on hitting in the post-season. Jason's seven hits against Tampa Bay included a home run, a double and four runs batted in. The Red Sox couldn't resist the Tampa Bay wave but Boston and Jason Bay have good reason to look forward to many more happy endings in the years to come.

Boston teammates all want to touch the hand of Jason Bay (No. 44) after his three-run home run against the Los Angeles Angels of Anaheim in the 2008 playoffs. (AP Photo by Chris Carlson)

Justin Morneau, Canada's $80-Million Man in Minnesota

When Larry Walker retired after the 2005 season, it didn't take long to identify his successor as the best Canadian player in baseball. He even wore the same uniform number - 33! Justin Morneau of the Minnesota Twins was just 25 years old and playing in only his fourth season when he was named the Most Valuable Player in the American League for 2006. And like Larry Walker in 1997, there was no doubt that Morneau deserved it.

Justin Morneau played 157 games, batted .321, hit 34 home runs and drove in 130 runs to help Minnesota win the Central Division title in 2006. In the voting for MVP honours, Morneau beat out two more famous stars, Derek Jeter of the Yankees and David Ortiz of the Red Sox.

At six feet, four and 225 pounds, Justin Morneau is slightly bigger than Walker. He also got off to a quicker start than Larry did. Walker didn't hit more than 30 home runs or drive in 100 runs until his sixth full season in the big leagues.

Morneau also hit the salary jackpot quicker than Walker did. After his second straight season of more than 30 home runs, in 2007, the Twins signed Justin to a six-year, $80-million contract. For a seven-month baseball season, that is almost $2 million a month.

Justin Morneau, born May 15, 1981, in New Westminster, British Columbia, played hockey and basketball as a high-school student. Like Larry Walker, he was a goaltender in hockey. Justin chose uniform number 33 out of admiration for Patrick Roy, the goalkeeper of the Colorado Avalanche. Justin was the third-string goalie for the Portland Winter Hawks when they won the Memorial Cup as Canadian junior champions in 1998, although he is quick to point out he didn't play in any of the championship games.

Morneau was offered college scholarships when he graduated from high school in 1999, but chose to pursue a baseball career instead. He signed with Minnesota and began his apprenticeship in Florida's Gulf Coast rookie league. Justin had been a catcher in high school and that's where he started with the Twins. He also played first base and the outfield and was used as a designated hitter during his first two years.

Justin became a full-time first baseman in 2001 at Davenport, Iowa, while playing for the Quad City River Bandits in the Midwest League. He batted .356 and hit 12 home runs in 64 games. Jason Bay was also playing in the Midwest League with the Expos farm team at Clinton, Iowa. Bay, who is two years older than Morneau, won the batting championship with a .362 average.

The two players from British Columbia again played against each other briefly in 2002 in the Eastern League. Morneau spent the whole year at New Britain, Connecticut, while Bay played in three different leagues, with St. Lucie, Binghamton, and Mobile. Their paths took different directions in 2003. Jason Bay went to the National League San Diego Padres and Morneau was called up to Minnesota in the American League.

An $80-Million Smile. Justin Morneau talks to the media after signing a six-year contract January 25, 2008. (AP photo by Hannah Foslien)

Justin Morneau's first game in the major leagues was against Larry Walker and the Colorado Rockies on June 10, 2003, at Minneapolis. Justin was the designated hitter. Another Canadian, Corey Koskie, played third base for the Twins.

Morneau hit a single to centre field off Jason Jennings his first time at bat. He struck out in the fourth inning, singled to right in the sixth inning, and grounded out in the eighth. A week later, Justin hit his first home run, as a pinch-hitter in Kansas City, off Albie Lopez.

Morneau split the 2004 season between Minnesota and Rochester, New York, in the International League. He hit 22 home runs at Rochester and 19 for Minnesota. In the American League playoffs, Justin had two doubles and two singles in four games.

Justin Morneau started his first full season with the Twins in 2005. In just the third game of the season, April 6 in Seattle, Morneau was hit on the head by a pitch from Ron Villone, and missed two weeks because of dizziness. Justin returned to the lineup April 22 and played 141 games. His batting average was only .239, but Justin hit 22 home runs and batted in 79 runs.

After a slow start in 2006, Morneau burst loose. He was hitting just .208 at the end of April, but socked a home run May 1 in Seattle to start a steady surge. His batting average went to .243 on June 1, and to .288 on July 1. Justin went over .300 July 15 at Cleveland with a home run off C.C. Sabathia. Morneau had five hits at Fenway Park in September, and ended the season with an average of .321, with 34 home runs and 130 runs batted in.

Justin also batted .417, with five hits, in the Twins' three playoff games against Oakland. His selection as the American League's Most Valuable Player eased the disappointment of a playoff defeat.

Morneau's 2007 season was almost as good as the previous year. Justin hit 31 home runs and drove in 111 runs. He was chosen to the American League All-Star Team and became the highest-paid player in Minnesota history with a new six-year contract.

In 2008, Justin Morneau added to his impressive record by winning the All-Star Game home run contest, and then scored the winning run in the All-Star Game to ensure the American League would have home field advantage in the World Series. Morneau played in every one of Minnesota's 163 games. He batted .300 with 23 home runs and 129 runs batted in. The Twins lost a sudden-death playoff to the Chicago White Sox and had to watch the post-season games on television.

Justin Morneau has established himself as not merely the rightful successor to Larry Walker, but, if he stays healthy, potentially the all-time Canadian batting champion.

Chapter 7

For the Record

Alphabetical List of Canadians Who Have Played in the Major Leagues, 1871 to 2008

At least 230 Canadians have played in the major leagues since 1871. You'll find an alphabetical list of every Canadian who played in the majors between 1871 and 2008 on the following pages.

Larry Walker, Ferguson Jenkins and Phil Marchildon were born in Canada and developed their skills in Canada. George Selkirk, Jeff Heath and Kirk McCaskill were born here but grew up in the United States. Kevin Reimer was born in Macon, Georgia, where his father Gerry was playing in the Southern League. Kevin grew up in Enderby, British Columbia, and is a proud Canadian.

For the purposes of this book, a person is a Canadian if he or she was:
a) born in Canada, as were Jason Bay and Olga Grant;
b) born abroad of Canadian parents, e.g., Kevin Reimer; or
c) born abroad but grew up in Canada, such as Jimmy Archer.

Mike Brannock, a third baseman from Guelph, Ontario, played for Chicago of the National Association in 1871, and he is the starting point for the alphabetical list of Canadian major league players that begins on the next page.

Terry Puhl was born in Melville, Saskatchewan, learned baseball there and left home at 17 to pursue his career. Terry's home is in Texas but his roots are in Saskatchewan. "I am a Canadian," he says. "My children have dual citizenship."

Larry Walker, the greatest all-around player Canada ever produced, wore a Canada T-shirt under his Colorado Rockies uniform. "I am proud to be a Canadian," he said, "and proud to tell other young Canadians that they can make a career in sport if they listen to their coaches, watch other players and work hard."

The achievements of the Canadians described in this book are part of Canada's sports history; but they are not just about the past. These stories are proof that Canadians play baseball with the best in the world, now and in the future.

Alphabetical List of Canadians Who Played in the Major Leagues

The following is a list of 230 Canadians who have played in baseball's major leagues up to and including the 2008 season. Biographical information and major league performance records of players can be found in *The Baseball Encyclopedia*; also in *Total Baseball*, and in the *Canadian Players Encyclopedia* by Neil Munro and STATS Inc., Skokie, Illinois. On-line sources include http://www.retrosheet.org and http://www.baseball-reference.com.

NAME	PLACE OF BIRTH	FIRST YEAR IN MAJORS
A		
Alexander, Bob	Vancouver, BC	Baltimore, AL, 1955
Andrus, Wiman	Orono, ON	Providence, NL, 1885
Archer, Jimmy	Dublin, Ireland*	Pittsburgh, NL, 1904
Atkinson, Bill	Chatham, ON	Montreal, NL, 1976
Aucoin, Derek	Lachine, QC	Montreal, NL, 1996
B		
Bahr, Edson	Rouleau, SK	Pittsburgh, NL, 1946
Balaz, John	Toronto, ON	California, AL, 1974
Barnwell, Chris	Jacksonville, FL*	Milwaukee, NL, 2006
Barton, Vince	Edmonton, AB	Chicago, NL, 1931
Bay, Jason	Trail, BC	San Diego, NL, 2003
Bedard, Erik	Navan, ON	Baltimore, AL, 2002
Bertoia, Reno	Italy*	Detroit, AL, 1953
Biasatti, Hank	Italy*	Philadelphia, AL, 1949
Boucher, Denis	Montreal, QC	Toronto, AL, 1991
Bowsfield, Ted	Vernon, BC	Boston, AL, 1958
Brannock, Mike	Guelph, ON	Chicago, NL, 1871
Braun, Ryan	Kitchener, ON	Kansas City, AL, 2006
Burgess, Tom	London, ON	St. Louis, NL, 1954
Burnside, Sheldon	South Bend, IN*	Detroit, AL, 1978
Butler, Rich	Toronto, ON	Toronto, AL, 1997
Butler, Rob	East York, ON	Toronto, AL, 1993
Buxton, Ralph	Weyburn, SK	Philadelphia, AL, 1938

BOWMAN

ROB BUTLER

Rob Butler is the only Canadian ever to play for a Canadian team in the World Series. (Bowman baseball card, 1993)

C

Calvert, Paul	Montreal, QC	Cleveland, AL, 1942
Cameron, Jack	Sydney, NS	Boston, NL, 1906
Carlin, Luke	Silver Springs, MD*	San Diego, NL, 2008
Casey, Bob	Adolphustown, ON	Detroit, NL, 1882
Clapp, "Stubby"	Windsor, ON	St. Louis, NL, 2001
Clarke, Justin	Amherstburg, ON	Cleveland, AL, 1905
Cleveland, Reggie	Swift Current, SK	St. Louis, NL, 1969
Cockman, Jim	Guelph, ON	New York, AL, 1905
Collins, Chub	Dundas, ON	Buffalo, NL, 1884
Colman, Frank	London, ON	Pittsburgh, NL, 1942
Congalton, William	Guelph, ON	Chicago, NL, 1902
Cook, Earl	Stouffville, ON	Detroit, AL, 1941
Cormier, Rheal	Moncton, NB	St. Louis, NL, 1991
Cort, Barry	Toronto, ON	Milwaukee, AL, 1977
Craig, Pete	LaSalle, ON	Washington, AL, 1964
Crain, Jesse	Toronto, ON	Minnesota, AL, 2004
Crosby, Ken	New Denver, BC	Chicago, NL, 1975
Currie, Clarence	Glencoe, ON	Cincinnati, NL, 1902
Cyr, Eric	Montreal, QC	San Diego, NL, 2002

D

Daly, Tom	Saint John, NB	Chicago, AL, 1913
Daviault, Ray	Montreal, QC	New York, NL, 1962
Davidson, David	Richmond Hill, ON	Pittsburgh, NL, 2007
Dee, Maurice	Halifax, NS	St. Louis, AL, 1915
Demarais, Fred	Montreal, QC	Chicago, NL, 1890
Dempster, Ryan	Sechelt, BC	Florida, NL, 1998
Dickson, Jason	London, ON	California, AL, 1996
Dorsey, Jerry	Canada	Baltimore, UA, 1884
Doyle, John	Halifax, NS	Pittsburgh, AA, 1882
Ducey, Rob	Toronto, ON	Toronto, AL, 1987
Dugas, Gus	St-Jean-de-Matha, QC	Pittsburgh, NL, 1930
Dunn, Steve	London, ON	St. Paul, UL, 1884

E

Emslie, Bob	Guelph, ON	Baltimore, AA, 1883
Erautt, Joe	Vibank, SK	Chicago, AL, 1950

F

Fisher, Harry	Newbury, ON	Pittsburgh, NL, 1951
Ford, Gene	Milton, NS	Detroit, AL, 1905
Ford, Russ	Brandon, MB	New York, AL, 1909
Fowler, Dick	Toronto, ON	Philadelphia, AL, 1941
Francis, Jeff	Vancouver, BC	Colorado, NL, 2004
Frobel, Doug	Ottawa, ON	Pittsburgh, NL, 1982

G

Gagné, Eric	Montreal, QC	Los Angeles, NL, 1999
Gardiner, Mike	Sarnia, ON	Seattle, AL, 1990
Gardner, Alex	Toronto, ON	Washington, AA, 1884
Gibson, George	London, ON	Pittsburgh, NL, 1905
Gladu, Roland	Montreal, QC	Boston, NL, 1944
Gorbous, Glen	Drumheller, AB	Cincinnati, NL, 1955
Graney, Jack	St. Thomas, ON	Cleveland, AL, 1908
Green, Jason	Port Hope, ON	Houston, NL, 2000
Green, Steve	Greenfield Park, QC	Anaheim, AL, 2001
Guiel, Aaron	Vancouver, BC	Kansas City, AL, 2002

H

Handrahan, Vern	Charlottetown, PEI	Kansas City, AL, 1964
Hannifan, Pat	Halifax, NS	Brooklyn, NL, 1897
Harden, Rich	Victoria, BC	Oakland, AL, 2003
Hardy, Alex	Toronto, ON	Chicago, NL, 1902
Harkness, Tim	Montreal, QC	Los Angeles, NL, 1961
Harris, Billy	Duguayville, NB	Brooklyn, NL, 1957
Harrison, Tom	Trail, BC	Kansas City, AL, 1965
Heath, Jeff	Fort William, ON	Cleveland, AL, 1936
Hill, Shawn	Mississauga, ON	Montreal, NL, 2004
Hiller, John	Toronto, ON	Detroit, AL, 1965
Hodgson, Paul	Montreal, QC	Toronto, AL, 1980

Frank Colman hit a home run his first time at bat for the New York Yankees. (National Baseball Hall of Fame Library, Cooperstown, NY)

Peter Hoy pitched five games for the Boston Red Sox in 1992. (Courtesy Boston Red Sox)

Hooper, Bob	Leamington, ON	Philadelphia, AL, 1950
Horsman, Vince	Halifax, NS	Toronto, AL, 1991
Hoy, Peter	Brockville, ON	Boston, AL, 1992
Humphries, John	North Gower, ON	New York, NL, 1883
Hunter, Bill	St. Thomas, ON	Louisville, AA, 1884
Hyndman, Jim	Hamilton, ON	Philadelphia, AA, 1886

I

Irwin, Arthur	Toronto, ON	Worcester, NL, 1880
Irwin, John	Toronto, ON	Worcester, NL, 1882

J

Jenkins, Ferguson	Chatham, ON	Philadelphia, NL, 1965
Johnson, Albert	London, ON	Louisville, NL, 1896
Johnson, John "Spud"	Canada	Columbus, AA, 1889
Johnson, Mike	Edmonton, AB	Baltimore, AL, 1997
Jones, Bill	Hartland, NB	Boston, NL, 1911
Jones, Mike	Hamilton, ON	Louisville, AA, 1890
Judd, Oscar	Rebecca, ON	Boston, AL, 1941

K

Kellum, Win	Waterford, ON	Boston, AL, 1901
Kerr, Mel	Souris, MB	Chicago, NL, 1925
Kilkenny, Mike	Bradford, ON	Detroit, AL, 1969
Klassen, Danny	Leamington, ON	Arizona, NL, 1998
Knight, Joe	Point Stanley, ON	Philadelphia, NL, 1884
Knowles, Jim	Toronto, ON	Pittsburgh, AA, 1884
Korince, George	Ottawa, ON	Detroit, AL, 1966
Koskie, Corey	Anola, MB	Minnesota, AL, 1998
Kottaras, George	Scarborough, ON	Boston, AL, 2008
Krakauskas, Joe	Montreal, QC	Washington, AL, 1937
Kyle, Andy	Toronto, ON	Cincinnati, NL, 1912

L

LaForest, Byron	Edmundston, NB	Boston, AL, 1945
LaForest, Pierre-Luc	Hull, QC	Tampa Bay, AL, 2003
Lake, Fred	Cornwallis, NS	Boston, NL, 1891
Landreth, Larry	Stratford, ON	Montreal, NL, 1976
LaRocque, Sam	St-Mathias, QC	Detroit, NL, 1888
Law, Ron	Hamilton, ON	Cleveland, AL, 1969
Lawrence, Jim	Hamilton, ON	Cleveland, AL, 1963
LePine, Pete	Montreal, QC	Detroit, AL, 1902
Lines, Dick	Montreal, QC	Washington, AL, 1966
Lisi, Ricardo	Halifax, NS	Texas, AL, 1981
Loewen, Adam	Surrey, BC	Baltimore, AL, 2006
Long, Nelson	Burlington, ON	Boston, NL, 1902
Lyons, Pat	Belleville, ON	Cleveland, NL, 1890

M

MacKenzie, Eric	Glendon, AB	Kansas City, AL, 1955
MacKenzie, Ken	Gore Bay, ON	Milwaukee, NL, 1960
Magee, Bill	New Brunswick	Louisville, NL, 1897
Maranda, Georges	Levis, QC	San Francisco, NL, 1960
Marchildon, Phil	Penetanguishene, ON	Philadelphia, AL, 1940
Martin, Russell	East York, ON	Los Angeles, NL, 2006
Mathieson, Scott	Aldergrove, BC	Philadelphia, NL, 2006
Maysey, Matt	Hamilton, ON	Montreal, NL, 1992
McCabe, Ralph	Napanee, ON	Cleveland, AL, 1946
McCaskill, Kirk	Kapuskasing, ON	California, AL, 1985
McGovern, Art	Saint John, NB	Boston, AL, 1905
McKay, Cody	Vancouver, BC	Oakland, AL, 2002
McKay, Dave	Vancouver, BC	Minnesota, AL, 1975
McKeever, Jim	Saint John, NB	Boston, UA, 1884
McLean, Larry	Fredericton, NB	Boston, AL, 1901
McMillan, George	Ontario	New York, NL, 1890
Mead, Charlie	Vermilion, AB	New York, NL, 1943
Mears, Chris	Ottawa, ON	Detroit, AL, 2003
Miller, Doc	Chatham, ON	Chicago, NL, 1910
Moore, Jerrie	Windsor, ON	Altoona, UA, 1884
Morneau, Justin	New Westminster, BC	Minnesota, AL, 2003
Morrison, Jon	London, ON	Indianapolis, AA 1884

Larry Landreth of Stratford, ON, pitched six shutout innings in his major league debut to beat the Cubs. (Montreal Expos)

Kirk McCaskill won more games than any Canadian-born pitcher except Ferguson Jenkins. (John Klein photo)

Mountjoy, Billy	London, ON	Cincinnati, AA, 1883
Mullin, Henry	Saint John, NB	Washington, AA, 1884
Murphy, Larry	Toronto, ON	Washington, AA, 1891
Myette, Aaron	New Westminster, BC	Chicago, AL, 1999

N

Nicholson, Kevin	Vancouver, BC	San Diego, NL, 2000

O

O'Brien, John	Saint John, NB	Brooklyn, NL, 1891
O'Connor, Dan	Guelph, ON	Louisville, AA, 1890
O'Halloran, Greg	Toronto, ON	Florida, NL, 1994
O'Hara, Bill	Toronto, ON	New York, NL, 1909
O'Neill, Fred	London, ON	New York, AA, 1887
O'Neill, Harry	Lindsay, ON	Philadelphia, AL, 1922
O'Neill, James "Tip"	Woodstock, ON	New York, NL, 1883
O'Neill, William John	Saint John, NB	Boston, AL, 1904
O'Rourke, Frank	Hamilton, ON	Boston, NL, 1912
Orr, Peter	Richmond Hill, ON	Atlanta, NL, 2005
Osborne, Fred	Canada	Pittsburgh, NL, 1890
Ostrosser, Brian	Hamilton, ON	New York, NL, 1973
Owens, Frank	Toronto, ON	Boston, AL, 1905
Oxley, Henry	Covehead, PEI	New York, NL, 1884

P

Pagan, Dave	Nipawin, SK	New York, AL, 1973
Pfann, Bill	Hamilton, ON	Cincinnati, NL, 1894
Phillips, Bill	Saint John, NB	Cleveland, NL, 1879
Piche, Ron	Verdun, QC	Milwaukee, NL, 1960
Pinnance, Elijah	Walpole Island, ON	Philadelphia, AL, 1903
Pirie, James	Ontario	Philadelphia, NL, 1883
Pladson, Gordon	New Westminster, BC	Houston, NL, 1979
Pond, Simon	North Vancouver, BC	Toronto, AL, 2004
Puhl, Terry	Melville, SK	Houston, NL, 1977

Q

Quantrill, Paul	London, ON	Boston, AL, 1992

R

Radmanovich, Ryan	Calgary, AB	Seattle, AL, 1998
Randall, Newton	New Lowell, ON	Chicago, NL, 1907
Raymond, Claude	St-Jean, QC	Chicago, AL, 1959
Reid, Billy	London, ON	Baltimore, AA, 1883
Reimer, Kevin	Macon, GA*	Texas, AL, 1988
Reitsma, Chris	Minneapolis, MN*	Cincinnati, NL, 2001
Richmond, Scott	North Vancouver, BC	Toronto, AL, 2008
Riley, Jim	Bayfield, NB	St. Louis, AL, 1921
Robertson, Sherry	Montreal, QC	Washington, AL, 1940
Rosen, Goody	Toronto, ON	Brooklyn, NL, 1937
Ross, Ernie	Toronto, ON	Baltimore, AL, 1902
Rowan, David	Elora, ON	St. Louis, AL, 1911
Roy, Jean-Pierre	Montreal, QC	Brooklyn, NL, 1946
Rutherford, John	Belleville, ON	Brooklyn, NL, 1952

S

Scanlan, Patrick	Nova Scotia	Boston, UA, 1884
Selkirk, George	Huntsville, ON	New York, AL, 1934
Shank, Harvey	Toronto, ON	California, AL, 1970
Shields, Vince	Fredericton, NB	St. Louis, NL, 1924
Shipanoff, Dave	Edmonton, AB	Philadelphia, NL, 1985
Siddall, Joe	Windsor, ON	Montreal, NL, 1993
Sinclair, Steve	Victoria, BC	Toronto, AL, 1998
Sincock, Bert	Barkerville, BC	Cincinnati, NL, 1908
Sketchley, Bud	Virden, MB	Chicago, AL, 1942
Smith, Charles "Pop"	Digby, NS	Cincinnati, NL, 1880
Smith, Frank	Fonthill, ON	Pittsburgh, AA, 1884
Smith, Tom	Guelph, ON	Brooklyn, NA, 1875
Snyder, Cooney	Toronto, ON	Louisville, NL, 1898
Spoljaric, Paul	Kelowna, BC	Toronto, AL, 1994
Stairs, Matt	Fredericton, NB	Montreal, NL, 1992
Steele, Bob	Cassburn, ON	St. Louis, NL, 1916

OVER THE FENCE IS OUT!

Terry Puhl played 182 consecutive games without an error, including the entire 1979 season. (Houston Astros)

Joe Siddal played for Montreal, Florida and Detroit. He hit his only home run against former teammate Jeff Fassero. (Montreal Expos)

Stern, Adam	London, ON	Boston, AL, 2005
Stewart, Andy	Oshawa, ON	Kansas City, AL, 1997
Summers, William	Toronto, ON	St. Louis, NL, 1893
Swindle, R.J.	Vancouver, BC	Philadelphia, NL, 2008

T

Taylor, Ron,	Toronto, ON	Cleveland, AL, 1962
Teahan, Mark	Redlands, CA*	Kansas City, AL, 2005
Thompson, John	London, ON	Cincinnati, AA, 1882
Thorman, Scott	Cambridge, ON	Atlanta, NL, 2006

U

Upham, John	Windsor, ON	Chicago, NL, 1967

V

Vadeboncoeur, Gene	Louiseville, QC	Philadelphia, NL, 1884
Van Brabant, Ossie	Kingsville, ON	Philadelphia, AL, 1954
Vickers, Harry	St. Marys, ON	Cincinnati, NL, 1902
Votto, Joey	Toronto, ON	Cincinnati, NL, 2007

W

Wainhouse, David	Toronto, ON	Montreal, NL, 1991
Walker, George	Hamilton, ON	Baltimore, AA, 1888
Walker, Larry	Maple Ridge, BC	Montreal, NL, 1989
Ward, Pete	Montreal, QC	Baltimore, AL, 1962
Watkins, Bill	Brantford, ON	Indianapolis, AA 1884
Weber, Joe	Hamilton, ON	Detroit, NL, 1884
Whitehead, Milton	Toronto, ON	St. Louis, UA, 1884
Wilkie, Aldon	Zealandia, SK	Pittsburgh, NL, 1941
Wilson, Nigel	Oshawa, ON	Florida, NL, 1993
Wilson, Steve	Victoria, BC	Texas, AL, 1988
Wingo, Ed	Ste-Anne-de-Bellevue	Philadelphia, AL, 1920
Wood, Fred	Dundas, ON	Detroit, NL, 1884
Wood, Pete	Dundas, ON	Buffalo, AA, 1885

Y

Z

Zimmerman, Jeff	Kelowna, BC	Texas, AL, 1999
Zimmerman, Jordan	Kelowna, BC	Seattle, AL, 1999

Notes:

* *Jimmy Archer was born in Ireland and came to Canada as a baby.*
* *Chris Barnwell was born in the U.S.A.; but his parents are Canadians.*
* *Reno Bertoia and Hank Biassati were born in Italy but grew up in Canada.*
* *Sheldon Burnside was born in the U.S.A. but grew up in Toronto.*
* *Luke Carlin was born in the U.S.A. but came to Canada at age two.*
* *Kevin Reimer was born in Georgia while his father, Gerry, was playing for Macon of the Southern League. Father and son Reimer are both Canadians from Enderby, BC.*
* *Chris Reitsma was born in the U.S.A. but grew up in Calgary.*
* *Mark Teahan was born and raised in the U.S.A.; his parents are Canadians.*

Pete Ward was the American League Rookie of the Year in 1963, when he batted .295 with 22 home runs. (National Baseball Hall of Fame Library, Cooperstown, NY)

Canadian Baseball Hall of Fame
St. Marys, Ontario, Near Stratford

The Canadian Baseball Hall of Fame and Museum has been dedicated to preserving Canada's rich baseball heritage since its inception as a non-profit, charitable foundation in October, 1983. Originally located in Toronto, the Hall opened in its current location in St. Marys, Ontario, a 30-minute drive from London and 15 minutes from the festival city of Stratford, in 1998.

The museum's exclusive collection of artifacts tells the story of the players, builders, teams and leagues that have shaped Canada's baseball history. The museum is located on a 32-acre parcel of land donated by the St. Marys Cement Plant, which includes three ball fields and is home to the Hall's "Kids On Deck" program, a unique summer camp for boys and girls.

The St. Marys Rotary Club was the first organization to pledge support for the Hall and continues to provide numerous volunteer hours and cash donations.

For more information about the Canadian Baseball Hall of Fame and Museum, please call (519) 284-1838, or visit their website at: http://www.baseballhalloffame.ca.

The Canadian Baseball Hall of Fame Museum in St. Marys, Ontario.

Aerial view of the Canadian Baseball Hall of Fame Museum in St. Marys, Ontario.

Canadian Baseball Hall of Fame Inductees, 1983 to 2008

Selection Criteria for the Canadian Baseball Hall of Fame

1. Selection is not restricted to Canadians but is open to anyone who has contributed to baseball in Canada, whether on the field or in an administrative capacity or a combination of both.
2. Open to both amateur and professional candidates.
3. Players must be retired at least three years.
4. Candidate must receive 75% of the vote to be inducted.

INDUCTEES, YEAR BY YEAR

1983

John Ducey, Edmonton, AB, player, umpire and official.

Phil Marchildon, Penetanguishene, ON, Philadelphia pitcher.

"Tip" O'Neill, Woodstock, ON, 19th century batting champion.

George Selkirk, Huntsville, ON, New York Yankees outfielder.

Frank Shaughnessy, Manager, President, International League.

Lester Pearson, former Prime Minister, honorary member.

1984

Andrew Bilesky, British Columbia Little League coach.

Charles Bronfman, Owner, Montreal Expos.

Jack Graney, London, ON, Cleveland outfielder, broadcaster.

Claude Raymond, St. Jean, QC, major league pitcher.

Goody Rosen, Toronto, ON, major league outfielder.

1985

Carmen Bush, Toronto, ON, amateur baseball builder.

Jack Kent Cooke, Toronto, ON, baseball team owner.

Dick Fowler, Toronto, ON, only Canadian no-hit pitcher.

John Hiller, Toronto, ON, Detroit Tigers pitcher.

Ron Taylor, Toronto, ON, major league pitcher.

1986

Reggie Cleveland, Swift Current, SK, major league pitcher.

Bob Emslie, London, ON, major league pitcher and umpire.

Oscar Judd, Rebecca, ON, major league pitcher.

Bob Prentice, Toronto, ON, infielder and scout.

1987

Ferguson Jenkins, Chatham, ON, major league pitcher.

George Gibson, London, ON, major league catcher and manager.

Rocky Nelson, International League first baseman, Montreal and Toronto.

1988

Reno Bertoia, Windsor, ON, major league infielder.

Ted Bowsfield, Penticton, BC, major league pitcher.

Jeff Heath, Thunder Bay, ON, major league outfielder.

Bill Phillips, Saint John, NB, 19th-century major league infielder.

Ron Piche, Verdun, QC, major league pitcher.

1838 Beachville and Zorro, ON teams, first game in Canada.

1989

Robert Brown, Vancouver, BC, Vancouver's Mr. Baseball.

Russell Ford, Brandon, MB, New York Yankees pitcher.

Arthur Irwin, Toronto, ON, 19th century player and manager.

1990

Jimmy Archer, Dublin, Ireland, major league catcher.

1991

Pete Ward, Montreal, QC, major league third baseman.

Jimmy Williams, Toronto, ON, outfielder and Baltimore coach.

Jackie Robinson, Montreal Royals second baseman.

1992

Tom Burgess, London, ON, major league outfielder.

Team Canada, 1991 World Youth Champions, honorary members.

1993 - 1994 *No inductees.*

1995

Terry Puhl, Swift Current, SK, major league outfielder.

1996

Justin Jay Clarke, Amherstburg, ON, major league catcher.

Father Ronald Cullen, Windsor, ON, amateur baseball organizer.

Frank O'Rourke, Hamilton, ON, major league player and scout.

1997

Pat Gillick, general manager, Toronto Blue Jays.

John McHale, first President, Montreal Expos.

1998

Canadian-born players, All-American Girls Professional League.

George (Knotty) Lee, Toronto, ON, player, umpire, official.

Ron Roncetti, Toronto, ON, amateur baseball player and official.

1999

Frank Colman, London, ON, major league outfielder.

Bobby Mattick, Toronto Blue Jays manager and scout.

George Sleeman, Guelph, ON, 19th-century baseball owner.

2000

Jim Fanning, Montreal Expos manager and executive.

2001

Gary Carter, Montreal Expos catcher.

Dave McKay, Vancouver, BC, major league player and coach.

2002

Paul Beeston, Welland, ON, major league executive.

Cito Gaston, Manager, World Champion Toronto Blue Jays.

Don McDougall, Charlottetown, PEI, baseball executive.

Dave Shury, Wilkie, SK, Provincial Administrator.

Harry Simmons, International League statistician.

Bill Slack, Petrolia, ON, minor league pitcher and manager.

2003

Richard Belec, Montreal, QC, Provincial Administrator.

Joe Carter, Toronto Blue Jays outfielder.

Kirk McCaskill, Kapuskasing, ON, major league pitcher.

Vancouver Asahi baseball team, British Columbia champions.

2004

Andre Dawson, Montreal Expos outfielder.

Peter Hardy, London, ON, President, Toronto Blue Jays.

Joseph Lannin, Lac Beauport, QC, owner, Boston Red Sox, 1913-1917.

Jim McKean, Montreal, QC, major league umpire.

2005

Steve Rogers, Montreal Expos pitcher.

Charles "Pop" Smith, Digby, NS, 19th-century player.

Dave Stieb, Toronto Blue Jays, no-hit pitcher.

Harold "Doc" Younker, trainer, Baseball Canada.

2006

Ron Hayter, Regina, SK, Provincial Administrator (Alberta).

Tommy Lasorda, Montreal Royals pitcher.

Larry McLean, Fredericton, NB, major league catcher.

Ron Stead, London, ON, Intercounty League pitcher.

2007

George "Sparky" Anderson, player, manager Montreal, Toronto.

John Haar, Vancouver, BC, Provincial Administrator.

Sherry Robertson, Montreal, QC, player, coach.

2008

Tony Fernandez, Toronto Blue Jays shortstop.

Billy Harris, Duguayville, NB, pitcher.

Gladwyn Scott, Hamiota, MB, Provincial Administrator.

Peter Widdrington, Toronto, ON, Toronto Blue Jays executive.

Canadians Who Played for the Blue Jays and the Expos

Sixteen Canadians played for the Montreal Expos and 14 Canadians have played for the Toronto Blue Jays. Pitcher Denis Boucher and outfielders Rob Ducey and Matt Stairs are the only Canadians to play for both the Expos and the Blue Jays. The first Canadian to play for Toronto was third baseman Dave McKay of Vancouver who drove in the winning run in the very first game the Blue Jays ever played, April 7, 1977, in the snow at Exhibition Stadium, Toronto.

Canadian Blue Jays

NAME	BIRTHPLACE	POSITION	FIRST YEAR
Dave McKay	Vancouver, BC	INF	1977
Paul Hodgson	Montreal, QC	OF	1980
Rob Ducey	Toronto, ON	OF	1987
Denis Boucher	Montreal, QC	LHP	1991
Vince Horsman	Halifax, NS	LHP	1991
Rob Butler	Toronto, ON	OF	1993
Paul Spoljaric	Kelowna, BC	LHP	1994
Paul Quantrill	London, ON	RHP	1996
Rich Butler	Toronto, ON	OF	1997
Steve Sinclair	Victoria, BC	LHP	1998
Simon Pond	North Vancouver, BC	OF	2004
Corey Koskie	Anola, MB	3B	2005
Matt Stairs	Saint John, NB	OF	2007
Scott Richmond	Vancouver, BC	RHP	2008

Dave McKay drove in the winning run in the Blue Jays' first game. (National Baseball Hall of Fame Library, Cooperstown, NY)

16 Canadians Played for the Expos

Claude Raymond was the first Canadian to play for a Canadian team in the major leagues. When Raymond joined the Montreal Expos in August 1969 from the Atlanta Braves, he went from first place to last place but says he was thrilled to be going home.

NAME	BIRTHPLACE	POSITION	FIRST YEAR
Claude Raymond	St-Jean, QC	RHP	1969
Billy Atkinson	Chatham, ON	RHP	1976
Larry Landreth	Stratford, ON	RHP	1976
Doug Frobel	Ottawa, ON	OF	1985
Larry Walker	Maple Ridge, BC	OF-1B	1989
David Wainhouse	Toronto, ON	RHP	1991
Matt Stairs	Saint John, NB	OF	1992
Matt Maysey	Hamilton, ON	RHP	1992
Mike Gardiner	Sarnia, ON	RHP	1993
Joe Siddall	Windsor, ON	C	1993
Denis Boucher	Montreal, QC	LHP	1994
Derek Aucoin	Lachine, QC	RHP	1996
Rheal Cormier	Moncton, NB	LHP	1996
Mike Johnson	Edmonton, AB	RHP	1997
Rob Ducey	Toronto, ON	OF	2001
Shawn Hill	Mississauga, ON	RHP	2004

Claude Raymond was the first Canadian to play for the Expos. (Montreal Expos)

OVER THE FENCE IS OUT!

Three Played for Both Jays and Expos

Matt Stairs, Denis Boucher and Rob Ducey played for both the Expos and the Blue Jays. Stairs began his career with the Expos in 1992. He went to Japan in 1993 and played for Boston, Oakland, Milwaukee, Kansas City, Detroit, Texas and Detroit before joining the Blue Jays in 2007.

Boucher was traded by Toronto to Cleveland in 1991 and came to the Expos in 1993. Ducey started with Toronto but played for California, Texas, Seattle and the Phillies before joining the Expos in 2001.

Canadian Brothers in the Major Leagues

Arthur Irwin, a shortstop from Toronto, played 1,010 games for five teams. John Irwin was a third baseman. The Irwin brothers played one game together with Worcester (Mass.) in 1882. John also played for five other major league teams.

Fred and Pete Wood, of Hamilton, formed a pitcher-catcher battery for the final game of the 1885 season with Buffalo of the National League.

Gene Ford, born in Milton, Nova Scotia, pitched seven games for Detroit in 1905. His brother, Russell, born in Brandon, Manitoba, won 99 games, from 1909 to 1915.

The Butler brothers from Toronto, Rob and Rich, both played for the Blue Jays; but not together. Rob Butler played for Toronto in 1993 and 1994. Rich joined the Blue Jays in 1997.

Pitchers Jeff Zimmerman and Jordan Zimmerman of Kelowna, British Columbia, are the only Canadian brothers who ever played for opposing teams in the same major league game.

McKay, Father and Son

Dave McKay, of Vancouver, played eight seasons in the American League. His son, Cody McKay, who was also born in Vancouver, was a catcher for Oakland in 2002, and for the St. Louis Cardinals in 2004. The McKays are the only Canadian-born father and son combination in major league history.

Canadian Baseball Records

Outstanding performance records for career, season and game by Canadian-born players in the major leagues, 1871-2008.

Games Played, Career
1,988 Larry Walker
1,662 Matt Stairs
1,531 Terry Puhl
1,402 Jack Graney
1,383 Jeff Heath
1,213 George Gibson
1,131 Frank O'Rourke
1,112 Charles Smith
1,054 James "Tip" O'Neill
1,038 Bill Phillips

Games Played, Season
163 Justin Morneau, 2008
162 Jason Bay, 2005
159 Jason Bay, 2006
157 Pete Ward, 1963
157 Terry Puhl, 1979
157 Justin Morneau, 2006
157 Justin Morneau, 2007
155 Jack Graney, 1916
155 Jason Bay, 2008
155 Russell Martin, 2008
154 Frank O'Rourke, 1929
153 Larry Walker, 1997
153 Corey Koskie, 2001
151 Jeff Heath, 1941
151 Russell Martin, 2007
151 Joey Votto, 2008

Hits, Career
2,160 Larry Walker, 1989-2005
1,447 Jeff Heath, 1936-1949
1,386 "Tip" O'Neill, 1883-1892
1,361 Terry Puhl, 1977-1991
1,313 Matt Stairs 1992- 2008
1,178 Jack Graney, 1908-1922
1,130 Bill Phillips, 1878-1888
1,032 Frank O'Rourke, 1912-1931
941 Charles "Pop" Smith, 1880-1891
936 Corey Koskie, 1998-2006
934 Arthur Irwin, 1880-1894

Hits, Season
225 "Tip" O'Neill, 1887
208 Larry Walker, 1997
199 Jeff Heath, 1938
197 Goody Rosen, 1945
192 Roy "Doc" Miller, 1911
190 "Tip" O'Neill, 1886
190 Justin Morneau, 2006
187 Justin Morneau, 2008
186 John "Spud" Johnson, 1890
183 Jason Bay, 2005

Hits, Game
6 Kevin Reimer, August 24, 1993
5 Pete Ward, July 24, 1965
5 Kevin Reimer, June 6, 1991
5 Justin Morneau, September 19, 2006
4 Goody Rosen, 1945
4 Larry Walker, 34 times
4 Jason Bay, 4 times in 2004
4 Jason Bay, July 24, 2006

Hits, Consecutive Games
21 Larry Walker, 1999
20 Larry Walker, 1998
18 Pete Ward, 1963
18 Terry Puhl, 1978
18 Larry Walker, 1999
17 Terry Puhl, 1977
16 Jeff Heath, 1938
16 Dave McKay, 1978
16 Larry Walker, 1997
16 Justin Morneau, 2006

Batting Average, Season
.435 "Tip" O'Neill, 1887
.379 Larry Walker, 1999
.366 Larry Walker, 1997
.363 Larry Walker, 1998
.350 Larry Walker, 2001
.346 "Spud" Johnson, 1890
.343 Jeff Heath, 1938
.340 Jeff Heath, 1941

Runs, Career

1,355 Larry Walker, 1989-2005
880 "Tip" O'Neill, 1883-1892
777 Jeff Heath, 1936-1949
737 Matt Stairs, 1992-2008
706 Jack Graney, 1908-1922
676 Terry Puhl, 1977-1991
643 "Pop" Smith, 1880-1891
562 Bill Phillips, 1879-1888
552 Arthur Irwin, 1880-1894
547 Frank O'Rourke, 1912-1931

Runs, Season

167 "Tip" O'Neill, 1887
143 Larry Walker, 1997
126 Goody Rosen, 1945
123 "Tip" O'Neill, 1889
113 Larry Walker, 1998
112 "Tip" O'Neill, 1890
112 "Tip" O'Neill, 1891
111 Jason Bay, 2008
110 Jason Bay, 2005
108 Larry Walker, 1999

Runs, Game

5 Jeff Heath, August 20, 1938
5 Larry Walker, July 27, 2000
5 Larry Walker, September 24, 2001

Runs Batted in, Career

1,311 Larry Walker
887 Jeff Heath
864 Matt Stairs
757 "Tip" O'Neill
576 George Selkirk
523 Justin Morneau
506 Corey Koskie
491 Jason Bay
435 Terry Puhl
430 Frank O'Rourke

Runs Batted in, Season

130 Larry Walker, 1997
130 Justin Morneau, 2006
129 Justin Morneau, 2008
123 "Tip" O'Neill, 1887
123 Jeff Heath, 1941

123 Larry Walker, 2001
115 Larry Walker, 1997
113 "Spud" Johnson, 1890
112 Jeff Heath, 1938
110 "Tip" O'Neill, 1889
109 Jason Bay, 2006

Runs Batted in, Game

8 George Selkirk, 1935
8 George Selkirk, 1938
8 Larry Walker, 1999
8 Jason Bay, 2003
8 Jason Bay, 2004
6 Matt Stairs, 1996
6 Larry Walker, 1996
6 Matt Stairs, 1998
6 Corey Koskie, 2003
6 Larry Walker, 2003
6 Justin Morneau, 2006
6 Justin Morneau, 2007

Runs Batted in, Inning

6 Matt Stairs, July 5, 1996
  vs. California, first inning

Home Runs, Career

383 Larry Walker
254 Matt Stairs
194 Jeff Heath
149 Jason Bay
133 Justin Morneau
124 Corey Koskie
108 George Selkirk
98 Pete Ward
62 Terry Puhl
52 "Tip" O'Neill
52 Kevin Reimer

Home Runs, Season

49 Larry Walker, 1997
38 Matt Stairs, 1999
38 Larry Walker, 2001
37 Larry Walker, 1999
36 Larry Walker, 1995
35 Jason Bay, 2006
34 Justin Morneau, 2006
32 Jason Bay, 2005
31 Justin Morneau, 2007

31 Jason Bay, 2008
27 Jeff Heath, 1947
27 Matt Stairs, 1997

Home Runs, Rookie Season

26 Jason Bay, 2004
24 Joey Votto, 2008
22 Pete Ward, 1963
19 Larry Walker, 1990
18 Jeff Heath, 1938

Home Runs, Game

3 Larry Walker, April 5, 1997
3 Larry Walker, April 28, 1999
3 Larry Walker, June 25, 2004
3 Justin Morneau, July 6, 2007

Home Runs, Consecutive Games

5 Matt Stairs, July 30-August 3, 1998
5 Larry Walker, June 18-23, 1999
4 Jeff Heath, September 25-29, 1938
4 George Selkirk, September 18-22, 1940
4 Larry Walker, three times

Bases-loaded Home Runs, Career

10 Matt Stairs, 1992-2008
7 Larry Walker, 1989-2005
5 Jeff Heath, 1936-1949
4 George Selkirk, 1934-1942
4 Pete Ward, 1962-1970
3 Terry Puhl, 1977-1991
3 Justin Morneau, 2003-2008
2 Corey Koskie, 1998-2006
2 Jason Bay, 2003-2008

Bases-loaded Home Runs, Season

3 Pete Ward, Chicago, AL, 1964
2 Jeff Heath, St. Louis, AL, 1947
2 Matt Stairs, Oakland, AL, 1998
2 Larry Walker, Colorado, NL, 1998
2 Larry Walker, St. Louis, NL, 2004

Triples, Season

20 Jeff Heath, 1940
19 "Tip" O'Neill, 1887
18 "Spud" Johnson, 1890
18 Jeff Heath, 1938
17 "Pop" Smith, 1883
16 "Tip" O'Neill, 1890
15 Bill Phillips, 1886
14 "Tip" O'Neill, 1886
14 Jack Graney, 1916
13 "Pop" Smith, 1885
13 Jeff Heath, 1941
12 George Selkirk, 1935
11 Goody Rosen, 1945

Doubles, Season

52 "Tip" O'Neill, 1887
47 Justin Morneau, 2008
46 Larry Walker, 1997
46 Larry Walker, 1998
44 Larry Walker, 1994
44 Jason Bay, 2005
41 Jack Graney, 1916
40 Frank O'Rourke, 1925
40 Larry Walker, 2002
37 Jeff Heath, 1942
37 Larry Walker, 1999
37 Corey Koskie, 2001
37 Corey Koskie, 2002

Bases on Balls, Career

913 Larry Walker
712 Jack Graney
674 Matt Stairs
593 Jeff Heath
486 George Selkirk
458 Corey Koskie
421 "Tip" O'Neill
397 Jason Bay
371 Pete Ward
325 "Pop" Smith
314 Frank O'Rourke

Bases on Balls, Season

105 Jack Graney, 1919
103 George Selkirk, 1939
102 Jack Graney, 1916
102 Jason Bay, 2006

Jeff Heath batted .340, hit 24 home runs, and batted in 123 runs for the Cleveland Indians in 1941. (Cleveland Plain Dealer)

98 Larry Walker, 2003
95 Jason Bay, 2005
94 Jack Graney, 1917
94 George Selkirk, 1936
90 Russell Martin, 2008

Bases on Balls, Game
4 Terry Puhl, September 25, 1989
4 Larry Walker, five times
4 Matt Stairs, September 8, 2002

Hit by Pitch, Career
138 Larry Walker
60 "Pop" Smith
56 Corey Koskie
54 Matt Stairs
53 Frank O'Rourke

Hit by Pitch, Season
14 Larry Walker, three times
13 Aaron Guiel, 2003
12 Corey Koskie, twice

Strikeouts, Career
1,231 Larry Walker
1,037 Matt Stairs
795 Corey Koskie
734 Jason Bay
670 Jeff Heath
539 Pete Ward
507 Terry Puhl
447 Justin Morneau

Strikeouts, Season
156 Jason Bay, 2006
142 Jason Bay, 2005
141 Jason Bay, 2007
137 Jason Bay, 2008
131 Mark Teahen, 2008
129 Jason Bay, 2004
127 Corey Koskie, 2002
127 Mark Teahen, 2007
124 Matt Stairs, 1999
122 Matt Stairs, 2000

Strikeouts, Game
4 Matt Stairs, 1998
4 Matt Stairs, 2001
4 Jason Bay, 4 times
3 Larry Walker, 30 times
3 Kevin Reimer, 9 times

Stolen Bases, Career
230 Larry Walker
217 Terry Puhl
169 "Pop" Smith
161 "Tip" O'Neill
148 Jack Graney
101 Frank O'Rourke

Stolen Bases, Season (Since 1900)
33 Larry Walker, 1997
32 "Doc" Miller, 1911
32 Terry Puhl, 1978
30 Terry Puhl, 1979
29 Larry Walker, 1993
27 Jack Graney, 1913

Consecutive Games Without Error
182 Terry Puhl, Houston, September 3, 1978 - April 18, 1980

Highest Fielding Average, Season, Minimum 125 Games
1.000 Terry Puhl, Houston, 1979, 152 games
.993 Goody Rosen, Brooklyn, 1945, 145 games
.993 Larry Walker, Montreal, 1992, 139 games

Canadian Pitching Records

Outstanding performances for career, season and game by Canadian-born pitchers in the major leagues, 1871-2008.

Games Pitched, Career

841 Paul Quantrill, 1992-2005
683 Rheal Cormier, 1991-2007
664 Ferguson Jenkins, 1965-1983
545 John Hiller, 1965-1980
491 Ron Taylor, 1962-1972
449 Claude Raymond, 1963-1971
428 Reggie Cleveland, 1969-1981
420 Ryan Dempster, 1998-2008
402 Eric Gagné, 1999-2008
380 Kirk McCaskill, 1985-1996

Games Pitched, Season

89 Paul Quantrill, Dodgers, 2003
86 Paul Quantrill, Dodgers, 2002
86 Paul Quantrill, Yankees, 2004
84 Rheal Cormier, Phillies, 2004
82 Paul Quantrill, Toronto, 1998
80 Paul Quantrill, Toronto, 2001
77 Paul Quantrill, Toronto, 1997
77 Eric Gagné, Dodgers, 2002
77 Eric Gagné, Dodgers, 2003
75 Jesse Crain, Minnesota, 2005

Games Won, Career

284 Ferguson Jenkins, 1965-1983
106 Kirk McCaskill, 1985-1996
105 Reggie Cleveland, 1969-1981
99 Russell Ford, 1909-1915
87 John Hiller, 1965-1980
76 Ryan Dempster, 1998-2008
71 Rheal Cormier, 1991-2007
68 Phil Marchildon, 1940-1950
68 Paul Quantrill, 1992-2005
66 Dick Fowler, 1941-1952

Games Won, Season

32 Bob Emslie, Baltimore, 1884
26 Russell Ford, Yankees, 1910
25 Ferguson Jenkins, Texas, 1974
24 Ferguson Jenkins, Chicago, 1971
22 Ferguson Jenkins, Chicago, 1970

21 Russell Ford, Yankees, 1911
21 Ferguson Jenkins, Chicago, 1969
20 Russell Ford, Buffalo, 1914
20 Ferguson Jenkins, 1967, -69, -72

Games Lost, Career

226 Ferguson Jenkins, 1965-1983
108 Kirk McCaskill, 1985-1996
106 Reggie Cleveland, 1969-1981
81 Ryan Dempster, 1998-2008
79 Dick Fowler, 1941-1952
78 Paul Quantrill, 1992-2005
76 John Hiller, 1965-1980
75 Phil Marchildon, 1940-1950
71 Russell Ford, 1909-1915
64 Rheal Cormier, 1991-2007

Games Lost, Season

21 Russell Ford, Yankees, 1912
19 Rube Vickers, 1908
19 Kirk McCaskill, California, 1991
18 Russell Ford, Yankees, 1913
18 Ferguson Jenkins, Texas, 1975
17 Bob Emslie, Baltimore, 1884
17 Paul Calvert, Washington, 1949
16 Dick Fowler, Philadelphia, 1946
16 Phil Marchildon, Philadelphia, 1946

Shutouts, Career

49 Ferguson Jenkins, 1965-1983
15 Russell Ford, 1909-1915
12 Reggie Cleveland, 1969-1981
11 Dick Fowler, 1941-1952
11 Kirk McCaskill, 1985-1996
7 Rube Vickers, 1902-1909
6 Phil Marchildon, 1940-1950
6 John Hiller, 1965-1980

Shutouts, Season

8 Russell Ford, Yankees, 1910
7 Ferguson Jenkins, Chicago, 1969

6 Rube Vickers, 1908
6 Ferguson Jenkins, Texas, 1974
5 Russell Ford, Buffalo, 1914
5 Ferguson Jenkins, Chicago, 1972
4 Dick Fowler, Philadelphia, 1949
4 Ferguson Jenkins, Texas, 1975
4 Ferguson Jenkins, Texas, 1978
4 Kirk McCaskill, California, 1989

Strikeouts, Career
3,192 Ferguson Jenkins, 1965-1983
1,194 Ryan Dempster, 1998-2008
1,036 John Hiller, 1965-1980
1,003 Kirk McCaskill, 1985-1996
930 Reggie Cleveland, 1969-1981
760 Rheal Cormier, 1991-2007
725 Paul Quantrill, 1992-2005
718 Eric Gagné, 1999-2008
711 Erik Bedard, 2002-2008

Strikeouts, Season
274 Ferguson Jenkins, Chicago, 1970
273 Ferguson Jenkins, Chicago, 1969
264 Bob Emslie, Baltimore, 1884
263 Ferguson Jenkins, Chicago, 1971
260 Ferguson Jenkins, Chicago, 1968
236 Ferguson Jenkins, Chicago, 1967
225 Ferguson Jenkins, Texas, 1974
221 Erik Bedard, Baltimore, 2007
209 Russell Ford, Yankees, 1910
209 Ryan Dempster, Florida, 2000
202 Kirk McCaskill, California, 1986

Strikeouts, Game
15 Erik Bedard, July 7, 2007
14 Ferguson Jenkins, 3 times
13 Ferguson Jenkins, twice
12 Ferguson Jenkins, 9 times
12 Kirk McCaskill, twice
12 Erik Bedard, 3 times

Bases on Balls, Career
997 Ferguson Jenkins, 1965-1983
707 Ryan Dempster, 1998-2008
684 Phil Marchildon, 1940-1950
665 Kirk McCaskill, 1985-1996
578 Dick Fowler, 1941-1952

543 Reggie Cleveland, 1969-1981
535 John Hiller, 1965-1980

Bases on Balls, Season
141 Phil Marchildon, 1947
140 Phil Marchildon, 1942
131 Phil Marchildon, 1948
129 Bill Magee, 1898
118 Phil Marchildon, 1941
115 Dick Fowler, 1949

Bases on Balls, Game
10 Joe Krakauskas, April 25, 1939
10 Phil Marchildon, June 14, 1948

Complete Games, Career
267 Ferguson Jenkins, 1965-1983
126 Russell Ford, 1909-1915
85 Bob Emslie, 1883-1885
82 Phil Marchildon, 1940-1950
75 Dick Fowler, 1941-1952
69 Bill Magee, 1897-1902
57 Reggie Cleveland, 1969-1981
56 Billy Mountjoy, 1883-1885

Complete Games, Season
50 Bob Emslie, Baltimore, 1884
32 Billy Mountjoy, Cincinnati, 1884
30 Russell Ford, Yankees, 1912
30 Ferguson Jenkins, Chicago, 1971
29 Bill Magee, Louisville, 1898
29 Russell Ford, Yankees, 1910
29 Ferguson Jenkins, Texas, 1974

Saves, Career
187 Eric Gagné, 1999-2008
125 John Hiller, 1965-1980
87 Ryan Dempster, 1998-2007
83 Claude Raymond, 1963-1971
72 Ron Taylor, 1962-1972

Saves, Season
55 Eric Gagné, Dodgers, 2003
52 Eric Gagné, Dodgers, 2002
45 Eric Gagné, Dodgers, 2004
38 John Hiller, Detroit, 1973

John Hiller was the Sporting News Relief Pitcher of the Year in 1973. John pitched 65 games for Detroit. He won 10 and saved 38, with an earned runs average of 1.41. In one game, Hiller struck out 10 batters. (National Baseball Hall of Fame Library, Cooperstown, NY)

World Series Records

Outstanding performances by Canadians in the World Series, 1903-2008.

Games Played

21 George Selkirk, 1936-1942
7 George Gibson, 1909
5 Larry McLean, 1913
4 Jimmy Archer, 1907, 1910
4 Ron Taylor, 1964, 1969
4 Larry Walker, 2004
3 Jack Graney, 1920
3 Reggie Cleveland, 1975
2 John Hiller, 1968
2 Rob Butler, 1993
1 John O'Neill, 1906
1 John Rutherford, 1952
1 Jeff Francis, 2007
1 Eric Gagné, 2007
1 Matt Stairs, 2008

World Series Hits

18 George Selkirk, 1936-1942
6 George Gibson, 1909
6 Larry McLean, 1913
5 Larry Walker, 2004
2 Jimmy Archer, 1907, 1910
1 Rob Butler, 1993

World Series Home Runs

2 George Selkirk, 1936-1942
2 Larry Walker, 2004

World Series Runs Batted In

10 George Selkirk, 1936-1942
3 Larry Walker, 2004
2 George Gibson, 1909
2 Larry McLean, 1913

Bases on Balls

11 George Selkirk, 1936-1942
2 George Gibson, 1909
2 Larry Walker, 2004

Games Pitched

4 Ron Taylor, 1964, 1969
3 Reggie Cleveland, 1975
2 John Hiller, 1968
1 John Rutherford, 1952
1 Jeff Francis. 2007
1 Eric Gagné, 2007

Innings Pitched

7 Ron Taylor, 1964, 1969
6.2 Reggie Cleveland, 1975
4 Jeff Francis, 2007
2 John Hiller, 1968
1 John Rutherford, 1952
1 Eric Gagné, 2007

Hits Allowed

0 Ron Taylor, 1964, 1969
0 Eric Gagné, 2007
1 John Rutherford, 1952
6 John Hiller, 1968
7 Reggie Cleveland, 1975
10 Jeff Francis, 2007

Strikeouts

5 Ron Taylor, 1964, 1969
5 Reggie Cleveland, 1975
3 Jeff Francis, 2007
1 John Rutherford, 1952
1 John Hiller, 1968
1 Eric Gagné, 2007

Bases on Balls

0 Eric Gagné, 2007
1 John Rutherford, 1952
2 Ron Taylor, 1964, 1969
3 John Hiller, 1968
3 Reggie Cleveland, 1975
3 Jeff Francis, 2007

"Tip" O'Neill Award Winners
Outstanding Canadian Player
of the Year

The "Tip" O'Neill Award is presented to the outstanding Canadian player of the year, chosen by the Canadian Baseball Hall of Fame. The award is named for the 19th-century outfielder from Woodstock, Ontario who set a major league record in 1887 when he won the batting championship with an average of .492 playing for the St. Louis Browns of the American Association.

1984 - Terry Puhl
1985 - Dave Shipanoff
1986 - Rob Ducey
1987 - Larry Walker
1988 - Kevin Reimer
1989 - Steve Wilson
1990 - Larry Walker
1991 - Daniel Brabant
1992 - Larry Walker
1993 - Rob Butler
1994 - Larry Walker
1995 - Larry Walker
1996 - Jason Dickson
1997 - Larry Walker
1998 - Larry Walker
1999 - Jeff Zimmerman
2000 - Ryan Dempster
2001 - Corey Koskie and Larry Walker
2002 - Eric Gagné and Larry Walker
2003 - Eric Gagné
2004 - Jason Bay
2005 - Jason Bay
2006 - Justin Morneau
2007 - Russell Martin
2008 - Justin Morneau

Index

Fox, Helen, 142
Francis, Jeff, 68, 254
Gagné, Eric, 204-207
Galvin, "Pud", 72
Gentry, Ruth, 142
George, Gene, 143
Gibson, George, 95-97
Gilchrist, Jeanne, 142
Gillick, Pat, 162, 240
Gladu, Roland, 144-145
Gormely, Charlie, 107-108
Gossage, "Goose", 186
Graff, Emil, 110-111
Grambo, Thelma, 142
Grant, Olga, 142
Grissom, Marquis, 55-65
Haine, Audrey, 142
Handrahan, Vern, 152-155
Hanna, Marjorie, 142
Harris, "Bucky", 124-126
Harvey, Doug, 146-150
Heath, Jeff, 128, 245-249
Heim, Kay, 143
Hickey, Lillian, 142
Hill, Ken, 55-60
Hill, Shawn, 80, 243
Hiller, John, 30, 67, 253
Holmes, Agnes, 142
Howe, Steve, 56
Hundeby, Thelma, 142
Hunter, "Catfish", 154, 166
Hunter, Dorothy, 142
Igali, Daniel, 29-30
Jacks, Sam, 29
Janowski, Alice, 142
Jenkins, Ferguson, 158-177
Jewitt, Christine, 142
Johnson, Arleene, 143
Jones, Jeff, 153
Jones, Marguerite, 142
Judd, Oscar, 110-115
Junor, Daisy, 142
Karpuk, Peter 149
Key, Dorothy, 143
Key, Jimmy, 56-60

King, Clyde, 164-165
Knezovich, Ruby, 143
Koufax, Sandy, 168
Krakauskas, Joe, 124-127
Kustra, Mary, 143
Lajoie, Napoleon, 98-99
Lanier, Max, 144
Leyritz, Jim, 59-62
Little, Olive, 140, 143
MacEachan, Allan, 156
MacLean, Lucella, 143
MacLeod, Donnie, 153
Maglie, Sal, 144
Managers, Canadians, 97
Mandeville, Jack, 183-184
Manning, Martha, 143
Mantle, Mickey, 67, 182
Marchildon, Phil, 29, 136-139
Martin, Russell, 208-211
Martinez, Pedro, 14, 55-63
Martz, Ruby, 143
Mason, Ruth, 143
Mattingly, Don, 60-62
Maxwell, Margaret, 143
Maysey, Matt, 190, 243
McAuley, Mildred, 143
McCreary, Ethel, 143
McCulloch, Colleen, 143
McDaniel, Kay, 143
McFaul, Gene, 143
McGraw, John, 83, 97, 104
McIntyre, Bill, 107-108
McKean, Jim, 58, 241
McLean, Larry, 102-104
Measner, Hazel, 143
Melvin, Doug, 162-165
Merkle, Fred, 83-85
Metzig, Bill, 148-149
Middleton, Ruth, 142
Morneau, Justin, 202, 214-216
Moroz, Evelyn, 143
Mountjoy, Billy, 80-82
Nelson, Helen, 143
Newcombe, Don, 128
Nicol, Helen, 142